SACRIFICE *and* SURVIVAL

SACRIFICE *and* SURVIVAL

Identity, Mission, and Jesuit Higher Education in the American South

R. Eric Platt

THE UNIVERSITY OF ALABAMA PRESS
Tuscaloosa

Typeface: Garamond and Corbel

Cover photographs: *Above*, Jesuit Faculty, St. Charles College, 1875; courtesy of Archives of the New Orleans Province, Society of Jesus, Loyola University Monroe Library. *Below*, Early St. Charles College, 1838; courtesy of Archives of the New Orleans Province, Society of Jesus, Loyola University Monroe Library
Cover design: Todd Lape/Lape Designs

∞

The paper on which this book is printed meets the minimum requirements of American National Standard for Information Sciences—Permanence of Paper for Printed Library Materials, ANSI Z39.48-1984.

Library of Congress Cataloging-in-Publication Data

Platt, R. Eric, 1981–
Sacrifice and survival : identity, mission, and Jesuit higher education in the American South / R. Eric Platt.
pages cm
Includes bibliographical references and index.
ISBN 978-0-8173-1819-2 (trade cloth : alk. paper) — ISBN 978-0-8173-8742-6 (e book) 1. Jesuits—Education (Higher)—Southern States. 2. Catholic universities and colleges—Southern States. I. Title.
LC493.P53 2014
378'.0712—dc23

2013049869

For my grandparents—all of them.
AMDG

What we call the beginning is often the end. And to make an end is to make a beginning. The end is where we start from.

—*T. S. Eliot*

Contents

Acknowledgments

As any author will tell you, a book is never really singly authored; numerous persons aid in its construction, review, and final publication. So it was with this book. As I reflect upon the creation of this work, research performed in archives, and the numerous conversations that prompted its development, a host of thanks come to mind that need to be paid. First and foremost, I would like to thank my parents Robert and DeWanda Platt for providing the love, affection, and upbringing that all children deserve and was given to my sister and me. Likewise, I wish to thank my sister, Robin Haney, for always believing in me. My parents, sister, brother-in-law, Kent, and nephews, Holton and Hayes, serve as a constant reminder that family is worth having and cherishing. For that I am deeply grateful. I would also like to issue a heartfelt thanks to all of my grandparents, both living and deceased, for the unlimited amount of love and support they showed throughout my life and continue to show today. This book is dedicated to their lives and memories.

In the course of creating this book, numerous friends have been along for the ride. My thanks go to my former roommates Adam and Katie Yates for a mountain of laughs, random afternoon road trips, and some of the best home-cooked food in Louisiana. To Daniel Eiland, his wife, Vanessa, and daughters, Charity and Zoe, I wish to express my gratitude for shared afternoon dinners and long walks taken while deep in conversation about Jesuits, higher education, and all things New Orleans. To my colleagues—particularly Gabe Radau, Jola Smolen, Steven McCullar, Takea Vickers, and Daniel Roberts and his wife, Kim—thanks for being dear friends and an unending source of support. Also, I would like to thank my longtime friend Ann Harrington and her father, Jim, for providing constant encouragement, fellowship, a place to sleep, and bowls of chicken soup whenever I needed to stay the night in New Orleans to partake in additional days of prolonged archival research. Ann, Jim, and I wandered the French Quarter many a night, discussing the finer points of Catholicism. In addition, I would like to extend my gratitude to my former supervisor, Lynn Evans, who provided support and encouragement during the initial research for this book.

The writing of this book could not have been accomplished without the aid of Rhonda Lott, Erica Daigle, and Sarah Lee Weeks. These three painstakingly reviewed early versions of this book and provided a plethora of welcome comments and critique. Words alone cannot express how much I appreciate all of you. To Joseph Powell, Dan Waterman, Jon Berry, and the staff of the University of Alabama Press, thanks for your tireless help with this project. Joseph, Dan, and Jon were always available to answer numerous questions and did an excellent job of demystifying the book publication process. In addition, I would like to thank Joslyn Zale at the University of Southern Mississippi for the construction of the map located within this text. Joslyn's skills as a cartographer added a level of visual geographic clarity that would have been otherwise lost.

As any historian will tell you, we can accomplish nothing without an archivist or two. This study could never have come to fruition without the inestimable guidance and assistance of Joan Gaulene and Paul Powell, administrators for the Jesuit Archives of the New Orleans Province. Joan and Paul not only tirelessly retrieved the all-important data for this study but they also contributed their thoughts on the Society of Jesus, the New Orleans Province, and life in the South. I give special thanks to both Joan and Paul and wish them a happy life. Thanks is also due to the New Orleans Province of the Society of Jesus for granting me permission to research in their archives and reproduce several wonderfully preserved images. As well, a particular debt of thanks goes to Brad Petitfils, director of Campus Planning and Assessment at Loyola University New Orleans, for introducing me to the Jesuit archives, Joan, and Paul. Brad's introduction to the archival staff at Loyola made all the difference. Thanks also to Art Carpenter and the archival staff at Loyola University New Orleans, the alumni office at Jesuit High School New Orleans, and the library administrators of Spring Hill College in Mobile, Alabama, for allowing me access to the many documents stored at each institution.

In addition to thanking family, friends, colleagues, and archivists, I would like to express my sincere appreciation for Ray Brown and his diligent collection of facts related to colleges and universities that have closed, merged, or changed their names. Ray has been an excellent friend, a fathomless well of knowledge, and a much appreciated fellow researcher of institutional closure and survival. From Ray's online database, I was able to locate former Jefferson College, now the Manresa House of Retreats in Convent, Louisiana, and its director Tim Murphy. Tim was kind enough to take a day off from his busy schedule to tour me through the beautiful buildings and grounds of Manresa. Tim not only guided me through the well-preserved college buildings but also introduced me to Jesuit education and Ignatian spirituality. Tim, I had no idea that this book would be the result of our conversations, but I believe you knew that St. Ignatius Loyola and Manresa would be a part of it and so they are. At the conclusion of this study, I was allowed to participate in a silent retreat at Manresa. It was one of the most reflective times in my life and allowed me the chance to immerse myself in *The Spiritual Exercises*. I am forever grateful for this experience. To the staff and priests of Manresa, I offer my thanks.

Last, but certainly not least, I want to give a very special thanks to my pup Jolie. Jolie has made me laugh, comforted me, and has been a constant companion from the first words put down in this book to the completion of its final chapter. There are other dogs in this world, but, Jolie, you are the best.

SACRIFICE
and
SURVIVAL

Introduction

Defining Survival

> It is false to assume that there is a one-to-one correlation between what goes on in the university and the needs of outside society. . . . All the institutions of society are partly functional and partly antiquated, vestigial, or even frankly "dysfunctional." This is because they all have a history and a life of their own, and their response to outside pressure is consequently imperfect, stumbling, tardy, even reactive.
>
> —Lawrence Stone

How does a university survive? What factors keep the lights on in one college and permanently closes the doors at another? As Stone mentions above, a university has its own history and life, and it possesses the ability to perform functionally or act in such a manner as to be considered outdated and incongruent with its surroundings. But what foundational catalytic factors affect its ability to survive? Consider the history of American higher education. The social communities surrounding American colleges and universities have played a historic role in their progress and survival. From the colonies of the New World to our present society, external social pressures have influenced the development of these institutions. These societal pressures, such as external perceptions of administrative decisions or the perceived need for practical job-related curricula, take a distinct form when influencing religiously affiliated colleges and universities, and more specifically, Catholic institutions of higher education in the American South. The religious identity and mission of these colleges and universities functions as foundational concepts that influence interactions between internal and external social environs to directly impact survival. Among the most enduring Catholic colleges and universities are those administered by the Society of Jesus, also known as the Jesuits. This religious organization manages an expansive global network of educational institutions with a distinct identity and mission. Jesuits have experienced the failure and success of their colleges and universities worldwide. Within this system, some Jesuit colleges have closed, while others have managed to survive with their Jesuit identity intact and continue to exist even in largely Protestant regions.

The interaction between Jesuit institutions and their surrounding social milieu presents a unique opportunity to examine the effects of institutional identity, mission, and environment on higher education survival. These factors raise a series of questions: Can the institutional identity and mission of Jesuit colleges and universities affect their ability to survive? What responses to historically hostile or hospitable social environments contributed to the survival of particular Jesuit institutions of higher education? How does the relationship between a Jesuit college or university and its surrounding social environment contribute to its ability to persist? Ultimately, can an examination of these factors, in tandem with historic examples, help explain how identity and mission contribute to the survival of institutions as they subsist in surrounding societies? With these questions in mind, this book will illustrate how concepts of institutional identity and mission, regarding Jesuit colleges and universities in the New Orleans Province of the Society of Jesus, had, and can have, catalytic effects on the interaction between local populations and an institution of higher education, otherwise known as the "town and gown," resulting in the death or survival of a college or university.

This book, therefore, is an exploration of foundational issues relating to the origin, development, and sustainability of southern Jesuit colleges and universities. The following chapters trace the roots of Jesuit education from the rise of Ignatius Loyola in the mid-sixteenth century through the European development of the Society of Jesus, Jesuit educational identity and mission, the migration of Jesuits to colonial New Orleans, the expulsion of Jesuits by papal mandate, the reorganization of Jesuit education, the attempt to establish a network of Jesuit colleges and universities across the South, and the final closure of all but two southern Jesuit colleges and a set of high schools.

This study also explores the effects of several events, including the Galveston Hurricane of 1900, yellow fever, Georgia floods, devastating fires, the American Civil War, the expansion of New Orleans due to the Cotton Centennial Exposition of 1884, curricular adaptations, ties between "town and gown," as well as anti-Catholic and anti-Jesuit sentiment as the Society of Jesus pushed forward to create a system of southern institutions. This work ultimately argues that institutional identity and mission critically impacted the survival of Jesuit education in the American South from the 1830s through the early twentieth century.

In general, there is little research that directly illustrates how institutions of higher education, with a strong mission and established identity, endure within an ever-changing societal context that may or may not be supportive. Literature concerning institutional and societal interactions indicates that the relationship between higher education and society does indeed have a direct effect on institutional progress.[1] The existing published research also notes that colleges and universities respond to changing societies,[2] and when external forces compromise the identity of an institution, members of the institutional organization respond actively. Even more disappointing is the dearth of literature that explains the evolution of the New Orleans Province system of higher education. It is the goal of this book to illustrate how concepts that influence institutional closure and survival affected the failure of some Jesuit colleges, the survival of others, and the redevelopment of the Jesuit educational system of the New Orleans Province.

It is easy to locate single institutional histories that chronicle the difficulties and ultimate success of large public universities. Books such as *To Foster Knowledge: A History of the University of Tennessee, 1794–1970* by James Montgomery, Stanley Folmsbee, and Lee Greene or *History of the University of Georgia* by Thomas Walter Reed serve as popular examples of institutional history. Even so, there is little research that examines the survival of an entire system of higher education. One such example is *The California Idea and American Higher Education: 1850 to the 1960 Master Plan* by John Aubrey Douglas. Douglas admits that there are few studies that detail the history of a statewide higher education system.[3] However, Douglas's study does not address how a singular group of individuals attempt to create a system of unified educational institutions that spans a large geographic region encompassing several states. Beyond literary examples of institutional and system histories, there is minute literature that details the interaction between social environs and institutional failure. However, some work has been accomplished regarding survival tactics for struggling colleges. One such book, *Cautionary Tales: Strategy Lessons from Struggling Colleges* by Alice Brown and contributors, details the attempts of several college administrations as they confront institutional decline.[4] Even with the publication of *Cautionary Tales*, literature is lacking that tracks the progression of Catholic and Jesuit higher education in the American South and how the relationship between Jesuit educational identity and mission and the southern social environment affected the survival of this unique form of Catholic education.

This lack of literature, concerning the history and survival of southern Jesuit colleges and universities, led my research to a string of intriguing resources. The first is an electronic database titled *List of Colleges and Universities that Have Closed, Merged, or Changed Their Names* created by Ray Brown, director for institutional advancement at Westminster College in Missouri. Brown maintains the database and divides relevant information according to state.[5] Prior to Brown's work, two studies were published regarding closed colleges. The first is Donald Tewksbury's 1932 survey of institutional movement known as *The Founding of American Colleges and Universities Before the Civil War* and the second is Colin B. Burke's 1982 book *American College Populations: A Test of the Traditional View*.[6] Burke critiques Tewksbury's text as insufficient and argues that the record and analysis of closed colleges has been underreported. Burke attempts to fill this gap by providing copious, although admittedly incomplete, lists of closed institutions and the reasons behind their demise.[7] Building from Tewksbury to Brown via Burke, one can get a sense of the enormity of data concerning closed colleges and universities throughout the United States. Following Burke, Alice Brown's book, published in 2012, highlights the rate at which colleges are closing. According to Brown: "Current estimates of the number of colleges closing annually range from three to five; many more are struggling to change to avoid closure."[8] While perusing the southern states via the aforementioned studies, I noticed a relatively high number of closed Catholic colleges (approximately forty-six from the southern region of the United States: Alabama, Arkansas, Florida, Georgia, Louisiana, Mississippi, North Carolina, South Carolina, Tennessee, Texas, and Virginia).[9] Such a high number of closures related to the Catholic Church led me to question the foundational nature of such institutions and whether the very identity of said colleges could be detrimental in regions that historically have not supported the Catholic faith.

Following an in-depth examination of Ray Brown's database, I found that the physical campus of a defunct Catholic college in Louisiana, Jefferson College in Convent, Louisiana, still stands. Now known as the Manresa House of Retreats, this former college turned spiritual retreat has been owned and operated by the Society of Jesus since 1931. Jefferson College, founded in 1831 as a college for the sons of wealthy Louisiana planters, has a unique history.[10] Situated on the Mississippi River between Baton Rouge and New Orleans, the college held four separate administrations, each with its own identity and mission. The first, second, and third administrations ended in failure and temporary closure of the college. The Society of Mary (Marists) governed the final years of Jefferson College until the administration's collapse and subsequent campus closure in 1927.[11] These administrational closures are especially fascinating because of their separate and unique time periods all within one physical campus and geographic location.

After reviewing Manresa's website, I contacted the retreat's administrative office and was offered the chance to tour the facility. On a rainy day, I drove from Baton Rouge to an oak-lined portion of Louisiana's River Road where Manresa stands reflecting Greek revival architecture infused with Catholic symbols. Tim Murphy, the director of Manresa, escorted me through the halls of the old college. The conversation quickly turned from the history of Jefferson College to the nature of spiritual retreats, the Catholic ideals of spirituality and education, the Jesuit perspective, and finally the specifics of Jesuit higher education.

This experience at former Jefferson College laid the groundwork for this study. In one location I was allowed to tour a defunct college that had experienced four administrative failures, the last of which occurred under Catholic management. Following the tour of Manresa, I turned to the Jesuit archives of the New Orleans Province and discovered a variety of documents germane to the historic development and closure of several Jesuit colleges and universities throughout the southern states. It was here that I discovered the Society of Jesus's educational documents and spiritual material, which provide a framework that governs their institutions' identity and mission and influences the way in which their colleges and universities interact with society. As such, I began to investigate concepts of institutional identity and mission, as well as survival methods of colleges and universities, all within the context of the southern United States. This book, therefore, will describe the history and evolution of southern Jesuit higher education and hypothesizes that the identity and mission of Jesuit colleges and universities directly affected institutional survival or failure via social relationships.

Further exploration of literature pertaining to Jesuit education illustrates the instructional and administrative methods of the Society of Jesus and the continued existence of Jesuit higher education in the United States as well as the South. Archival data revealed that southern expectations, originating from middle- and upper-class individuals, as demonstrated by the societal want to attain professional job-related higher education, along with sentiments of anti-Catholicism and anti-Jesuitism from Protestant organizations, created a challenging environment for Jesuits who wished to provide a system of sustainable Catholic liberal arts colleges for regional students. At the same time, Jesuits forged alliances with other religious orders, maintained colleges for men only (female religious orders such as the Ursulines or the Sisters of the Sacred Heart educated women), and joined accrediting associations to aid in the development and enhanced legitimacy of southern Jesuit higher education. In addition, the Society of Jesus, like their southern clerical and lay peers, had to contend with a geographic region imbued with racial tension, slavery, and segregation. As a result, all Jesuit colleges, until the formal integration of Loyola University New Orleans in 1950 and Spring Hill College in 1954, barred admittance to African Americans.[12] However, students from South America, Mexico, and Cuba were granted admittance to some southern Jesuit institutions such as St. Charles College, the College of the Immaculate Conception, and Spring Hill College.[13] Even so, skin color was important, and immigrant students, whose skin was too dark, were prohibited from enrolling.[14] R. Bentley Anderson, in his book *Black, White, and Catholic: New Orleans Interracialism, 1947–1956*, discusses the historic exclusion of African Americans from Catholic education in New Orleans and the South. While Anderson addresses educational exclusion and the fight for religious integration, he also carefully unravels the role Jesuit educators played in the New Orleans civil rights movement.[15] Though racial ideologies permeated southern and religious mindsets, the Jesuit institutions featured in this study enrolled white male students and excluded both female and black students. As such, the focus of this study is primarily concerned with the religious administrations of southern Jesuit colleges and universities in regard to their persistence and addresses the role of Jesuit and Catholic educational identity, educational mission, and the interaction between heavily Protestant populations and Catholic educational viability. So how did this predominantly Protestant ideological climate affect the liberal arts educational system of the Society of Jesus? How did the Society of Jesus sustain institutions of higher education consistent with Jesuit identity and mission in a region typified by periods of anti-Jesuitism, and what decisions were made in order to maintain an educational presence in the American South?

In their constant endeavor to fulfill an expansive educational mission, members of the Society of Jesus founded St. Charles College in Grande Coteau, Louisiana, in 1837 as part of the Mission of Lyon.[16] Later, in 1847, they took charge of Spring Hill College in Mobile, Alabama (founded in 1830 by the first bishop of Mobile, Michael Portier).[17] The order established a territory and engaged in educational pursuits that covered a geographic territory from Galveston, Texas, to Tampa, Florida, that spread northward into Georgia. The region became known as the New Orleans Mission in 1880 and later the New Orleans Province in 1907, encompassing much of the Gulf South, including New Orleans and Mobile, Alabama.[18] The order's higher educational advancement continued in Mobile and grew throughout Louisiana until the start of the Civil War in 1861. Unlike many southern institutions, Jesuit colleges managed to remain open during the war by promoting their identity and mission via preparatory departments. In the years that followed, the Society of Jesus delegated its efforts, further developing the order's southern institutions of higher education. Ultimately, the Jesuits of the South added professional programs of study to their liberal holistic curricula to meet growing demands for agricultural and industrial change in southern higher education. This institutional expansion, conjoined with the growing need for curricular revision, led to a questioning of the order's educational purposes in the South. In an effort to maintain the Jesuit nature of their colleges and universities, as well as meet the needs of changing social environments, the Society of Jesus issued a set of harsh decisions to adapt and fortify its southern system of higher education in the early twentieth-century.

Faced with a low population of priests and brothers in the southern states, low student enrollments, institutional competition, and changing curricular foci, the Jesuits of the New Orleans Province embarked on a series of educational projects that would revise their network of colleges and universities and ultimately reduce their presence to a more manageable pair of institutions: Loyola University New Orleans and Spring Hill College in Mobile. Considering archival data and existing literature regarding institutional identity, mission, societal relationships, and survival, this book chronicles a lineage of singular institutions and societal events that forced the Society of Jesus to sacrifice several southern colleges and adapt southern Jesuit higher education in order to promote the survival of their regional educational practices.

The historical cases presented in this book relate to a series of defunct and existing Jesuit colleges in the New Orleans Province. These cases, which include St. Charles College, Grand Coteau, Louisiana; St. Mary's University, Galveston,

Institution	Founding	Closure
St. Charles College, Grand Coteau, Louisiana	1837	1922
Spring Hill College, Mobile, Alabama	1830	Currently open
The College of the Immaculate Conception, New Orleans, Louisiana	1849	1912
St. Mary's University, Galveston, Texas	1854	1922
College of the Sacred Heart, Augusta, Georgia	1900	1917
Loyola College, New Orleans, Louisiana	1904	1912
Loyola University, New Orleans, Louisiana	1912	Currently open

Texas; the College of the Sacred Heart, Augusta, Georgia; the College of the Immaculate Conception, New Orleans, Louisiana; Loyola College, New Orleans, Louisiana; Spring Hill College, Mobile, Alabama; and Loyola University New Orleans, provide a construct for researching and understanding how Jesuit institutional identity, mission, and societal relations affect survival. Also, pertinent information regarding Jefferson College in Convent, Louisiana; the College of Saints Peter and Paul in Baton Rouge, Louisiana; St. Johns College in Shreveport, Louisiana; and Sacred Heart College in Tampa, Florida, is included to illustrate various transformational decisions made by the southern Jesuits. Throughout each college or university case, the identity and mission of the Society of Jesus, as well as influential interactions with local social environs, is apparent.

Primary documents, used to construct each case were often inscribed with Jesuit symbols and phrases. At the top or bottom of many letters, journal entries, or handwritten reports composed by Jesuit priests and brothers are the letters *AMDG*. These letters stand for the motto of the Society of Jesus, *Ad Majorem De Gloriam*, translated as "For the Greater Glory of God."[19] The identifiable Jesuit seal that encloses the letters *IHS* (a third-century symbolic monogram of the name of Jesus Christ)[20] encircled by the sun's rays adorns many books and journals on Jesuit education and spirituality. Even the physical campuses of defunct and existing Jesuit colleges are ornamented with such symbols. This constant iconographic representation of the Society of Jesus's identity, along with the Jesuit theme *magis*, meaning "to do more,"[21] is ubiquitous. So too was the ever-present mission of the Society of Jesus. The *Constitutions of the Society of Jesus* provide a premise for establishing Jesuit colleges and their religious purpose. Finally, the Jesuit method of instruction, the *Ratio Studiorum*, provides an even greater insight into the mission of Jesuit colleges as it concerns instructional principles. All of this information and representation is elucidated in the following chapters to better illustrate the individual college and university cases.

Identity, Mission, Society, and Survival

An undeniable fact about colleges and universities is that they are located within concentric circles of society: city, state, country.[22] Jeffrey Pfeffer and Gerald Salancik explore this concept in their book *The External Control of Organizations: A Resource Dependence Prospective.* Pfeffer and Salancik explain that societal environs react to organizations such as educational institutions, are not always dependable due to ideological changes, and have the potential to constrain an organization's ability to survive via resource dependence. These societal changes and dependences create tension when ideological differences between society and a college or university do not coincide.[23] Societal ideals develop alongside changing societal demands, and the pressure to provide externally perceived "useful" education forces higher education to reexamine instructional practices and respond accordingly.[24] Such reexaminations influence the success of a college, university, or academic department. Jesuit colleges and universities in the New Orleans Province, like any other physical form of higher education, existed within social surroundings that influenced their ability to garner resources. Negative external perceptions about an institution might hinder the transaction of resources, thus hindering institutional success; however, does *success* mean the same as *survival*? For this study, it does not.

Institutional *success* may determine an institution's standing, performance, or (in some cases) the influence of effective leadership.[25] These aspects may be connected with survival but *survival*, for this study, relates entirely to a college's or university's ability to remain operational and in existence. Existing literature concerning institutional success does not directly address how an organization with a developed identity and mission, such as a college administered by the Society of Jesus, adapts to survive given environmental influences. Also, literature pertaining to organizational identity rarely examines the concept of whole institutional identity, especially in regard to institutional survival. Rather, identity is presented as an internal cultural force developed by individuals within an institution that influences success but not survival.[26]

Indeed, as this study shows, surrounding social environs do have a direct impact on a college or university as a result of perceptions concerning an institution's identity and purpose. Despite societal and institutional changes, colleges and universities maintain some form of relationship with surrounding societies (negative or positive). As a result, interactions with social environs have significant effects on the development of an institution of higher education.[27] Unfortunately, most research regarding societal effects on higher education is conducted with a focus on leadership or resource exchange and has precluded the possible effects of identity and mission on the survival of colleges and universities. In other studies, it has been proposed that the maintenance, expansion, and beautification of college facilities play a large role in institutional success.[28] Still others suggest that institutional leadership molds the adaptive processes of an institution in an attempt to promote longevity.[29] According to Pfeffer and Salancik, the key component to organizational survival is the ability to acquire and maintain resources, not foundational issues that influence societal relationships such as identity and mission.[30] Pfeffer and Salancik may be correct; however, what causes resource acquisition to become difficult? Are there foundational issues that hinder resource exchange? No study has gone so far as to question the role of institutional identity and mission in the acquisition of resources, and thereby college and university survival. James Bess and Jay Dee come close by stating that institutions of higher education operate as complex systems engaging in administrative and academic functions to fulfill their missions.[31] Bess and Dee's claim aids in the establishment of the key question of this study: Can institutional identity and mission affect survival? Given this research perspective, it is therefore pertinent to examine a series of colleges and universities whose well-established and externally perceived identity and mission affected their survivability. Such is the case with the Jesuit colleges and universities in this book.

While attempting to understand factors that affect institutional survival, it is important in this case to define aspects of institutional identity, mission, and the interaction between an institution of higher education and the surrounding social environment. Generally, institutional *mission*, in regard to higher education, relates to the overall purpose and function of a college or university. Mission manifests itself in goals, purpose, and educational products, such as the granting of degrees, community outreach, and academic service. On the other hand, institutional *identity* refers to a shared set of ideals that represent the whole organization.[32] These ideals can include the institution's mission, physical expressions, and symbols that contribute to a juxtaposition of attributes that culminate in characteristics and formative beliefs upon which internal individuals agree and institutional leaders support.[33] For a Jesuit institution, these symbols may include previously mentioned mottoes such as *AMDG* or the seal of the Society of Jesus. Together, identity and mission define what an institution wants for itself and how it will interact with its environment. Likewise, the identity and mission perceived by outsiders may or may not be congruent with an institution's perception of itself. Institutional identity and mission, therefore, collectively define and provide governing concepts concerning what an institution *is* and *does*. While regarding identity and mission as having an effect on survival, we must also consider "town and gown" relationships, which will be defined below. Ultimately, how surrounding social environments perceive institutional identity and mission had a direct impact on southern Jesuit higher education.

Regarding *institutional identity*, there is much research pertaining to its definition. Penelope Eckert and Etienne Wenger define institutional identity as the understanding and enactment of organizational practices in conjunction with their external perception.[34] Dennis A. Gioia, Majken Schultz, and Kevin G. Corely add to this definition with their notion that identity is a construct defined by the members of an organization, linkage to core values, history, traditions, and the potential to resist change.[35] Also, the identity of an organization shapes the way acting members engage in institutional mission. Institutional identity can serve as the justification for managerial strategies and tactics aimed at acquiring financial, human, and/or material resources.[36] Identity, above all, is the central, enduring, and distinctive character of an organization.[37] Ultimately, researchers agree that identity is a construct of internal members, external perception, and is established in order to promote the purpose of an institution such as a college or university.

S. Albert and D. A. Whetten identify three key concepts related to the establishment of institutional identity. The first refers to the features that contribute to the essence or foundational concepts of an organization. Members of an institution must believe that these features are essential for organizational subsistence. The second concept is distinctiveness, which refers to the factors that distinguish an institution from its competitors and justify its existence. The final identity concept is temporal continuity. Characteristics of an institution that have withstood the test of time enhance identity permanence and represent associated members' commitment to overarching purposes.[38] These three components are important to consider when analyzing the surviving Jesuit institutions of Loyola University New Orleans and Spring Hill College. Faculty and staff of Loyola University and Spring Hill College consist of Jesuit and non-Jesuit members (fourteen Jesuits work at Loyola, thirteen at Spring Hill);[39] however, all employed are encouraged to follow Jesuit principles governing the administration and instructional techniques of both institutions. This attempt to adhere to Jesuit educational philosophy creates an internal environment that is discernibly different from other colleges or universities. These features at Loyola University and Spring Hill College are based on the same educational principles established by the Society of Jesus during the administration of their first colleges in the sixteenth century.[40]

At times, institutional identity may be characterized by competing dualities. In Jesuit higher education, a fundamental identity duality would be that of the university and the church.[41] Jesuit institutions must maintain their educational practices while supplying religious services to students, staff, and faculty. This duality can create disunity with surrounding environs. If this duality runs contrary to the surrounding environment, the institution may react assertively to protect itself, thereby ensuring the continued sustainability of the institution's identity within the larger societal milieu. In fact, the loss or deterioration of an institution's identity can threaten survival by weakening supportive social networks and decreasing the reception of critical resources.[42] External pressures that threaten institutional identity may increase the likelihood that institutional members will explicitly concentrate on maintaining a continuity of identity while making adaptations for survival.[43] When environmental pressures arise, institutional identity must be made explicit, reevaluated, or adapted in order to sustain an institution;[44] however, as Gioia, Schultz, and Corely state, "the notion of an identity that is enduring implies that identity remains the same over time—that it has permanency. An identity with a sense of continuity, however, is one that shifts in its interpretation and meaning while retaining labels of 'core' beliefs and values that extend over time and context."[45] Because institutions of higher education must adapt or close in response to changing environs, there is a need to study and better understand the role of institutional identity, particularly as colleges and universities deal with tumultuous environments.[46]

Like identity, *institutional mission* has a great deal of literature devoted to it. John Scott, in his work on the transformation of university missions, relates that a clear understanding of the history of an institution and its mission can benefit policy makers and legislators.[47] It is also important to note that institutional mission is a separate concept from the publically disseminated college or university mission statement. In a 1979 issue of *Science*, Richard Chait adapted an article from the *Chronicle of Higher Education* in an effort to inform readers about the nature of college mission statements. Reasons listed for the development of mission statements included the need for a public declaration of institutional purpose, direction for future institutional goals, and the fulfillment of regional accreditation standards. According to Chait, however, most mission statements remain overly global and rhetorical, and they can be exaggerated during times of institutional identity crisis. The actual mission of an institution is greater than the mission statement. Institutions are driven by and adapt to the market, and predominantly, "the mission will always be, in some sense, survival." Chait concludes that "the best way to survive, even flourish, may be to worry a little less about mission statements and a little more about actions."[48] If anything, a mission statement is a publicly consumable token of an institution's projected purpose; however, the actual mission of an institution is more expansive and encompasses the history, strategic goals, and actions of a college or university.

Because published statements do not always reflect the actual mission of a college or university, this study does not rely on mission statements in the construction of historical cases. Carrying out the purpose and goals that align with an institution's actual mission is crucial to the longevity of a college or university.[49] Therefore, mission statements alone are not effective enough to promote institutional survival; they simply act as a point of public reference. Rather, the purpose, goals, objectives, beliefs, and values of an institution are the driving force behind institutional mission.[50] Nancey Fjortoft and John C. Smart argue that an institution with a highly distinctive mission will strive to adhere to the beliefs and goals connected with said mission; however, such a mission could also be a detriment to the overall institution. Institutional mission harbors the possibility of creating difficulties as a college or university considers adapting to changing external environments. Fjortoft and Smart state that, "in effect, institutions that limit themselves to choices that are consistent with their agreed upon mission may not be able to adapt fully to changing environmental conditions."[51] As such, a college or university with an overly stringent and rigid mission may have difficulty adapting to changing social environments.

In order to better understand the mission of Jesuit higher education, we must analyze those documents that elicit the purpose behind the formation and existence of a Jesuit college or university. According to H. G. Good, textbooks and other forms of written material that describe the instructional practices of an educational institution are invaluable.[52] Good's idea takes shape in this study, which relies on formative Jesuit texts. For example, the *Constitutions of the Society of Jesus* include an annotated section on the identity, mission, and administrational practices of Jesuit colleges. Also, the *Ratio Studiorum* provides a prescribed methodology for teaching in Jesuit institutions. These documents are extremely important when attempting to establish the practices of historically Jesuit institutions in the southern states, but it is the use of primary sources and archival materials that serves as the chief data component in this study.

Archival data examined for this historical study reveal that each Jesuit college's or university's identity and mission played a sizeable role in its establishment and administration. The seminal texts of the Society of Jesus also indicate that, in addition to institutional identity and mission, Jesuit colleges and universities must consider their surrounding environments and adapt accordingly. In *The Constitutions of the Society of Jesus*, Ignatius Loyola writes that "since the Society endeavors to aid its fellowmen not merely by traveling through diverse regions but also by residing continually in some places, for example, in the houses and colleges, it is important to have learned the ways in which souls can be helped in those places, in order to use that selection of these ways which is possible for the glory of God our Lord."[53] This quote illustrates the importance of understanding environments in which Jesuit colleges and universities have been established. Furthermore, I argue that the guiding identity and mission of an institution can influence communal relationships that determine how well an institution functions within a given place. Pfeffer and Salancik state that "what happens in an organization is not only a function of the organization, its structure, its leadership, its procedures, or its goals. What happens is also a consequence of the environment and the particular contingencies and constraints deriving from that environment."[54] I take this concept further by illustrating that the Society of Jesus understood this connection long before any modern research would indicate.

As an institution attempts to adapt to the needs of its environment, the mission may be shaped by external factors causing alterations in internal programs; however, these developments may spawn disunity rather than a focused institution driven by a unified purpose. Paul L. Dressel points out that an overarching institutional mission may aid in the development of objectives and determines the clientele that an institution wishes to serve. Nevertheless, in order to remain consistent with the institutional mission yet survive within a larger social environment, a supportive leadership and rallying faculty must buttress the mission of a college or university in order to maintain solidarity.[55]

As has been previously indicated, the relationship between a college or university and its surrounding environment, also known as "town and gown," plays an essential role in an institution's survival. The institution's ability to respond to the demands of the contiguous social climate allows for progression and survival, but these demands can conflict with the purpose of an institution and can prevent a college or university from achieving its established goals. Therefore, institutions cannot both respond to every demand and remain true to their purpose. Complete responsiveness to all environmental demands would cause the institution to fail in time.[56] As presented by the Academy of Arts and Sciences, "universities are expected to engage in a vast number of public service activities; in particular, they are urged to respond to the pressing needs of the wider community in which they are located."[57]

By neglecting to provide some form of public service that addresses social demands, an institution of higher education will fail to form a positive town and gown relationship, which could result in tension between the institution and its social surroundings. The failure to develop and maintain a lasting communal relationship can be attributed to a lack of conflict resolution regarding the outlook and behavior of the two groups: college and community.[58] Edward Shils argues that universities need to attend to the affairs of surrounding communities but must first attend to their own intellectual responsibilities, thus maintaining an autonomous identity and mission.[59] With the need to maintain a unique status as an autonomous college or university, survival for many institutions depends on the ability to acquire support from like-minded individuals and organizations that agree with the overall purpose of the institution.[60] Colleges and universities, public or private, have conformed to national regulations issued by central governments. With the cost of research and teaching high, colleges and universities rely on government subsidies, which in turn make educational institutions responsive to political forces for financial support.[61] A method of conforming to national standards is through the admission of an institution into an accrediting body or application for a state charter. This process is known as legitimacy.

Pfeffer and Salancik explain that organizations are mere components of larger social systems and depend on those surrounding systems for their continued existence. In order to justify an organization's existence to the larger social environment, it must become "legitimate" in the view of the environment. This process of becoming legitimate is bound to social norms and values and does not always correlate with economic viability.[62] However, the ability of an organization to become legitimate via regional means of accreditation or certification can improve an institution's standing in the surrounding environment. Overall, externally perceived legitimacy, at some level, is required for the survival of any institution.[63] Governing bodies outside of an institution control this conferred status of legitimacy, and it becomes a survival issue when an institution is performing in a manner disapproved of by the local social environment. When organizational legitimacy is a problem for survival, a college or university may adapt to expectations placed upon it by a larger organization or achieve legitimacy through the approval of the surrounding environment. According to Pfeffer and Salancik, "while organizational survival is enhanced by legitimacy, it is also enhanced by economic viability in the case of private organizations."[64] An example of legitimacy would be the application and admittance of institutions of higher education to accrediting bodies such as the Southern Association of Colleges and Schools (SACS). Such accreditation standards as those issued by SACS provide an excellent point of termination for this study: When the two surviving college cases presented in this book (Loyola University New Orleans and Spring Hill College) received SACS accreditation, they were recognized as possessing legitimate forms of curricula required to operate and maintain a thriving form of higher education in the purview of secular peer institutions. As such, this study ends following the accreditation of the aforementioned institutions.

In addition to understanding institutional survival and the development of colleges and universities administered by the Society of Jesus, this research is a response to a call for expanded historical research concerning southern higher education and how it has been influenced by southern ideologies. The historian Thomas G. Dyer states that "scholars have zealously studied virtually every aspect of southern history. Thus when a topic seems underexploited or, in the parlance of contemporary politics, underdeveloped, it should come something of a surprise to those who study the region. Such is true of the history of higher education in the South. Although much has been written about episodes or cases, the field has not been assiduously studied . . . scholars have not focused their energies on attempting to understand this complex and important aspect of the region's past."[65] This study seeks to address a portion of Dyer's claim via the analysis of southern Jesuit institutions of higher education. This study goes further, not only in examining southern colleges and universities in light of redeveloping social environments but also in examining the pertinence of institutional identity and mission as they relate to higher education subsistence. Such exploration leads to a fuller understanding of how higher education must remain responsive to society while enduring as an autonomous entity.

This conceptual overview regarding institutional identity, mission, and town and gown relationships illustrates how the aforementioned factors mesh and affect a college or university's ability to function and thrive. Survival can be influenced by issues relating to leadership, resource attainment, and institutional maintenance, but a college's identity, its mission, and how it interacts with society must be examined as catalysts that have the ability to restrict supportive resources, explain the reasons behind administrative decisions, and determine how an institution persists or why a college or university closes its doors. The cases presented in this study depict the institutional histories of seven Jesuit colleges and universities in the American South in order to illustrate the catalytic, and sometimes detrimental, affect of identity, mission, and town and gown relationships. Ultimately, this study demonstrates that through individual and collective case analysis, as well as the use of a conceptual framework comprising formative organizational elements, we can generate a historical interpretation that attempts to explain the closure of several southern Jesuit institutions and the adaptation and reconfiguration of higher education within the New Orleans Province of the Society of Jesus. Generally speaking, this study allows educational researchers and administrators a greater insight into the early and effective stages that may cause a college or university to fail or survive.

1
Tracing the Society of Jesus and Jesuit Higher Education

> [The] fruit sought in colleges may be spread more universally through the branches taught, the number of persons attending, and the degrees which are conferred in order that the recipients may be able to teach with authority elsewhere what they have learned well in these universities of the Society for the glory to God our Lord.
>
> —Saint Ignatius Loyola

In order to fully understand how institutional identity, mission, and town and gown relationships affect the survival of Jesuit colleges and universities, it is important to become familiar with the history of the Society of Jesus, the Jesuit method of instruction, and the order's expansion into the American South. In his book *Contending with Modernity: Catholic Higher Education in the Twentieth Century*, Philip Gleason provides a justification for understanding Jesuit history and education: "Without understanding Catholic educators' religious and intellectual convictions we cannot possibly understand what they did or why they did it."[1] Such is the case with the Society of Jesus and its founder Ignatius Loyola.

To better understand the life and educational actions of Ignatius Loyola, I turned to Thomas Clancy. Father Clancy (1923–2009), former Jesuit provincial for the New Orleans Province, professor of history, vice president of Loyola University New Orleans, and archivist for the New Orleans Province, passed away while this study was in its formative stages. His writing on the Society of Jesus is formidable. He and his surviving colleagues would most likely agree that Ignatius Loyola is at times a mystery. In his book *An Introduction to Jesuit Life: The Constitutions and History through 435 Years*, Clancy makes an illustrative statement about the life of Loyola:

> Beginning in the last years of the nineteenth century there has been an enormous amount of scholarly production and popular diffusion concerning Ignatius' life and ideas. Indeed he might be said to be among the dozen most thoroughly investigated humans in history. . . . A veritable library of learned and popular books has been published by dedicated and erudite authors. But the enigma still remains. Loyola has never been a popular saint.

> The faithful have found other Jesuits more appealing. . . . One of the most delightful things about visiting the Province of Guipuzcoa in the Spanish Basque Country is to discover the extraordinary popularity of the saint among the people of his native country.
>
> For the rest he remains an enigmatic figure.[2]

Ignatius's position as the founder of the Society of Jesus adds a crucial layer to this study. The life and history of Ignatius Loyola, his spiritual mission, educational experiences, and administrative identity, are important to consider when examining any portion of Jesuit higher education. The details provided here are not presented as an interpretation of his life but rather to provide a historical framework for the formation and spread of the Society of Jesus through the establishment of the New Orleans Mission and later Province.

Ignatius was the last of thirteen children and grew up at the end of the Moslem wars, a time of Spanish discovery.[3] Names such as Columbus and Cortez were on the lips of well-to-do Spaniards. In his youth, Ignatius studied the practices of the gentry and nobles.[4] When he was approximately fifteen years old, Ignatius was sent by his family to study as a page in the court of Don Juan Valasquez de Cueller and entered a life of both military training and clerical studies. Ignatius prided himself on his martial expertise and felt that he was fit for "more" than the duties of a country pastor.[5]

In 1512, at the Battle of Pamplona, Ignatius utilized his military training and fought in defense of Spain; however, a cannonball shattered Ignatius's right leg and wounded his left.[6] When he was discovered lying in his own blood, the French honored him as a gallant foe, had their doctors operate on his shattered leg, and sent Ignatius home to the Castle of Loyola.[7] As Ignatius recuperated from his injuries, he read books concerning the lives of Christ and the saints.[8] These books had an immense effect on Ignatius and produced in him a keen awareness of the importance of religious study that fanned the flames of his spiritual devotion.[9] Once well enough, he journeyed to a monastery in Montserrat in hopes of making a pilgrimage to Jerusalem. Ignatius made a general confession and replaced his noble clothing with that of a beggar. Ignatius's pilgrimage to the Holy Land was delayed due to plague, and he remained in Montserrat, where he was to be treated by God "like a schoolboy."[10] During the following eleven months, Ignatius rejected the worldliness of his former life, helped the sick, attended daily Mass, spent hours on his knees in prayer, and often retreated to a cave in Manresa near the monastery. Here, Ignatius produced *The Spiritual Exercises*, his first and most influential writing that established the identity of his future religious order.[11]

The Spiritual Exercises are a series of meditations, prayers, and examinations of personal conscience for the purpose of determining God's will for an individual's life and are divided into what Ignatius called "weeks."[12] According to James Brodrick, "the central aim and purpose of *The Spiritual Exercises* is to bring the mind and heart of the person who makes a retreat into ever closer conformity with the mind and heart of Christ, so that out of love of Christ and a desire to be more like Him, they may learn to prefer and embrace poverty with Jesus Christ poor, rather than riches; shame and insults with Jesus Christ reproached and insulted, rather than honours; the reputation of a fool with Jesus Christ mocked and scorned, rather than a great name for wisdom among men."[13] In essence, the intention of this spiritual contemplation is to create a closer conformity with the mind of Christ.[14] Through this process, a person chooses of his or her own volition to embrace Christ through a closer self-educated and meditative understanding of Jesus. As such, *The Spiritual Exercises* remain key to the spiritual and educational apostolate of the Society of Jesus. In fact, it is within *The Spiritual Exercises* that Ignatius fully develops the principle of the *magis* (more) and the inclination that he and others must pursue "more" for the glory of God.[15]

Departing Manresa, Ignatius traveled to Jerusalem and attempted to join the Franciscan order. Despite his efforts, the Franciscans could not accept Ignatius due to financial hardships.[16] As a result, Ignatius traveled to Barcelona to further his own education. Ignatius studied grammar and Latin at a school in Barcelona under the guidance of Jerome Ardavalo. Learning alongside children, Ignatius convinced himself that through further studies he could become a useful instrument for God.[17] This formative experience shaped ideologies governing the earliest educational courses for young laymen in Jesuit colleges. From Barcelona, Ignatius traveled to the University of Alcala in 1526 where he studied dialects, physics, and theology. In 1528, he enrolled at the University of Paris. At the age of thirty-seven, Ignatius excelled in Latin and devoured humanist philosophy; however, he believed that all this study was nothing unless its purpose was to glorify God through service for others.[18]

On August 15, 1534, Ignatius and six other men gathered in a church at Montmartre, attended Mass, and formed their own religious society founded on the life and teachings of Jesus. Other than the connection forged by their desire to lead a religious life, these men were also connected by their similar liberal arts educations. Ignatius and his fellows had completed multiple levels of college education. Ignatius himself had received a Bachelor of Arts in 1532, a Licentiate of Arts in 1533, and a Master of Arts in 1534.[19] His studies in the liberal arts shaped the method by which he and his fellow Jesuits would develop schools, colleges, and universities. Not only would the liberal arts be of chief import in European Jesuit colleges and universities but they would also spread to American Jesuit colleges and universities as well.

On September 14, 1540, Pope Paul III gave his approval for Ignatius and his followers to establish and call themselves the Company of Jesus in the Papal Bull *Regimini Militantis Ecclesiae*.[20] At the pontiff's request, the Company of Jesus, later known as the Society of Jesus, accommodated the pope's edicts, always serving for the greater glory of God. When asked to provide teachers for schools, the Society of Jesus answered the call. Ignatius and the other members of the order had received advanced degrees from prestigious European universities. This education was never intended to be an individual honor, but rather a means of helping the company do more for others. This apostolic endeavor allowed for another opportunity to pursue the driving force of the magis through education.[21] Ignatius later regarded education as a priority for the Society of Jesus; he deemed the work of education as a seminal tool in the salvation and perfection of students through the *cura personalis* (care of the whole person). These holistically trained students would go forth from the order's colleges and universities and spread Catholicism throughout society.[22]

With the religious identity and spiritual mission of education affixed to the order, Ignatius wrote the governing document that directed the religious missions of the Society of Jesus as well as the organization of Jesuit colleges and universities around the world in 1554, *The Constitutions of the Society of Jesus*.[23] This guiding book establishes the Jesuit identity, lays down crucial aspects regarding the mission and purpose behind different Jesuit apostolates, and governs the hierarchy and responsibilities of the Society of Jesus. In the *Constitutions*, Ignatius writes concerning Jesuit educational pursuits and their spiritual underpinnings:

> Through a motive of charity colleges are accepted and schools open to the public are maintained in them for the improvement of learning and in living not only for our own members but even more especially of those from outside the Society. Through this same motive the Society can extend itself to undertaking the works of universities, that through them this fruit sought in the colleges may be spread more universally through the branches taught, the number of persons attending, and the degrees which are conferred in order that the recipients may be able to teach with authority elsewhere what they have learned well in these universities of the Society for the glory of God.[24]

As Ignatius points out, institutions were not only built by but also given to the Society of Jesus fully constructed. Whole colleges were turned over to the order in hopes that the Jesuits would govern and strengthen instructional methods. Such instances occur in two of the cases presented in this book.

Ignatius, a strict superior general of the Society of Jesus, documented in the *Constitutions* the exact branches that should be taught at Jesuit colleges and universities. The principle area of study was to be theology but would also include

Latin, Greek, and Hebrew. The Jesuits also taught grammar, rhetoric, poetry, and history, along with natural sciences. At the same time, courses in logic, physics, metaphysics, and moral philosophy were offered.[25] All in all, the curriculum was a liberal education interwoven with Catholic principles. Ignatius remained fervent about maintaining a liberal arts curriculum, and regarding professional branches of education such as law or medicine, he stated that "the study of medicine and laws, being more remote from our institute, will not be treated in the universities of the Society, or at least the Society will not undertake this teaching through its own members."[26] The Society of Jesus did not prefer to engage in professional forms of instruction, but if such professional education were to be provided within a Jesuit institution, then it would be taught by a layperson with experience in the particular professional field.

As the religious order expanded throughout Europe, Jesuits established colleges and continued to promote liberal education. In 1599, forty-three years after the death of Ignatius, the order produced its own method of instructional practices for their educational institutions. This text is known as the *Ratio Atque Institutio Studiorum Societatis Iesu*, otherwise referred to as the *Ratio Studiorum*, or simply "the method of studies." Through the use of this document, Jesuits all over the world possessed a universal technique for teaching. How one Jesuit taught, another could also. Following its publication, the *Ratio Studiorum* was used in 245 Jesuit institutions. By 1626, the number of Jesuit colleges had risen to 441 and in 1749 to 669, and the Jesuit system of education had spread from Europe to India, Cuba, Mexico, and the Philippines largely due to the instructional methods of the *Ratio Studiorum*.[27] As one reads the *Ratio Studiorum* in conjunction with the order's *Constitutions*, it becomes apparent that the Society of Jesus considered a liberal education to be the most holistic and developmental form of instruction.

The Jesuit educational system grew to span all of Europe and eventually branched into Asia. But what made this system so prosperous aside from the well-developed method of studies? John W. O'Malley, in his book *The First Jesuits*, provides a description of qualities that made early Jesuit education not only expansive but also successful. In brief, early Jesuit institutions charged no tuition; welcomed students from all social classes; capitalized on character formation; developed a balanced educational plan consisting of the study of languages, philosophy, and science; implemented divisible classes based on subjects; encouraged public orations, disputations, and plays; and promoted a religious education for all students that could be applied to everyday life. In a further effort to enhance fraternity, Jesuits created a network of institutions that maintained constant communication with each other. As well, every Jesuit instructor was highly educated and tried to influence his students more through actions than words.[28]

In short, members of the Society of Jesus were well prepared to teach in early schools fashioned by their own hands. The Jesuit parish school grew out of the need to provide basic education for boys in rural areas and eventually expanded into private colleges. The first major and still existing establishment of a Jesuit university in the United States is Georgetown University, opened in 1789.[29] Schools of business, law, medicine, dentistry, engineering, nursing, journalism, and ultimately graduate education followed in American Jesuit colleges and universities. In fact, many other Catholic colleges and universities drew from Jesuit educational philosophy and practice chiefly because the Society of Jesus had created a discernable methodology for instruction and was renowned as effective educators.[30] Herein lies the major difference between Catholic and Jesuit education. The Society of Jesuit had developed a universal instructional method utilized in all of its colleges to form a worldwide curricular practice. Other Catholic educators did not, as of yet, have such a model. William Leahy reflects this juxtaposition by stating "other Catholic colleges and universities drew from Jesuit educational theory and practice because Jesuits had articulated a definite philosophy of education and because they had a reputation as effective educators since their founding."[31] Thus, Catholic educational institutions borrowed the organizational and administrative strategies of the Society of Jesus, including the *Ratio Studiorum*, to enhance their curricula and instructional practices.[32]

Jesuit institutions spread, maintaining a standard curricular structure from one Jesuit college to another. As students studied in a Jesuit college they were instructed to search for truth and thus develop a sense of spirituality. As individuals partook in this form of education they were encouraged to serve as teachers to others and unto themselves. Jean-Marc Laporte, a Jesuit priest and writer on Ignatian identity and mission, assists in the understanding of how such an identifiable system of education came about and how it guides the order's colleges and universities. Laporte illustrates certain Jesuit identities through the foundational actions and life of Ignatius Loyola and the history of the order. Second, the mission governing the order is established through its identity. Finally, it is the duty of the Society of Jesus to imbue their apostolic work with their own spirituality so that laypersons may partake in communal education.[33]

The passion of the Jesuits for college and university instruction sent them across the globe and eventually to the Americas. In the New World, the Jesuits continued their practices of liberal education and kept in contact with Jesuits in other countries, learning from each other's experiences as they advanced in the apostolate of education. Ignatius made it clear in the *Constitutions* that the best way to keep the order unified was to write and communicate among priests, brothers, and superiors in the different countries and regions inhabited by the Society of Jesus.[34] In the New World, most Jesuits partook in missionary work. Few functioned as educators in the traditional sense; however, with the growth of American colonies, Jesuits began performing more classroom duties than mission work.[35] Focusing on the life of Ignatius, as well as the ideologies behind the cura personalis and the magis, Jesuits in the New World hastened to establish an educational regime that would promote the spread of Catholic doctrine.

Jesuits in the New World

The Society of Jesus has held a position of significance in America since 1566, when twenty-four Jesuits arrived in the Spanish territory of Florida.[36] Later, in 1634, a second group of English Jesuits settled in St. Mary's City, Maryland. In the following years, additional members of the order made their way to North America to aid in the exploration and colonization of America.[37] As has been stated in *The Jesuit Relations and Allied Documents*: "Not a cape was turned, nor a river entered, but a Jesuit led the way."[38] As the American colonies grew, the Society of Jesus grew alongside them. Jesuits accompanied pioneers into new regions of the American frontier and settled in geographic areas that eventually became heavily populated in order to spread Catholicism.

Groups of Jesuits already existed in Quebec and Mexico, and eventually these groups would connect through the expansion of the United States of America. Despite many unsuccessful attempts by the Jesuits to aid pioneers in the search for pathways westward or southward, the Jesuit Père Jacques Marquette undertook a daring venture with explorers Louis Jolliet and Jean Talon in 1673. Their goal was to expand the colonial territory for France southward via the Mississippi River.[39] Traveling along the shore of Lake Michigan to Green Bay, Marquette and his fellow travelers eventually came across the Fox River, which connected the explorers to the Wisconsin River. The explorers, after much paddling to avoid rapids and whirlpools, arrived at the Mississippi River, where they canoed southward. During their exploration of the Mississippi, they discovered a direct route to the Louisiana Territory. As a result, Marquette and his companions proved that Louisiana could be reached via the Mississippi River, a fact that played in favor of American expansion and Jesuit progress in the South.[40]

Since 1700, Jesuits had expanded their endeavors in small groups toward the colony of New Orleans and the Gulf of Mexico as part of the Quebec Mission.[41] Alongside the Jesuit presence in Quebec, the well-known Le Moyne family had risen in prominence as settlers and explorers. The two most noted members of the family were Pierre Le Moyne d'Iberville, known as Sieur d'Iberville, and Jean-Baptiste Le Moyne de Bienville, known as Sieur de Bienville. On one of these trips south, Iberville, the first governor of New Orleans, brought with him the Jesuit Paul du Ru as the expedition's chaplain, perhaps out of a loyalty to the order. After arriving in New Orleans, du Ru traveled northward on the Mississippi River covering the area that Marquette had not.[42] Despite Sieur d'Iberville's work to develop a colony in the Louisiana Territory, the French government, concerned with public health and strategic placement, decided to move the inhabitants of the colony, including the Jesuits, from New Orleans to the western shore of Mobile Bay. Although he was disappointed at the relocation, du Ru became the first resident priest of Mobile, Alabama, in 1702. However, Mobile was under the control of Bishop Jean-Baptiste de La Croix de Chevriéres de Saint-Vallier of Quebec, whose jurisdiction covered the Mississippi valley. After his transfer to Mobile, Father du Ru and Bishop Saint-Vallier had a strained relationship. After much consideration, du Ru's provincial, Reverend Julien Baudran, decided that du Ru and the small group of Jesuits working alongside the Mobile Bay should return to France in 1704. Following the egress of du Ru and the Mobile Jesuits, several members of the order traveled to the Gulf Coast colonies, thus increasing the presence of the Society of Jesus in the South.[43]

Despite du Ru's removal, Jesuits persisted in exploring the American South. In 1720, Father Jean Laval attempted to visit the southern region to conduct a survey of the Mississippi coast, but the trip was cut short due to the presence of plague aboard Laval's ship. Only two years later, in 1722, the Jesuit historian Father Pierre Francois-Xavier de Charlevoix made a short visit to the Louisiana Territory and gave the colony a negative review based on the harsh living conditions of the swampland; however, he would later write about his hope for the future prosperity of the colony.[44] The comings and goings of so many Jesuits throughout the Louisiana Territory and Mobile indicate that no Jesuit held permanent residence in the southern territory. Even so, the Jesuits were not prepared to give up their missionary efforts along the Gulf Coast. With the aid of the Le Moyne family, particularly the younger brother of Iberville, Sieur de Bienville, the Society of Jesus became prominent in the New Orleans colony.

In Canada the Le Moyne family was closely associated with and had witnessed the work of the Jesuits. Bienville, like his brother, wanted to see the order return to the southern colonies. Bienville was convinced that only an efficient organization like the Society of Jesus could survive and flourish among the hardships of colonial missionary life.[45] At the time of Bienville's New Orleans governorship, the Quebec Mission still controlled all religious decisions related to the Louisiana Territory; however, in 1723, the Holy See detached the Louisiana Jesuits from the Canadian province. In that same year, the Society of Jesus placed all Jesuits serving in the Louisiana Territory under the jurisdiction of the Lyon Province in France, thus creating the New Orleans Mission of Lyon. Father Joseph Francois de Kereben acted as its first superior, and in 1724, Nicholas de Beaubois was named to succeed Kereben and journeyed to New Orleans with six other Jesuits. De Beaubois's first objective was to establish an agreement with the French government to support the creation of a permanent Jesuit rectory in New Orleans. The Jesuits' sanctioned purpose in New Orleans was to perform missionary work among the Native American tribes of the Mississippi valley.[46] Bienville and the Jesuits shared a peaceful relationship based on the advancement of the New Orleans colony. As Bienville strove to promote the Society of Jesus in the colony, the Jesuits returned the favor by defending him whenever his gubernatorial administration came into question.[47]

Bienville's close relationship with the Jesuits became apparent during the French administration of New Orleans. Due to the inability of the French government to cover missionary expenses, the Jesuits of New Orleans decided to form a working plantation equipped with livestock, crops, and slaves.[48] The proceeds of the plantation maintained the missionaries and their work with the Native American populations. The first concession of land for the plantation was on the east side of the Mississippi River, opposite the colony, a tract considered undesirable due to its inconvenient location. The Jesuits resolved to secure a more suitable site on the western side of the river. Aware of their needs, Bienville passed an act on April 11, 1726, that transferred a large tract of his own land to the Jesuits adjacent to the colony. The land measured 3,600 feet wide by 9,000 feet long and lay between what is now known as Tchoupitoulas, Annunciation, and Terpsichore Streets and the edge of Bayou St. John. Two subsequent purchases resulted in an expansion that ultimately extended the land from the river to Broad Street and from Common Street to Felicity Road.[49]

In order to obtain this new concession of land, Father de Beaubois, as the leader of the New Orleans Jesuits, sailed to France in 1726. The voyage to France had a secondary motive: When the need for hospital managers in New Orleans increased, the colonial administration had written to the Company of the Indies, a banking and trading firm, to ask for help in the acquisition of the Daughters of Charity. To the colonial administration's disappointment, the Daughters of Charity were not in a position to send any of their members. In response, de Beaubois, envisioning an opportunity to do more for the colony, made contact with the Ursuline Sisters who agreed to nurse the colony's sick and provide educational services for young women. Though historically Jesuits and their colleges only offered courses for boys and young men, the order, so far, had been forbidden to establish and maintain any educational institution in New Orleans per the original religious edicts of the territory.[50] Through the Ursulines, the Jesuits had helped establish a formal regime of education in the colony though not for men.

Even though de Beaubois had envisioned a league of female educators traveling to the colony, the Ursulines were, in fact, primarily nurses. According to Emily Clark, editor of *Voices from an Early American Convent*, "the Company of the Indies crafted a contract with this group of nuns that stipulated the hospital as their primary responsibility, making clear that teaching would be supplemental and could only be undertaken if it did not interfere with or detract from their nursing duties."[51] This contract assured a position for the Ursulines within the colony. Through the procurement of the Ursulines, the Jesuits provided a solution for the colony's burgeoning educational and nursing needs. This group of Ursuline nuns, secured by Father de Beaubois, set sail on the *Gironde* from port L'Orient on February 22, 1727, and reached New Orleans on August 7 of that same year.[52]

Through the efforts of the Ursulines, the Jesuits had proven their usefulness by acquiring not only nurses but also skilled educators. The Jesuits and the Ursulines shared a variety of similarities. Both utilized forms of meditative spiritual retreats, and both religious orders were known for producing excellent educators. While the Ursulines' educational techniques provided a much-needed service for the colony, the primary objective of Father de Beaubois's trip to France was to ensure the Society of Jesus's place in the South through land promised by Bienville to form a plantation. The plantation that de Beaubois and the southern Jesuits constructed was carefully and methodically organized. The plantation financially supported the New Orleans Jesuits and provided a wide variety of crops, including corn, rice, potatoes, cotton, indigo, and sugar cane.[53]

Indeed, Father de Beaubois garnered enough land for an expansive, Jesuit-run plantation, as well as the aid of the Ursulines to help with hospital and educational needs in the colony. Even though the Jesuits had accomplished much in and for New Orleans, they, in the course of their missionary work, had trodden through territory overseen by the Capuchin Friars. The Capuchins had been granted pastoral rights to oversee the religious instruction of all within the walls of colonial New Orleans and argued with the Society of Jesus over geographic missionary territory.[54] The Jesuits had been granted missionary rights outside of the colony. We can theorize that with the expansion of the colony, clear demarcations of "spiritual boundaries" were blurred, thus resulting in heated disputes between the two religious orders. This localized issue, along with a series of dense political factors, would soon pose a risk to Jesuit progress in the South. Indeed, European powers had already aligned to undo the work of the Society of Jesus throughout Europe and the Americas.[55]

Despite the educational and religious identity of the Society of Jesus, the spiritual direction of the colony lay with the Capuchin Friars.[56] The Capuchins had arrived in 1723, and their apostolic work in New Orleans pertained to dispensing the sacraments of the Catholic Church and tending to the sick. In addition, the Capuchins were responsible for colonial education long before the Jesuits had established a college in the American South.[57] Having seen the need for an educational institution, the Capuchins purchased a house on St. Ann Street with a promise of reimbursement from the Company of the Indies. Father Raphael, the Capuchin superior, opened the first New Orleans school in 1725 to educate colonial boys and Native Americans. By September of that same year, the school was already too small. As plans were made to expand the school, the Jesuits criticized the educational efforts of the Capuchin Friars. Father de Beaubois directly criticized the intelligence of the colony's children and circuitously insulted the quality of instruction given at the Capuchin-run school. Historian Adam Hebert explains that this Jesuit criticism of the Capuchin school marked a breach of apostolate boundaries and fractured the already tense relationship between the two orders; however, hardships were not limited to verbal slings and arrows. Whether a result of public Jesuit criticisms or the Capuchin's difficulties in retaining teachers, acquiring schoolbooks from abroad, and, most important, making payments on the schoolhouse, the number of enrolled students dropped off in 1726. This decreased enrollment made it difficult to keep the school open.[58]

Regarding payments on the schoolhouse, the Capuchin priest, Father Raphael de Luxembourg, had entered into a contract with the Company of the Indies to reimburse the Capuchins for the purchase of the St. Ann Street property. When the Company of the Indies failed to make payment, a legal battle ensued to determine whether the company or the Capuchins should pay for the school. The French courts determined that the fault lay with the Company of the Indies and that it was their responsibility to cover the financial cost of the declining school. Two years later, payment still had not been made. With no form of reimbursement, the Capuchins did not possess the required finances to pay for the cost of the school property or its operation. As a result, the school closed in 1731.[59]

This public financial and contractual struggle may have been a factor that kept the Jesuits from pursuing the development of a college in New Orleans. As such, the Society of Jesus felt that the colony lacked sufficient lodgings for an educational institution and that materials required to construct and support such an institution were not readily available.[60] Because of this, the Jesuits ignored encouragement by the civil administration of New Orleans to found a colonial college as a means to end the educational migration of the colony's 561 children to colleges and universities in France. The Jesuits' main objective in the colony, per the religious mandate of the original Quebec Mission, was to perform missionary work outside of New Orleans.[61] The Society of Jesus did not have ecclesiastical permission to establish an educational institution, as it was part of the Capuchin's objectives to do so. However, once the legal battle over the St. Ann Street school had come to a dismal close, the Capuchins went out of the education business in New Orleans. Soon the Jesuits would find themselves out of work and out of the colony altogether.

While the Jesuits were maintaining their missions and plantation outside of New Orleans, all was not well concerning the status of the Society of Jesus in Europe. In 1762, a dispute concerning the courtly power and influence of the order raged between European monarchs and Pope Clement XIII. Several nations, including Spain and France, were attempting to suppress the Society of Jesus. These attempts at suppression originated from the belief that the Jesuits were causing civil unrest in Europe and abroad through court influence and land conquests. By April 1762, a formal suppression of the Jesuits was enacted in France and Portugal, and all colleges operated by the Society of Jesus in those countries were forced to close.[62] When King Charles of Spain vowed to remove all Jesuit priests from his country, neighboring heads of state sided with Charles and suppressed the Society of Jesus in their own countries despite public outcry in support of the order.[63] As France expelled their Jesuits in 1763, the citizens of New Orleans sided with the French government and expelled the Jesuits from the Louisiana Territory. The Capuchins filled all religious positions and spiritual responsibilities formerly held by the colonial Jesuits. By order of Louis XV, King of France, the large Jesuit plantation was now property of the French government.[64] In 1773, following the formal suppression of the Society of Jesus in Europe, Pope Clement XIV, bending to political pressure, dispatched the hardest blow to the Jesuit order. Clement decreed the global suppression of the Society of Jesus.[65]

The expulsion of the Jesuits from New Orleans was based on the belief that the order cared only for their plantation and not for their apostolic work.[66] It can be theorized that because the Jesuits were working outside of the colony walls, their missionary work was not as obvious as the work of the Capuchin Friars, who administered the Holy Sacrament to those living within the colony. Furthermore, the decree of suppression in the Louisiana Territory condemned the Jesuits without a proper trial. Their property and land were confiscated, divided, and sold; the Capuchins claimed all ornaments and sacred vessels that resided in the Jesuit's church; and the church was demolished. But the decree went further than seizing property: the Society of Jesus was now defunct. Jesuits were no longer allowed to demarcate themselves by that title and were commanded to don the garb of secular priests instead of the traditional Jesuit habit. In the end, the Jesuits were shipped back to France. Adding insult to injury, colonial officials forced Father Michael Baudoin, the New Orleans Jesuit superior, to attend the celebration feast following the suppression.[67] For fifty-one years, the Jesuits were silenced by the Holy See and their global network of colleges closed. Nevertheless, Jesuits persevered in small groups throughout the world. In countries such as Prussia, ruled by Fredrick the Great, and Russia, under the Empress Catherine, the remaining vestiges of the order found sanctuary, were allowed to practice *The Spiritual Exercises*, and kept their identity alive.[68]

After five decades of exile, the Society of Jesus was granted a reprieve. In August 1814, Pope Pius VII, in the Papal Bull *Sollicitudo Omnium Ecclesiarum*, restored the Society of Jesus. As the newly elected pontiff, Pius VII was determined to reinstate the Jesuits and return them to their apostolic work. Pius believed that the return of the Jesuits would herald a new awakening for the Catholic Church through the order's passion for education.[69] Despite the fervent support of the pope, the society's restoration was slow owing to a lack of manpower and lingering suspicions. But eventually, countries around the world reacquainted themselves with the order, accepted the Jesuit return, and allowed the order's educational work to begin anew.

Jesuit educational ideals, long defunct, were reinvigorated throughout Europe. With the election of Joannes Roothaan as superior general, the Society of Jesus revitalized its missionary efforts, spread the practice of *The Spiritual Exercises* to the lay population, and updated the *Ratio Studiorum* to include a wider range of languages, mathematics, philosophies, sciences, and geography. Despite the restoration, Jesuits experienced prejudice from various European governments for the next fifty years and were expelled temporarily from Italy, Spain, France, Germany, Switzerland, Guatemala, and Nicaragua. This prejudice did not dampen the Jesuit pursuit of the magis. To expand their spiritual and educational efforts, Jesuits journeyed en masse to the United States, where they built and fortified a large system of colleges and universities.[70]

Despite global suppression in the late eighteenth century, Jesuits had traveled to the northern United States since 1801 to teach at Georgetown University. By 1805, several Jesuits, although not publicly calling themselves so, had established a religious community at Georgetown and had appointed Father Robert Molyneaux as their superior.[71] In the American South, however, the Society of Jesus had absolutely no presence. Even so, conversations had taken place regarding the return of the Jesuits to New Orleans. According to Gilbert J. Garraghan, in his three-volume work titled *The Jesuits of the Middle United States*, Louis William Valentin Dubourg, bishop of Louisiana from 1823 to 1826, attempted to formulate a Catholic-based educational regime in Louisiana by way of the Society of Jesus. Dubourg had contacted the Jesuits at Georgetown in 1826 and offered them land in Opelousas, Louisiana, for the construction of a new Catholic college. Dubourg's offer was rejected and conversations with the Jesuits seemed to cease until Leo de Neckère was consecrated as bishop of New Orleans in 1830.[72]

In 1832, de Neckère, along with his vicar general Father Antoine Blanc, visited the St. Louis Jesuits and urged them to take the Opelousas land and build a college. After meeting with the New Orleans bishop, Father James Oliver Van de Velde wrote to Reverend John Roothaan, superior general of the Society of Jesus in Rome. Van de Velde explained that de Neckère "should die happy" if his request for a college was granted. However, before a decision was made, Bishop de Neckère died of yellow fever in 1833. As a result, the college plan was postponed until a new bishop could be installed. Two years after de Neckère's death, Antoine Blanc was elevated as archbishop of the newly established Roman Catholic Archdiocese of

New Orleans.[73] Blanc, eager to continue the educational work of his predecessor, traveled to Rome on November 22, 1835, and pled with Roothaan to send Jesuit educators to the New Orleans archdiocese in order to build a college. Roothaan conceded to Blanc's request. The first objective of the newly returned Jesuits would be to construct a church and college in Louisiana for the education of Catholic youth and provide for the religious needs of southern residents.[74]

Following the approval of Blanc's request, seven Jesuits priests and two brothers set sail from France and arrived in New Orleans on February 22, 1837. Once these Jesuits arrived, steps were immediately taken to find a site for a new college in Louisiana. Locations such as Houma, Donaldsonville, and Mandeville were considered but rejected due to financial constraints and local Jesuit opposition. The Jesuits ultimately choose Grand Coteau in St. Landry Parrish presumably due to its healthy environment and rare occurrence of yellow fever, a sickness prevalent in New Orleans.[75] One of the Jesuit priests, Father Nicholas Point, prepared the plans for the college, and on July 31, 1837, Archbishop Blanc laid the institution's corner stone amid an assembly of supporters.[76] The endeavors of Archbishop Blanc planted the seed of Jesuit education in southern soil, and it was called St. Charles College.

The new apostolate zeal of the Jesuits in the American South focused on the development of colleges for the instruction of southern boys and young men. In 1837, St. Charles College opened in Grand Coteau, Louisiana, and in 1847, a small group of French Jesuits assumed control of Spring Hill College in Mobile, Alabama. Soon, plans were announced to open a Jesuit church in New Orleans with an adjoining college. After discussing their southern educational mission, the Jesuits set their plans into motion. As a result, a college in New Orleans was established, ultimately called the College of the Immaculate Conception, and later a college in Baton Rouge, the College of Saints Peter and Paul.[77] After the Civil War, southern Jesuits expanded their educational mission and assumed control of a university in Galveston, Texas. The order's constant pursuit of the magis in the newly established New Orleans Mission encouraged the Jesuits to open educational intuitions in Shreveport, Louisiana; Augusta, Georgia; and Tampa, Florida. By the end of the nineteenth century, the Society of Jesus had reestablished their educational foothold and expanded their presence in the South.

Despite these expansions, prior to the Civil War and following it, hardships were plentiful for the growing southern mission. Protestant ideology had dominated American society since the arrival of Puritan settlers; however, with the rise of Catholic immigration to New Orleans and the larger American South in 1820, the social context was disrupted by nativism and blatant anti-Catholic sentiment. When Archbishop Blanc requested the return of the Society to New Orleans, the United States was experiencing a heightened period of anti-Catholic unrest. According to historian Andrew H. M. Stern, in his book *Southern Crucifix, Southern*

Cross: Catholic-Protestant Relations in the Old South, "The Jesuits bore the brunt of Protestant fear and hatred."[78] The Jesuits, unfortunately, returned to the South during this period. In describing the antebellum period of anti-Catholic sentiment, Donald Crosby states that "the sectional and social conflicts which arose during the administration of Andrew Jackson (1828–1836) spawned a . . . period of religious antagonism unparalleled in American history. Anti-Catholic societies and publications flourished, as nativists and Protestant groups organized to break the power of Rome."[79] This period of negativity toward Catholics and Jesuits was felt more strongly in some areas than others. Even so, the Jesuits were well aware of their situation.

This religious disruption affected the establishment of Catholic colleges. As well, conflicting educational ideologies placed a strain on Catholics who wished to attain pragmatic job-related higher education in lieu of liberal arts instruction. Also, anti-Catholic, as well as anti-Jesuit, sentiment had been etched into the American consciousness with the eighteenth-century Jesuit suppression and anti-Papist doctrine. Anti-Catholic movements took shape in organizations such as the Know-Nothing Party, the Ku Klux Klan, and the American Protective Association.[80] With the expansion of Jesuit institutions in America during the first half of the nineteenth century, Protestant groups exhibited steadily increasing fear in regard to the Society of Jesus and its educational institutions. One Protestant clergyman instructed his congregation as follows: "We must build College against College. . . . All experience has confirmed our anticipation, that America is a field on which the . . . Christian discipline of a Protestant College must annihilate the rival system of Jesuitical education."[81] Prior to the Civil War and during Reconstruction, anti-Catholic groups lead the battle against Catholics and Jesuits in particular. Waves of literature issued forth, depicting the Jesuits as corrupt and power-driven. Published encyclicals called for the removal of American Jesuit educational institutions.[82] College textbooks issued at secular colleges explained to students that the popes of Rome were using the Society of Jesus to stamp out Protestantism and take control of all nations through religious and political influence.[83] With the spread of publications denouncing the Society of Jesus in the South, the order combated anti-Jesuit organizations while attempting to address the linguistic issues facing their French fathers as they taught sons of English-speaking southerners. In regard to Catholic and Jesuit education, the historian Donald Howkins states that

> the middle decades of the nineteenth century were the worst possible time for Catholic schools for three reasons. First, there was a very unfriendly climate towards Catholics throughout the USA in the 1840s and '50s which saw the rise of nativism and the Know-Nothing Party. Maria Monk and ex-

> priests found fame and fortune lecturing on the evils of the Catholic Church in general and the Jesuits in particular. . . . In second place yellow fever epidemics periodically devastated the population of the Gulf South or wherever mosquito's flourished. . . . In the third place there was the Civil War and Reconstruction[, and] . . . the economic hardships that followed the war made education an unattainable luxury for many Catholic families.[84]

Even with the variety of hardships listed in the aforementioned quotation, not one had as much effect on American thought concerning the nature of Catholicism as the nineteenth-century book by Maria Monk.

Monk's book, *The Awful Disclosures of Maria Monk*, describes her Protestant upbringing, conversion to the Catholic faith, and ghastly details of her life as a sexually abused novice and later nun in the Hotel Dieu Nunnery in Montreal. First printed in 1836, Monk's book describes scenes of lechery, rape, chained imprisonment, and physical abuse at the hands of Catholic priests. Seduced by her confessor, Monk explains that her priest took sexual advantage of her and other religious women through his position of authority.[85] In a quote from the 1878 revised text, we can see how the publishers hoped that widespread readership would continue to fuel hatred and distrust of Catholics in the minds of US citizens: "Hoping that 'Maria Monk' will still continue to inspire a wholesome and practical hatred of Popery *and all that it means today in our very midst*, no less than what it meant forty years ago in Canada, we commend this little volume to all lovers of true American liberty, without distinction of sex, creed, sect, or previous nationality."[86] Even though the events described in Monk's book were later disproven by a series of investigations,[87] its ideological impact was lasting in the minds of American Protestants. As a direct result, American Catholics and Catholic immigrants were discriminated against across the United States, particularly in regions with large Protestant populations.

Hostility toward immigrants was fervent and difficulties multiplied for those of foreign birth who also claimed to be Catholic. In the 1880s, Father Francis Gautrelet and Father Theobald Butler acquired volunteers from Europe to serve the growing German and Irish Catholic populations. These Jesuit recruits spoke English and German more clearly than their French counterparts. As well, in 1880, Reverend Thomas O'Neil, ex-provincial of the Missouri Province, was sent to the New Orleans Mission as a father visitor. After due consideration, O'Neil encouraged the replacement of French superiors who had founded the New Orleans Mission with Irish superiors.[88] Through these actions, the leadership of the New Orleans Mission went from being French dominated to Irish controlled. This new leadership attempted, albeit slowly, to adapt the cultural climate of their colleges to a more "American friendly" regime centered on the commercial and professional curricular expectations of southern students instead of the liberal arts model Jesuit colleges followed in the past. The reliance on French in classrooms diminished due to the inculcation of English-speaking Jesuits. However, southern Jesuits were hesitant to reform their long-standing instructional model. Through the efforts of the Jesuit father general in Rome, Peter Jan Beckx, the Society of Jesus was further pressed to further adapt Jesuit colleges to social and linguistic norms in order to better meet the needs of American and immigrant populations.[89]

The renowned historian on the Catholic Church in Louisiana, Roger Baudier, indicates that negative sentiment against immigrants from Europe developed throughout the South and in particular along the Gulf Coast and in New Orleans where immigrants, many of them Catholic, settled. Baudier illustrates this prejudice against immigrants, Catholics, and particularly Jesuits in his book *The Catholic Church in Louisiana*: "Because of Irish and Italian immigrants being involved, nearly all Catholics, and Germans also, many also being Catholics, it was to be expected that the religious question would be thrust into the affair. And so it was. A violent anti-Catholic sentiment developed, including, during the fervor of native Americanism enthusiasm and demands that America be governed by Americans, all the old nonsense of Papal domination, Church interference in political affairs, Jesuitism, the baneful influence of Bishops and clergy, allegiance to a foreign potentate and similar ranting."[90] This general negative feeling toward Catholics, Jesuits, and immigrants was only worsened by its proliferation via political and Protestant groups. As Baudier makes clear, Protestant southerners were afraid of internal corruption by transatlantic regimes of Catholic hegemony dictated by the pope in Rome.

As a result of this fear, southerners' chief concern was the possible political rise of Catholics. Before and after the Civil War, New Orleans was flooded with violent anti-Catholic rhetoric warning against the election of Catholics to political offices. Handbills were dispersed defaming Catholic priests and the Society of Jesus, heralding that such a religious order should not be allowed to rule the city. In addition, the Know-Nothing Party in Louisiana was bitterly opposed to Catholicism and publicly castigated it. Called "Know-Nothings" due to the intense secrecy of the political party, the organization refused admittance to practicing Catholics or any man having a Catholic wife. Rumors persisted that the party allowed admittance to professors at Centenary College in Jackson, Louisiana, who taught students the negative implications of the rise of Catholicism in the South and promoted the destruction of Catholic churches in New Orleans.[91]

Another example of hardships faced by the Jesuits and their southern educational institutions is the tumultuous years of the College of Saints Peter and Paul in Baton Rouge, Louisiana. In 1847, the Jesuits purchased a parcel of land to construct a college in the capital city.[92] However, the college did not open until January 2, 1850, with an enrollment of twenty-five students. Prior to the construction of the first buildings, local anti-Catholic groups opposed the formation of the college. Despite the enthusiasm of Baton Rouge's Catholic population in welcoming the Society of Jesus, they did little to support the construction of the college. As in New Orleans, the Baton Rouge chapter of the Know-Nothing Party and members of the Methodist church publicly discouraged the educational plans of the Jesuits. In fact, communal uprisings against the college were so strong that local anti-Jesuit organizations, in an attempt to deter the college's construction, had a road laid through the campus property before construction on the site began. When Father John Cambiaso, the institution's rector, saw the new road, he retaliated, realigned the college plans, and constructed buildings on either side of the road, creating an easily accessible campus. As a result, a threatening letter was sent to Cambiosa.[93] Father Michael Kenny details the implications of the letter with the following: "When Father Cambiaso proceeded to build on one bisection and to clear the adjoining church premises for a new church, they [local anti-Jesuit representatives] sent him the message that they had a 5-barrel gun they would explode on him unless he quit forthwith. He [Father Cambiaso] replied that should they assail him they would find good shooting from his own single-barrel more effective. Without further assault he had a pair of two-story frame buildings set up."[94] Despite such disputes, the college was erected consisting of three two-story buildings that contained dorm rooms, classrooms, a chapel, and residential space for priests and brothers. The construction projects did not end there. The Jesuits were also responsible for rebuilding the Catholic church in Baton Rouge, St. Joseph Cathedral.[95]

In the end a combination of social and contextual issues led to the closure of the College of Saints Peter and Paul. Not only did local, social conflicts in Baton Rouge cause the Society of Jesus grief, an epidemic of yellow fever forced the temporary closure of the institution in 1853 and killed members of the Jesuit staff. In 1855, a second epidemic of yellow fever struck Baton Rouge killing several of the local Jesuit population and three of the college's students. In 1865, following the Civil War, the Jesuits decided to close the college due to epidemics, lack of community support, and the fear that if successful, the college would draw boarders away from other southern Jesuit institutions. Having made the decision to refortify existing colleges outside of Baton Rouge, the Jesuit population departed the Louisiana capital city in 1865.[96]

Like yellow fever, the American Civil War created a plethora of difficulties for the Society of Jesus. During the Civil War, southern Jesuit institutions, unlike several of their secular counterparts, remained open. Southern Jesuit colleges functioned throughout the war for a variety of reasons. First, these colleges relied heavily on preparatory departments that serviced younger boys who were not of age to enlist in the military. This practice helped to offset the number of enlisting "age-appropriate" students by continuing to provide an enrolled student population. Also, the institutions provided a residence for occupying troops in exchange for leaving the physical campuses unharmed. Finally, Father Gautrelet, president of Spring Hill College, visited Jefferson Davis and requested the cessation of Confederate Army recruiters to all southern Jesuit campuses.[97] With a decreased but secure student population and intact facilities, Jesuit colleges struggled throughout the war but remained open.

Despite hardships resulting from the Civil War, expansion was still on the minds of southern Jesuits. In the Civil War letters of Father Hippolyte Gache, former president of Spring Hill College in Mobile, it is evident that the Jesuits had plans to connect the mission work of the order's colleges in the South with those Jesuit institutions in the North. Father Gache believed that Columbia, South Carolina, was the ideal location to establish a college. He believed the apostolic work of a centrally located college, joined in forces with those Jesuit colleges in the North and South, would aid in the spread of education imbued with Catholic doctrine. This plan of connecting southern Jesuit institutions to northern colleges was short lived. After the war ended, the New Orleans Mission was strained financially and the plan was abandoned, leaving southern Jesuit colleges far removed from their northern counterparts.[98]

During Reconstruction and beyond, the South struggled to recuperate from war losses. Southern colleges and universities were focused on industrial and scientific education to improve the region's work force. Religious education, in particular Jesuit higher education, experienced a growing clash between liberal arts curricula and the rising social demand for scientific training. Catholic Americans and Catholic immigrants sought forms of higher education that would provide a better quality of life. This desired education included training in basic languages and technical skills culturally reinforced by American ideologies, not liberal arts curricula. American Catholics, and Catholic immigrants in particular, perceived higher education prior to and after the First World War as a luxury. During this period, impoverished Catholics made up 17 percent of college age students and were found to be the least likely denomination to pursue a college degree.[99] To compound social issues, southern Jesuit colleges and universities, due to their rigid historic foundations, limited resources, and social isolation, vehemently opposed innovation or simply could not respond to regional curricular changes due to a lack of materials and instructors. With a dearth of financial support from the Catholic Church, Jesuit higher education was extremely vulnerable to external forces, and conflict soon arose involving intellectual research in Catholic higher education. This research was produced by Catholic academics in the fields of psychology, philosophy, and the natural sciences in an attempt to reconcile science and theology, which roused the attention of Pope Pius X in 1907. Consequently, Pius X condemned modern philosophical and theological ideas. This forbiddance of intellectual inquiry established limits to Catholic academics and scholarship.[100]

Even with papal edicts limiting scholarship, social demands for pragmatic education, and anti-Catholic movements creating hardships for the Society of Jesus, southern Jesuits colleges and universities continued to progress. Though this progress was slow, and stubbornness hindered adaption efforts, the superior general of the Society of Jesus in Rome, Father Xavier Wernz, recognized the efforts and growth of the New Orleans Mission and in 1907 elevated the mission's standing to that of a province. In a letter to the fathers and brothers of the New Orleans Province, Wernz states the following:

> On this day [June 7, 1907], our New Orleans Mission . . . has been raised to the rank of a Province. . . . You are familiar with the saying "In union there is strength." Now in our Society there can be no union unless it consists of obedience and charity. Obedience will bind you to your superiors, and charity draw you closely one to another. . . . I am well aware . . . that many obstacles beset you in the service of God. Your Province composed of members from various nations, has within and without, men who are by nature opposed one to the other. This fact you cannot and should not forget in your labors, for the charity of God ought to urge you to have regard to the character of each . . . so treat those of other nations that all may see that great charity reigns among you everywhere, and moreover that, what is of rule in our Society, you give special proofs of love in the Lord, to those of other nations.[101]

Father General Wernz made a point to emphasize that continued progress and strength would only be possible through unity, understanding of social surroundings, and, most important to the Jesuits, the binding force of the vow of obedience. This vow served as the catalyst for many decisions, which had lasting impact on Jesuit higher education in the New Orleans Province.

Even though the Jesuit father general had faith in the New Orleans Province, more conflicts arose as Catholic higher education faced the curricular trends of larger secular and land-grant institutions that emphasized scientific training and deemphasized holistic liberal arts curricula. William P. Leahy explains that "the conflict and ensuing secularization, curriculum reform, accreditation, and standardization in education held particular significance for Catholicism and its schools, especially in the twentieth century. . . . Before World War II, Catholic colleges and universities in America had a clear and compelling sense of purpose: To protect the faith of Catholics and to make it possible for Catholics to obtain a college education."[102] With the rise of accreditation associations, Jesuit colleges and universities considered the benefits of joining; however, Jesuits themselves had difficulty earning American PhDs due to rigorous academic requirements. Consequently, without properly educated faculty, Jesuit institutions found it difficult to join accrediting bodies, attain larger student enrollments, and rise to the ranks of their secular peers. In addition, low student revenue hindered any upgrading of curricula, educational programs, and campus facilities.[103]

Discerning the need for a Catholic governing board, American Catholic educators established the Association of Catholic Colleges in 1899. Later, in 1904, this organization was renamed the Catholic Educational Association (CEA). This association supplied a much-needed method of rejuvenating Catholic colleges and universities. Methods of renewal involved adapting existing curricular models to the American four-year undergraduate curricula. In the 1920s, Jesuit institutions joined the CEA, as well as secular accrediting organizations, and enhanced scientific training for faculty and students. In addition, Jesuit colleges and universities expanded liberal and scientific curricula to include professional and business programs. Still, the Society of Jesus in the American South continued to herald an identifiable liberal arts curriculum and slowly added professional and graduate programs.[104] This hesitance to quickly adapt to changing educational trends would cost the order dearly and ultimately forced the retrenchment of the southern Jesuit system of higher education.

As the Society of Jesus expanded in the American South, issues regarding Jesuit educational identity and mission affected surrounding social groups. In return, Jesuit institutions met with hostilities regarding their method of instruction, the religious nature of their colleges, and their very presence in the South. Protestant populations and anti-Catholic/anti-Jesuit organizations criticized the Society of Jesus and called for their removal. Widespread anti-Jesuit sentiment hindered Jesuit educational growth and, in time, played a part in the redesign of Jesuit higher education in the New Orleans Province. As well, internal issues of academic legitimacy forced Jesuit college officials to reorganize the southern system to better accommodate students' educational needs while maintaining a Catholic educational presence in cities heavily populated with Catholic supporters. In essence, the very identity and mission of the Society of Jesus dictated the formation and reformation of Jesuit higher education in the American South. In order to survive, however, Jesuit college administrators recognized the need to adapt, maneuvered social reactions to their religious identity and educational mission, and slowly revised curricular structures and downsized the number of physical campuses to address academic and social expectations.

2

Jesuit Identity, Jesuit Mission, and Southern Locale

> A function of clear institutional identity, and its measure is the ability of institutions to withstand. . . . Viewed in the longer term, many . . . institutions are not favored by recent history. They were forced, early on, to learn survival skills.
>
> —Carnegie Foundation for the Advancement of Teaching

As with any history, context and interpretive concepts are essential. As such, chapter 1 illuminated the all-important foundation of the Society of Jesus, how Ignatius Loyola's own educational experiences factored into the development of Jesuit higher education, and the nineteenth- and early twentieth-century ideological and social climate of the South in regard to Catholics and Jesuit colleges and universities. Facing a societal landscape colored by anti-Catholicism, anti-Jesuitism, and nativism, the Society of Jesus experienced numerous hardships related to the identity and mission of its colleges and universities. As has been argued, the combination of Jesuit identity and mission and its overall impact on social environments influenced Jesuit institutional survivability in the American South. As such, it is important to understand Jesuit identity, mission, and interactions between Jesuit educational institutions and the southern ideological climate. This chapter presents an interpretive description of American and southern ideological developments concerning Catholics and Catholic education, as well as several examples of Jesuit educational experiences and administrative reactions to the progressions of colleges and universities in the New Orleans Mission and later Province. We begin first with pertinent factors that illuminate Jesuit educational culture, structure, identity, as well as curricular missions and move forward to interactions between Jesuit colleges and southern society.

Jesuit educational identity is typified by liberal arts curricula, which focused on developing community leaders and offering vocational or commercial education when the need arose.[1] Curricula were designed to impart students with knowledge and skills deemed worthy to promote graduates in the surrounding social milieu and carry the ideals of the institution forward into society.[2] As lay students were not intended to become clergy, the goal in their instruction through theology and philosophy was to mold them into leaders who would live out a faithful life serving

God and positively influencing others.[3] Concerning the religious curricular structure of Jesuit colleges and universities, John McKenzie states that "what theology can contribute to the trained mind is knowledge of the truth as it is apprehended by theology; and knowledge of the truth is not going to hamper anyone's thinking."[4] McKenzie's argument is that the study of theology promotes the search for truth, and truth itself is integral to learning. Therefore, Jesuit theological curricula are not harmful but bolster the search for intellectual and spiritual truth.

In order to prepare students for higher level courses and stock the college divisions of Catholic institutions, a crucial curricular aspect was the provision of classes relegated to the secondary level.[5] These preparatory classes were an identifiable trait of Jesuit education that lasted well beyond secular higher education's separation from this type of curricular coupling. Such a preparatory curriculum was comprised of literature and classical liberal arts courses with additional classes in literature, mathematics, natural science, economics, and languages. Combined with higher educational courses, these lower grades made up the instructional regime of Jesuit colleges and universities in the nineteenth and early twentieth centuries.[6] In order to prepare students to fully understand theologically based lectures, Jesuits followed Ignatius's command that primary instruction must include letters, languages, Latin, arts, philosophy, and finally theology.[7]

While the course structure was thorough, expansive, and in line with Ignatius's educational experiences at European institutions, the instructional methods utilized in Jesuit colleges were harsh, and the *Ratio Studiorum* was often criticized for being too demanding.[8] Even so, Jesuits were pleased with their method of studies and encouraged its use in their southern institutions and applauded those who incorporated it into their instructional designs, as Father Albert Biever indicates in his journal on teaching at Spring Hill College: "Father F. X. O'Connor, S.J. the Vice-President and Prefect of Studies at the meeting of the [Spring Hill College] teachers commended my method which after all was drawn from the 'Ratio Studiorum.' This little praise encouraged me greatly. I was young, only nineteen years, and inexperienced. At the end of the school year I was appointed teacher of the Third Grammar."[9] With such organizational support, it is not difficult to understand that the premier elements of the *Ratio Studiorum*, coupled with Ignatian spirituality and Jesuit identity and mission, established the driving force behind Jesuit curricula.[10] According to Eugene Devlin, "the *Ratio* was not concerned with providing an easy or effortless way to character. It required of the student persevering effort and the sacrifice of subjective impulses to the objective claims of morality."[11] This method was concerned with the formation of the whole person, *cura personalis*, not a simple pathway to a college degree.

Despite the *Ratio Studiorum*'s stringent teaching methodologies, the overarching identifiable factor of the Jesuit system of education was its proposed adaptability to regional practices. When comparing Jesuit institutions across the globe, great variety can be found in the geographically established curricula.[12] If anything, the system implemented by the Society of Jesus was labeled with a stalwart identity and regional selectivity. This regional selectivity was evident in Louisiana dating back to the days of Jean-Baptiste Le Moyne de Bienville and the small apostolic war between the Jesuits and Capuchins in New Orleans. The Jesuits, disregarding the colonial Capuchin school, observed that no educational institution would be successful in the colony due to student egress to Europe and the lack of acceptable materials to build and stock an educational institution. Therefore, they did not establish a college in early New Orleans.[13]

According to Miguel Bernard, "whatever accusations might be hurled against Jesuit pedagogy (and there have been many), it cannot be accused of being vague in its aims, or of wanting system in its methods."[14] The *Ratio Studiorum* established that all educational materials utilized in Jesuit colleges should be easily accessible to the public. As a result, Jesuit methods of instruction and administration were widely known though perhaps not completely understood. In fact, the curricular plan of studies at the Jesuit-administered College of the Immaculate Conception in New Orleans, Louisiana, adhered to the instructional direction of the *Ratio Studiorum*. All academic classes were imbued with moral and mental philosophy, and public advertisements detailed the benefits of following a method tested by years of practice and tradition.[15] Not only were religious instructional aspects of the college known, Biever also indicates that "the New Orleans church and college are said to be the first in the world thus officially dedicated to the Immaculate Conception [of Mary]."[16] This connection with a religious figure heralded by the Catholic Church clearly established the religious identity of this particular Jesuit institution.

The College of the Immaculate Conception was understood by the community to be a Catholic institution; however, Catholic and non-Catholic alike were allowed to enroll as long as they partook in Catholic worship.[17] Students assembled every morning in the adjoining church for mass, prayer, and communion before the day's classes began.[18] Even extracurricular activities focused on religious contemplation through spiritual social clubs, religious music, and literary societies. Some of these organizations were listed in college catalogs as the Sodality of the Blessed Virgin Mary, the Apostleship of Prayer in League with the Sacred Heart, and the Sanctuary Society of St. John Berchmans. Also, there was the St. Cecilia choir and orchestra, along with a variety of literary societies that provided students with opportunities to practice debate and oratory skills.[19] Even though non-Catholic students were admitted to the College of the Immaculate Conception,

Jesuit administrators and instructors made sure that such social organizations provided a Catholic element for all students regardless of denominational ties. Such religious student organizations were included at several historic Jesuit institutions.

Even though Jesuit colleges offered a variety of liberal arts courses, the academic focus did not meet the actual industrial and agricultural needs of the southern populous. The design flaw in southern Jesuit institutions lay in their antiquated curricular models. This model, which reflected a European liberal arts education, could not provide a practical instructional structure to match secular universities following the Civil War.[20] As such, it was difficult to adapt the *Ratio Studiorum* to the American South during and beyond Reconstruction. As Michael Kenny explains, the "[Civil] War and its 'Reconstruction' consequences . . . make the letter of the *Ratio Studiorum* inapplicable."[21] Thus, in order to survive, southern Jesuit colleges, during and after Reconstruction, often, though not always, deviated from the Society of Jesus's method of studies in order to adapt to changing curricular and accreditation trends. As Jesuit institutions attempted to adapt to the reforms of American higher education at the end of the nineteenth century, they complied with high school and university curricular standards promoted by the National Entrance Examination Board. This board's main objective was the establishment of testing services that filtered students to various institutions based on national college entrance requirements.[22] The board relegated students to separate high schools or colleges based on age and test scores. The Jesuit system, at this time, relied on the aforementioned curricular combination of preparatory/high school and college-level courses. The southern Jesuit system was no exception: all colleges, prior to the twentieth century enrolled students, younger preparatory boys as well as "college-age" students, in the same campus facility.[23] Kathleen Mahoney, in her book *Catholic Higher Education in Protestant America: The Jesuits and Harvard in the Age of the University*, comments on the eventual curricular split of Jesuit high schools and colleges: "While the Jesuits labored over the issue of dividing the seven-year course of studies into distinctive preparatory and collegiate-level programs, other Catholic educators accepted the . . . model and began to successfully push for the establishment of independent Catholic high schools."[24] Despite the fact that these curricular reformations were now required for regional academic accreditation, Jesuit provinces across the United States were slow to respond, and often the order resisted reform entirely through the beginning of the twentieth century; however, by the 1920s, Jesuit secondary and higher education had begun to more closely resemble secular institutions.[25]

With accreditation standards changing, two additional issues presented problems for the Society of Jesus regarding the Catholic identity of Jesuit institutions. This first issue was a subcurrent of Americanized Catholic populations that moved away from age-old identifiable characteristics of Jesuit colleges. Simply put, Jesuit colleges were not perceived as "American." The second was the increased adaptation of American Catholic institutions to secular curricula, thus weakening the overall Catholic identity of these colleges and universities.[26] One example of this secular movement in southern Jesuit colleges is the advisement of Father Visitor Thomas O'Neill, who was appointed by the Jesuit Father General Peter Jan Beckx to audit the practices of all southern Jesuit institutions. Thomas O'Neill, from the Missouri Province, had instituted curricular reformation at Spring Hill College in 1880. His visitation allowed for the restructuring of the New Orleans Mission's administration from an old regime of French priests and brothers to a set of Irish American Jesuits determined to progress the order's southern educational institutions. This administrative change allowed for the adaptation of southern Jesuit colleges and universities to better accommodate the curricular needs of their students while enrolled in a Catholic educational institution, thus promoting the continued, yet slightly adapted, educational mission of the order.[27]

From the identity of the Society of Jesus sprang forth the mission of Jesuit education. Aspects of institutional mission have shaped Jesuit colleges and universities around the world. The purposes governing institutional missions are publicly perceived and internally directed and ultimately resonate with the development and survival of a college or university. The mission of Catholic institutions of higher education is, as Melanie Morey and John Piderit explain, an institutional aspect shaped by the foundational nature of the college or university. Morey and Piderit state that "how *mission* is understood and implemented, however, will be greatly affected by the culture from which it emerges and the depth and breadth of the Catholic character of that culture."[28] As colleges and universities managed by the Society of Jesus are culturally formed by the order itself, Jesuit institutions take on the expressed mission of that religious order. With the inclusion of literature regarding institutional mission, this chapter will attempt to demonstrate the Catholic connection to institutional survival and the formation of Jesuit institutions.

Ignatius believed that a great mission of the Society of Jesus would be religious education, such as catechetical lessons;[29] however, it is incorrect to label the Society of Jesus primarily as a teaching order. The order's spiritual missions range from teaching to preaching and missionary work, but the greatest longitudinal mission expressed by all Jesuits working within each college and university is the salvation of souls.[30] Jesuits are aware that the Society of Jesus was not founded to develop colleges and universities. That directive came later. This is taught to novices with the understanding that preaching and mission work are imperative to the life of a Jesuit. As Gustave Weigel states, "the heart of the matter for Jesuits is that their schools are means, not ends." Jesuit education in and of itself is but a part of the greater mission of the Society of Jesus.[31] To help illustrate this concept, William Byron, in his book chapter titled "A Religious-Based College and University Perspective," states that "in the Jesuit view, higher education is a medium; it is not just a means. It has intrinsic value. Involving, as it does, the pursuit of wisdom, higher education is worth much in purely human terms and thus worthy of dedicated human effort. But the worth of higher education, as both means and medium, transcends the human and touches the divine."[32] In other words, Jesuit education is meant to impart knowledge for the greater glory of God. When the order began educational work, it was Ignatius's desire that all instruction focus on the cultivation of intellect and morality.[33] Rooted in humanism, these Jesuit institutions were intended to educate the whole person—mind, body, and spirit—and lead them toward moral lives of leadership aimed not only at aiding society but also at spreading Catholicism.[34]

For the Society of Jesus, an institutional mission that calls for the harmonious development of the whole person, cura personalis, typifies each college and university. Curricula selected for use in Jesuit institutions is intended to affect not only the intellect and the body but also the soul and conscience. In the eyes of Jesuits, such a system is impossible without including religion in all instructional aspects.[35] As Harold Attridge states, "the commitment to work for the reign of God is entirely compatible with the quest to know the truth and to live in conformity with it. Not to engage in the, oftentimes abrasive, quest for truth is, in fact, to run the risk of setting up idols. At a university, particularly a university that seeks to work for the kingdom of God, the quest for Socrates must be sacrosanct."[36] Spiritually based education and service to God are the hallmarks of Jesuit identity and are considered chief components of the educational mission. Despite adapting curricula and programs to changing times, the overall aims remain the same.[37] Jesuits traveled the world; carried with them the identity and mission of the Society of Jesus; promoted it in their colleges; and ultimately, were influenced by the social context of geographic location.

Clearly, when identity and mission coalesce and influence societal relationships, institutions of higher education must adapt to social expectations in order to survive. It was no different for Jesuit higher education. As the Society of Jesus established colleges and universities in the United States, the public noted their presence. Due to negative public perceptions, however, financial and resource assistance was often difficult to acquire, and anti-Jesuit criticism aimed at the order's system of education followed these Catholic colleges and universities. As a result, town and gown relationships were at times tenuous and difficult to maintain. In largely Catholic cities, however, the establishment of Jesuit institutions was relatively easier than in highly Protestant portions of the United States. These town and gown, or in this case town and cassock, relationships detail the struggles of Jesuit higher education in America. Mahoney argues that Catholic higher education's connection with Roman Catholicism set it vastly apart from the surrounding educational environment of American Protestant higher education. Moreover, students and faculty belonging to Catholic institutions have historically been set apart from the larger society, whether it was due to their Catholic heritage or, in several cases, their immigrant status. Despite these difficulties, Jesuits took up the pressing task of responding to new academic demands from surrounding communities, all the while holding to their educational ideals and religious identity, in part by reasserting their institutions' main objective: the communication of the faith through academic instruction.[38]

As previously illustrated, the public perception of the Society of Jesus was often negative. Jesuits even held a place in American dictionaries as authors of deceit and hypocrisy. According to Mahoney: "antebellum lexicographers sharpened Americans' understanding of the Jesuit. Those consulting Noah Webster's 1850 *American Dictionary of the English Language* learned that the Jesuit was a member of the Society of Jesus, a 'society remarkable for their cunning in propagating their principles; Hence . . . [a] crafty person; an intriguer,' and that Jesuitism meant 'cunning deceit, hypocrisy, prevarication, deceptive practices to effect a purpose.'"[39] Such dictionaries claimed that Jesuits were rooted in the past, irrelevant, and lacking in modern educational methods. As the age of the college gave way to that of the university during Reconstruction, Jesuit institutions in America were publicly defamed as being against liberty and unresponsive to the educational needs of the modern age. However, *The Constitutions of the Society of Jesus* mandated that the order's educational institutions should adapt and be responsive not only to suit the times but also to respond to the people of surrounding environments.[40] Despite the direction to adapt, it would seem that the American populace was unaware of the foundational principles guiding the formation of Jesuit colleges and universities. Even so, many southern Jesuits were hesitant to adhere to *The Constitutions* and the directive to adapt to social surroundings. Instead, southern Jesuits relied on familiar practices of European liberal arts instruction and adapted curricular structures only when directly ordered by superiors or when facing the pressing need to maintain an educational presence in the American South.

As Albert Biever has presented, "all works of God begin in lowliness and are beset by many tribulations. The work of the Society of Jesus . . . was not to prove any exception."[41] Criticism abounded regarding Jesuit higher education. Critics of nineteenth-century Jesuit education not only commented on the harsh instructional regime of the *Ratio Studiorum* but also claimed that Jesuit colleges and universities served as bastions for Catholic tyranny. Other criticism regarded the ambitious educational expansion of the order. Jesuits loomed large in the minds of American Protestants. Even in the early days of the Jesuit restoration to the United States, leeriness of the order permeated American society. Mahoney goes on to explain that, "for many, every Catholic steeple, every Catholic immigrant—every

Jesuit and his school—was cause for concern, providing incontrovertible evidence that the Protestant Kingdom of God [that is, America] was still in the making, its very existence tenuous."[42]

Robert Schwickerarth, author of *Jesuit Education: Its History and Principles Viewed in the Light of Modern Educational Practices* gives a series of factors that spurred anti-Jesuit sentiment in nineteenth-century America. It was propagandized that Ignatius Loyola was first a soldier and that military vestiges crossed into the Society of Jesus, creating a religious order bent on societal domination. Second, Jesuits were denounced as plotting to overthrow European governments, including England, and were accused of having had a direct connection to Guy Fawkes and the Gunpowder Plot of 1605. Preached against as the authors of war, the teachers of dishonesty, and held in suspicion by Puritans, the Jesuits seemed to have been viewed with contempt the world over.[43] Even Elizabeth I of England and other European monarchs condemned the Society of Jesus for being too powerful, religiously heavy-handed, and overly ambitious.[44]

This widespread crimination crossed the Atlantic Ocean and took root in America. Even members of the Catholic Church criticized the Jesuit order and their educational institutions; however, the mission of such Jesuit colleges and universities held fast to the religious apostolate of education. According to Schwickerath, "Religious [clergy and nuns], above all, try to impart a religious, a Christian education."[45] As has been noted, the goal of the Society of Jesus was to provide instruction permeated with religious theology that would expose students to a life devoted to participation in the Catholic Church. Despite attempts to impart such education, Jesuit priests and brothers in the American South had to navigate social surroundings with contextual ideologies incongruent with Catholicism and Catholic educational practices. Father Michael Kenny provides an example of this incongruence. According to Kenny, no postbellum Catholic educational institution in Alabama was free from Protestant criticism. In Mobile, Alabama, Spring Hill College was defamed by Protestant denominational leaders who preached against the existence of a Catholic college in south Alabama. Spring Hill College and the Visitation Academy of Mobile took the brunt of these criticisms, many of which came from Episcopalian populations in neighboring counties.[46] Another example of Protestant disdain for Jesuit higher education is the short-lived College of Saints Peter and Paul in Baton Rouge. As was mentioned in chapter 1, in 1851, the Jesuits opened a college in the capital of Louisiana, at the same time effectively taking control of the surrounding St. Joseph parish. The local Methodist population rallied against the Jesuit institution and attempted to prevent its opening. In 1865, the college was forced to close due to local opposition and the occurrence of yellow fever.[47] Regional opposition to Jesuit higher education also affected the ability to convert young men to Catholicism and enlist their aid as priests and brothers in the Society of Jesus.

Following the return of the Jesuits to the American South in the early nineteenth century until the start of the Civil War, less than 3 percent of all Jesuits who worked in southern states were listed as American by birth. The majority were immigrants from France or Ireland;[48] however, the need to "home grow" Jesuit priests and brothers forced southern Jesuit superiors to construct novitiates and import additional Jesuits from Europe for instructional purposes. By 1880, increases in southern Jesuit populations led to the separation of the New Orleans Mission from the supervision of the Province of Lyons. This separation made the mission independent and reliant on its own means to survive.[49] Despite this growth, Father Thomas Clancy, in a speech given at Georgetown University, admitted that one of the greatest struggles for Jesuit colleges throughout America was the ability to stock institutions with enough priests. This lack of "man power" made it difficult to maintain the essence of Jesuit higher education as the order moved its colleges and universities into the twentieth century.[50] Father Clancy's comments rang true throughout the American Assistancy; however, no region reflected Clancy's comment as much as the New Orleans Province.

According to the *Catalogues of the New Orleans Province*, southern Jesuits were slow to increase their numbers due to war, disease, and a lack of Catholic men interested in joining the order. With the expansive post–Civil War growth of the College of the Immaculate Conception in the heavily Catholic city of New Orleans, several Catholic males were introduced to the Society of Jesus and later joined the Jesuits. As a result, the Jesuit population in the New Orleans Mission began to increase. The provincial catalogues indicate that the period after Reconstruction through the 1930s was one of exponential growth as Jesuit populations in the South rose above 400 by 1935; however, the New Orleans Province was the largest geographic region out of eleven American provinces and included the states of Alabama, Arkansas, Florida, Georgia, Louisiana, Mississippi, New Mexico, South Carolina, Tennessee, and Texas.[51] Despite an increase in the number of Jesuit priests and brothers, their numbers were not large enough to properly administer the unwieldy geographic territory. Additionally, lay-Catholic numbers were decreasing in the American South. In 1915 the total number of southern Catholics was estimated at 550,000. By 1935 this number had dropped to 329,351.[52] As a result of expanded mission territory (expanded to increase the number of Catholics served by the Society of Jesus) and decreased Catholic populations, the Jesuits, though steadily increasing in numbers, found it difficult to recruit enough Catholic men to properly manage the expansive province.

Due to such limited numbers, superiors of the New Orleans Mission moved priests and brothers from location to location and from college to college to better serve the needs of the region. The following entries from the minister's diary at the Sacred Heart Church and College in Augusta, Georgia, illustrates relocation efforts made in order to meet the staffing needs of the college.

> November 14, 1902—Fathers Tyrell, Mattern, and Biever consulters of the Mission arrived here from Macon at 5:00 P.M.
> August 28, 1903—Father Kenny arrived from Grand Coteau to teach here.
> August 22, 1904—Fathers arrive from Spring Hill and Grand Coteau to help with the college.[53]

Such constant mobility was undoubtedly taxing and did not provide a form of instructional or administrative consistency.

By the late nineteenth century, many educational institutions affiliated with the Catholic Church were developing in regions with high Catholic populations instead or rural areas or cities with disproportionate Catholic to Protestant ratios. It can be argued that establishing Jesuit institutions in heavily Catholic regions fostered a greater identity agreement between the town and gown and perhaps increased the number of men willing to train to be clergy. Following the writings of Ignatius Loyola, the Society of Jesus established several of their colleges in urban settings. It was Ignatius's habit to locate the colleges of the Society of Jesus in highly populated, highly Catholic cities.[54] It was the same with most Jesuit institutions in the American South. The site of the College of the Immaculate Conception was located in the heart of the central business district of New Orleans. However, by the start of the twentieth century this area had become noisy, crowded, and polluted. As such this locale was no longer considered a beneficial temple to academic and religious life. Thus, the institution was closed and all college curricula and students were transferred to a new Jesuit university.[55] In essence, location affects Jesuit colleges as it does any other institution of higher education.

For Jesuit colleges and universities in the American South, location was important to acknowledge as it established geographic and political boundaries that influenced town and gown relationships. As has been suggested, such practices have been important for Catholic institutions in Protestant populated regions of America. As Mahoney states, "defining the boundaries of engagement with American Protestantism and Protestant America has shaped Catholic higher education, determining in large measure the degree to which it has been able to achieve respectability and social relevance in the American context while maintaining its Catholic character."[56] Even when Jesuits navigated the New Orleans business district, the College of the Immaculate Conception seemed to perform well. According to Roger Baudier, "the boys' college met with prompt success. . . . Students came from all parts of the city. The roster of the College of the Immaculate Conception in its early years, is virtually a directory of the leaders of New Orleans in the subsequent decades. The college did an untold amount of good in overcoming the chronic spirit of indifference to religion among men and in bringing up a more zealous and devout body of Catholic laymen, which heretofore, had been one of the saddest wants of New Orleans for more than a century."[57] From Baudier's quotation it is easy to ascertain the significance of such a Catholic institution in a city with a large Catholic population. Certainly the Society of Jesus took note of the effects that southern surroundings had on their institutions. The social relations between local communities, state governments, and the Jesuits spawned both friendships and hardships for the order.

Jesuit colleges and universities are chartered by state governments but owned by a corporation of Jesuits that determines the characteristic identity of each college or university. The distinctive identity of this corporation is important to understand when examining the larger institutional identity of a Jesuit institution.[58] In order to establish a Catholic university, a charter must be granted by both the state and papal authority.[59] The same is true with Jesuit institutions across the United States and in the American South. For example, Spring Hill College is one of the oldest Jesuit institutions in North America and was the first college established in Alabama.[60] Following his placement as superior of Spring Hill College, Father Jean Baptiste Maisonnabe secured a state charter for the instruction of students in religious and literary courses.[61] This charter accompanied a papal mandate, thus acknowledging the approval of state, regional, and clerical leaders. Not only did Spring Hill College receive a state charter and papal support, but Mobile's Catholic population, "a spillover from its historical ties to New Orleans,"[62] provided a consistent enrollment of young men.

The need for various forms of support (state, papal, social) was highly evident to the Jesuits. Following the establishment of St. Charles College in Grand Coteau, Louisiana, Archbishop Blanc turned his attention to the city of New Orleans and the need for an educational institute for Catholic boys. With the arrival of the Ursulines and various other female religious orders, young female New Orleanians had an established network of Catholic schools. Young men, on the other hand, had none. Once again, Blanc approached the Jesuits and invited them to establish a parish in New Orleans and open a college for young men. In June 1848, the foundation was laid for the College of the Immaculate Conception, an adjoining church, and a residence for the Jesuit fathers and brothers. Later, the state of Louisiana, as well as the Holy Father in Rome, issued their approval of the New Orleans college.[63]

Even though the College of the Immaculate Conception received endorsements from civic and clerical leaders, it was poorly supported by commercial agencies.

To counter this lack of financial support, the Jesuits petitioned their parishioners to provide assistance.[64] Published appeals for aid carried the sentiments of the order as its priests and brothers strove to build a college and adjoining church in New Orleans. Despite the solicitation for financial assistance, response was low, consisting of only two donations totaling $50. In response to low public support, the city's secular Catholic clergy provided $2,350. Topping all other donations was that of the Ursuline Sisters. The Ursulines, who had long supported the Society of Jesus both in New Orleans and abroad lent the Society of Jesus, interest free, $20,000.[65] As the College of the Immaculate Conception, Spring Hill College, and St. Charles College grew, the Jesuits were invited elsewhere to establish institutions of higher education.

Bishop Anthony Durier, seeing the further need for Catholic education in northern Louisiana, invited the Jesuits to establish an educational institution in Shreveport. Their response was the creation of St. John's College in 1902.[66] In 1874, the society was called to Augusta, Georgia, to manage a church and parish. In 1900 the Jesuits expanded their ecclesiastical work by opening a college. In 1884, the bishop of Galveston, Texas, gave St. Mary's University to the the Society of Jesus, and in 1889, the Right Reverend J. Moore, bishop of St. Augustine, called the Jesuit fathers and brothers to Florida. In Florida, the Jesuits established a church and educational institution in Tampa.[67] It is important to note that the Jesuits were invited to develop parishes, churches, and colleges across the South. The reputation of the Society of Jesus as a religious order with strong teaching practices and a growing number of southern colleges and universities kept them in the public eye of both lay and religious leaders.

A Catholic university, such as a Jesuit institution, stands for a long tradition of combining faith and reason; however, delving deeper into historic missions of Catholic higher education, one can find aspects regarding the safeguarding of Catholic students from the dangers of modernity.[68] Despite the adaptive efforts of the Jesuits, their attempts to emulate secular higher education were slow to formulate, and Catholic students in lower socioeconomic classes began to drift to forms of higher education that could provide practical job-related education and training. In the late nineteenth century, the Society of Jesus contended with edicts established by the New York State Board of Regents concerning the qualifiers for a higher education institution. In 1897, the American Assistancy of the Society of Jesus noted that the state of New York sought to formally demarcate the differences between high school and college level courses. Stress was mounting to separate lower levels of instruction from the collegiate level and to properly title all institutions based on the type of curricula offered. The regents of New York had determined that no institution offering any form of high school or college preparatory curricula should be called a "college."[69] Reports also claimed that no student should be admitted to a college or university without having completed four years of high school instruction. The curricula of Jesuit colleges across the country and in the American South were based on the *Ratio Studiorum*, however, which dictated that Jesuit institutions were to enroll students from the preparatory level all the way through the completion of college courses. The Jesuits slowly began to rectify their educational structures and physical campuses to remain competitive with their secular counterparts, but the concern was how to remain true to the identity and mission of the Society of Jesus as it was asserted in the *Ratio Studiorum*. The Jesuits realized that they would have to lengthen the terms of the lower grammar and college liberal arts courses to span four years instead of the three requested in the *Ratio Studiorum*.

The order, despite its difficulty with the decision of the New York regents, took this ruling as a sign to adapt, and across the nation, Jesuit colleges began to align more closely with Protestant and secular institutions. Despite its continued dedication to the spirit of the *Ratio Studiorum*, the southern American branch of the Society of Jesus echoed American educational trends, though gradually and at times grudgingly. Older, more stalwart Jesuits were often disinclined to "Americanize" their European system of colleges and universities. This further hindered the process of adapting the out-of-date educational system to new accreditation standards. Reflecting on this aspect of the New Orleans Province's history, a 1963 self-study committee at Loyola University New Orleans generated a report which states that "it appears, indeed, that [Jesuit administrators at the turn of the twentieth century] repudiated American higher learning of that period. The records indicate that these men clung to the notion of the traditional, intermediate, Jesuit, European educational system, and denigrated the existing American University system on the grounds that it was 'godless.'"[70] When Father Visitor Norbert de Boynes arrived in 1921 to assess the New Orleans Province and its collection of colleges and universities he disapproved of the slow curricular transition and strained human resources. In response, de Boynes ordered a system-wide revision, including the closure of several institutions.[71]

In a letter to Mike Alchediak regarding the history of the New Orleans Province, Thomas Clancy states that "one of the continual struggles in the history of the Province and Mission is the struggle of those who want to expand and those who want to concentrate on fewer apostolates. In general Provincials like to expand and Generals like to contract."[72] Clancy was correct in his statement concerning the decisions of provincial superiors and superior generals, especially as these actions related to the recommendations of father visitors. The recommendation of a father visitor was a powerful influence that determined the fate of several Jesuit institutions, and no visitor to the New Orleans Province was as stern or as thorough as Father Norbert de Boynes. In 1921, Father de Boynes was sent to review the New Orleans Province. De Boynes was greatly concerned with the order's overextended state in the South. De Boynes and Father Edward Cummings, the former president of Spring Hill College and, at that time, president of Loyola University New Orleans, were in agreement that the only way to ensure the sustained identity and ultimate survival of Jesuit higher education in the American South was to seek affiliation with the Southern Association of Colleges and Schools (SACS) and close all New Orleans Province colleges except Loyola University and Spring Hill College.[73]

Acting on behalf of the father general in Rome, Father de Boynes made a full inspection of the New Orleans Province and its Jesuit colleges and churches. After his inspection, de Boynes provided the Jesuits with a report of his visitation and his recommendations for improvement. De Boynes reminded the southern Jesuits that they were servants who worked for the greater glory of God through their vow of obedience. The following is an abbreviated account of the 1921 visitation report as it concerns the colleges of the province:

> A true Jesuit, trained in the school of the Spiritual Exercises, is a man of prayer, ever faithful to his daily spiritual duties and united by the bonds of the closest friendship to our divine Lord. Such a man's aim in life is summed up by our motto: 'Ad Majorem Dei Gloriam.' He is determined to fulfill, according to the measure of God's grace imparted to him, the solemn obligations he took upon himself on the day of his vows. . . .
>
> The apostolate of the Society must needs be greatly influenced by the conditions of Catholicity in the South. It had to adapt itself to such conditions and it has done so. . . . In such an immense territory where Catholics are so few and far between, there are not many cities in which a strong Catholic influence can be exercised on a larger scale. . . . This is the reason why it is so difficult to find suitable cities for flourishing day-schools and colleges. . . . The Province has not been able for long years to prepare specialists either for the classroom or the pulpit. . . . St. Ignatius founded the Society to promote the greater glory of God. . . . He wanted his sons to give a thorough college training to their students and impart an education that will form leaders. . . . It is clear that a few men prepared for such work will do more good for the glory of God than a host of men who have all the good will in the world but are lacking in the necessary preparation and knowledge. It is also evident that a few colleges or schools, furnished with an able faculty and the necessary equipment, and measuring up to the recognized standards, will be much better fitted for the good formation of Catholic boys and young men, and at the same time

reflect greater credit on the Society, than many colleges and schools that are deficient in teachers and in equipment. . . .

Under these conditions it is impossible to raise the studies of your colleges and schools to the standard required by the Ratio Studiorum and the College Associations. Hence in spite of great efforts you can not bring about proper development in your education activities, nor make them, as they should be, models for other colleges of the South to imitate. . . . To express my thought completely, why could not Loyola University be the center and focus of intellectual Catholic activity, advantageous both for Catholics and non-Catholics alike. . . . You should adapt your plans and your work to the possibilities and the needs of the South, and not dream impossible things or build castles in the air. Your share of work, such as we find it in the South, is splendid when we consider either the ordinary ministries of the Society among Catholics or the hard work of spreading the Faith among non-Catholics. It has been assigned to you by God Himself; do your work therefore with courage and zeal, and love it as you love the will of God. . . .

Commending myself to your holy Sacrifices and prayers, I am,
Your devoted servant in Christ,
N. deBoynes, S.J.
VISITOR OF THE NEW ORLEANS PROVINCE[74]

Father Cummings, after communicating with de Boynes, realized that the fate of Spring Hill College might be thrown in with other institutions such as St. Charles College and St. Mary's University.

Cummings acted quickly and convinced de Boynes that "the teaching powers of the Province must be centered on the development of Loyola University and Spring Hill College in compliance with the College Accrediting Associations, and to that necessity the smaller institutions must be sacrificed."[75] It is possible that Cummings was able to defend the Mobile institution due to his previous Spring Hill College presidency; however, no documentation has been found that describes the exact reasons why Cummings was able to sway de Boynes to spare Spring Hill College. Through Cumming's intercession, the de Boynes's visitation and recommendations led Jesuit superiors to focus the predominance of provincial human and material resources on Loyola University and Spring Hill College in order to strengthen the identity and mission of southern Jesuit higher education. This decision to strengthen the educational identity and mission of the New Orleans Province, in effect, forced the closure of all remaining southern Jesuit colleges, leaving a much-reduced system but one with a better chance of survival.[76]

In memorial notices concerning the recommendations of de Boynes, the Jesuits of the New Orleans Province were reminded that the religious mission of Jesuit colleges would be enhanced by the appointment of a spiritual father whose purpose was to serve only as a counselor to college students without the encumbering duties of teaching or administration. This spiritual father would be available at all times to counsel and guide any student who sought him out. In this capacity, the spiritual father would enhance the moral and religious education of young men and further the grand mission of Jesuit instruction by helping to prepare students for the spiritual battles they would confront after graduation.[77] Such provisions for spiritual direction had to be included in the balance of adapting curricula and maintaining the Jesuit identity of Loyola University and Spring Hill College. In the midst of the de Boynes's visitation, New Orleans Province superiors were invited to join an inter-province committee to address the changing face of American Jesuit higher education.

On April 20, 1921, provincials from across the United States assembled at Fordham College in New York to take part in the Inter-Province Committee on Studies. The primary objective of this committee was the accreditation of all Jesuit colleges and universities in the United States. The committee's secondary purpose was to foster inter-province educational efforts and promote a singular ideal of what American Jesuit higher education was and would become in order to attain new standards of academic legitimacy. The committee made several decisions. First, all high school and college curricula would be divided and reestablished on separate campuses; second, the name "college" would from that point forward only refer to institutions of higher education that did not offer high school or preparatory courses; third, standard Jesuit curricula would be promoted throughout all American Jesuit institutions; fourth, even though the "spirit of the Ratio Studiorum cannot be maintained with the present schedule of subjects," all Jesuit instructors should assume the same leadership and guiding qualities of *The Spiritual Exercises* to foster a sense of religious identity in all Jesuit institutions despite the increase of secular courses; and fifth, all colleges would sustain an enrollment of no fewer than one hundred students and provide no fewer than eight distinct departments of study from the following: ancient languages, English and literature, modern languages, mathematics, physics, chemistry, philosophy, history, political science, education, psychology, economics, and social sciences. Moreover, it was decided that no fewer than ninety course hours should be prescribed for a bachelor's degree and that each student must have a major with the option of at least one minor. The committee also took a stance on the continuation of physical training for all students. Finally, and most important, the committee decreed that lessons of morality should permeate all class instruction to some degree.[78]

The committee also made decisions on the professional and academic development of Jesuits to better serve in their colleges and universities. It was determined that all Jesuit instructors, regardless of their field of study, should partake in instructional training, that the *Ratio Studiorum* should be closely studied for implementation and adaptation in all Jesuit-taught classes, and that all Jesuits who teach or will teach should pursue a terminal degree in a predetermined area of study such as the sciences or languages. Also, Jesuit instructors should attempt to publish textbooks or other scholarly works to enhance the academic proliferation of Catholic scholarship. In addition, the committee decided that henceforth, all materials deemed important to the process of restructuring Jesuit higher education must be retained in archives for future study by other Jesuits.[79]

The American father provincials were pleased with the committee's decisions and issued the following statement: "The undeniable fact that the method of the Society of Jesus has achieved such marvelous success in the past warrants the conclusion that it is a most correct and efficacious method. We recommend therefore that the Ratio, wisely adapted to the times, be thoroughly explained and illustrated in practice to our young teachers in training. . . . The Jesuit system insists not only on the development of the intellect, but lays even more stress on the training of the will. The teacher, according to the Ratio, is not a mere instructor; he is an educator."[80] Even though new emphasis was placed on the teaching ability of Jesuit instructors, many Jesuit college administrators worried about their particular institution's survival due to the removal of preparatory departments and subsequent loss of younger students. In response to these concerns, Jesuit superiors issued the following statement: "Some of our colleges which twenty years ago stood the proud rivals of local colleges and universities, have lost their old prestige on account of this predominance of small boys. . . . But then there was not so exact a line of demarcation between the primary and secondary, and between the secondary and the collegiate courses. Even in this country fifty years ago these lines were not so exactly drawn."[81] This comment alone demonstrates the tardiness of the American Jesuit system of higher education to adapt to changing educational trends.

Following the inter-province meeting at Fordham College, the New Orleans Province Jesuits formed their own committee to reinforce adaptations deemed necessary by the American provincials. The following was taken from the minutes of the Committee on Studies of the New Orleans Province: "Attention is called to the recommendation of the INTER-PROVINCE COMMITTEE ON STUDIES regarding the use of the word COLLEGE or UNIVERSITY by schools not doing college or university work. It is recommended by this committee that this be carried into effect. In case the institution is chartered as a college, the High School should be known as HIGH SCHOOL DEPARTMENT of [the] College or University."[82] With lines of demarcation drawn by the inter-province committee, New Orleans Province superiors turned their attention to de Boynes's recommendation of submitting Loyola University and Spring Hill College to regional accrediting boards.

By 1924, the Department of Colleges and Secondary Schools for the Catholic Educational Association (CEA) enforced academic standards for all Catholic colleges. According to the association's admission guidelines, all colleges that request membership in the CEA must grant bachelor's degrees, accept only those students who have completed a four-year high school curriculum, require 120 hours for college graduation, not maintain a preparatory department (unless kept rigidly separate from the college), and place all emphasis on the Catholic character of the institution, its mission, identity, and instruction.[83]

In an effort to test the accrediting waters, a plan was hatched to submit Spring Hill College first to the rigors of the accrediting boards, to learn from the experience, and to ultimately submit Loyola University. A report of the Committee on the Revision of Studies states:

> Graduates of Spring Hill, having the B.S. degree, are admitted without condition into universities such as Pennsylvania, Mass. Institute of Technology; into West Point; and are given advanced standing in teaching by the Board of Regents, New York. . . . The plan . . . adopted was that Spring Hill should seek for general recognition of its courses and degrees with all Southern universities as well as with the Government and National Associations; reporting to the other Colleges what requirements are demanded and what deficiencies noted; then all Colleges having the same schedule approved of for Spring Hill will apply for like recognition and standing. It was urged that in the meantime all should try to gain as much recognition as possible with local schools, Colleges, and Associations.[84]

Following this plan, Spring Hill College and, later, Loyola University New Orleans were approved by SACS. This accreditation, as demonstrated via the Loyola University and Spring Hill College cases, illustrates the attempt to adapt southern Jesuit higher education to period legitimacy norms while retaining the Catholic identity of each institution per involvement with the CEA.

In time, academic legitimacy attained through accrediting organizations was not enough. Secular peer institutions (public and private) had to acknowledge that the academic teaching and scholarship of Jesuit instructors was on par with professors at secular colleges and universities. Father General Wlodimir Ledóchowski encouraged the attainment of academic and scholarly legitimacy in a letter the American Assistancy of the Society of Jesus. Ledóchowski states:

> The modern educational world, as we know, calls for more publicity, for greater exterior evidence of scholarship than in the past. Teachers must have degrees, they must write books and articles of scientific value, give conferences and lectures that interest people, keep in contact with learned organizations. We cannot afford to ignore these requisites of the modern teachers, though we must try to direct them to the spiritual and supernatural end proper to our vocation. . . . I cannot sufficiently emphasize my conviction that the success of your future educational work will depend very largely on the cooperation of all in carrying it forward; cooperation of the Provinces among themselves, cooperation of the several colleges of each Province, cooperation lastly of all the members of the Province, old and young, Superiors and subjects, each unselfishly looking to the general good.[85]

In the New Orleans Province, Loyola University and Spring Hill College continued their efforts to maintain academic legitimacy. As both institutions progressed through the twentieth century, the number of Jesuits teaching and researching at both institutions steadily increased while the number of Jesuits serving churches and parishes in the New Orleans Province decreased. In 1936, Father Michael Kenny wrote that "the hope of increasing vocations expressed in 1921 by Father Visitor de Boynes is being fulfilled, and they are almost entirely native and southern. . . . In 1907 there were but twenty-five novices and juniors, and thirty in 1921; now there are fifty-five. The relative fewness of native vocations for the Brotherhood [Jesuit brothers] is not peculiar in the South, but the scholastic increase gives gratifying promise for the future."[86] Despite the increased numbers of priests, brothers, and scholastics, there were still not enough Jesuits to manage the expanded geographic territory of the southern branch of the Society of Jesus following the promotion of the New Orleans Mission to the New Orleans Province. Also, the number of new Jesuits qualified to teach on the college level decreased due to a lack of graduate educational attainment. Such population and educational issues certainly taxed southern Jesuit institutions.

These overarching trends weave together the seven institutions presented in this book through a broader analysis of the administration and decision-making processes of the Society of Jesus. The Jesuit hierarchy, mission of adaptability, and Catholic identity played roles not only in the individual institutions presented in this study but also affected the Society of Jesus's ability to maintain their colleges and universities and thrive as a religious organization in the American South. Today, the two remaining Jesuit institutions of the New Orleans Province retain a highly Catholic identity. Upon walking onto either campus, visitors are struck with a myriad of visual Catholic symbols, statues, and Catholic phrases etched into stone. Jesuit centers for the promotion of Ignatian ideals and educational missions are located on both campuses. Even with declining Jesuit populations, both institutions still retain their Jesuit identity and maintain a link with their surrounding communities. Although highly adapted from southern antebellum Jesuit institutions, Loyola University and Spring Hill College stand as functional testaments to the educational efforts of the Society of Jesus in the American South.

Though the Jesuits of the New Orleans Province were slow to act on orders of adaptation, they still enacted curricular and system change for the betterment of southern Jesuit higher education. As such, they managed to maintain their educational identity and mission as promulgated through the order's instructional documents. As Morton Hill states, "when there is failure it is admitted. There are no coated enthusiasms. Most encouraging of all is this: nowhere do Jesuits blame the *Ratio* for their failures in education, any more than they would blame the *Exercises* for their failures in the things of the spirit. Jesuits have confidence in their heritage."[87] This would have been an excellent quotation for lay readers to take into account when reviewing Jesuit higher education's development throughout the United States; however, the publication in which this quote is printed, the *Jesuit Educational Quarterly*, was a confidential publication explicitly labeled "for private circulation" in Jesuit houses alone.[88] Likewise, the *Woodstock Letters*, originally conceived by Father Joseph E. Keller and published at Woodstock College in Woodstock, Maryland, from 1872 to 1969 was a periodical by Jesuits for Jesuits. These quarterly publications are filled with firsthand accounts and memories of fathers and brothers in the American Assistancy. The purpose of this compendium was to unify the American Assistancy of the Society of Jesus through communal understandings of experiences undertaken by members of the Society of Jesus. These publications recount the history of the order in the United States; its attempts at mission work and education; and include biographies, obituaries, novice descriptions, as well as curricula and enrollment data pertaining to Jesuit educational institutions. Printed for "Ours Only," these publications, when opened, included a small slip of paper explaining the clandestine nature of the *Woodstock Letters*: "Ours are reminded that *The Woodstock Letters* are for private circulation only, and hence should on no account be shown to externs, nor left where strangers visiting our houses may see them. This is the order of Rev. Father Provincial. Permission to publish extracts from *The Letters* can be given by Father Provincial alone, and when such permission is given the Editor should be notified, who will then supply sheets containing the matter required, so that the entire number may not be put into the hands of externs."[89] Although the Jesuits tried to communicate their educational identity and mission to the lay public via advertisements, college catalogues, and encyclicals, disseminating information in the *Jesuit Educational Quarterly* and the *Woodstock Letters* might have further demystified the Society of Jesus and enhanced town and gown relationships.

Though the Society of Jesus faced explicit hardships in the United States, particularly in the South, there is still global success to be recorded. At the end of the 1930s there existed some 244 Jesuit colleges and secondary schools, enrolling approximately 375,954 students worldwide.[90] However, the number of educational institutions in the American South remained low. Likewise, the number of Jesuits needed to properly administer those educational institutions and oversee the ecclesiastical endeavors of the New Orleans Province was difficult to attain. As has been argued, the relationship between town and gown is influenced by factors relevant to institutional identity and mission. The same is true with Jesuit higher education as it is imbued with Catholic ideologies and must function within larger social settings, Catholic or not. In the chapters that follow a series of cases are presented that illustrate the history of a variety of southern Jesuit institutions, their interactions with surrounding social environments, and how they adapted, merged, survived, or closed. Considering the institutional and contextual issues presented in each of the following cases it becomes apparent that the survival of each southern Jesuit college or university was influenced by the guiding culture and administrative actions of the Society of Jesus. As such, it can be noted that the concepts of identity and mission become viable or detrimental factors when they are congruent with or in contrast to surrounding societies.

3
Failure to Survive

> Closing has been a constant feature of the life of the [New Orleans] mission and province.
>
> —Father Thomas Clancy

Now that we understand how factors of institutional identity and mission affect societal relationships, thereby influencing college and university survivability, we can fully examine histories of individual southern Jesuit colleges and universities to determine how they functioned, evolved, adapted, failed, or survived. In the following cases, three college micro-histories are presented. Each case details an institutional closure brought about by the convergence of Jesuit institutional identity and mission reacting with social environments and contextual circumstances to affect survival. These micro-histories include St. Charles College, Grand Coteau, Louisiana (1837–1922); St. Mary's University, Galveston, Texas (1854–1922); and the College of the Sacred Heart, Augusta, Georgia (1900–1917). Each of these institutional histories highlights social factors in various southern states and explains how foundational efforts, institutional destruction, and redevelopment efforts contributed to local community reactions. In addition, these cases detail curricular developments, enrollment difficulties, geographic displeasure, and the final decisions of the Society of Jesus to shut down each college. Through the analysis of these three Jesuit institutions, singular and comparative, we can better understand social reactions to each institution, the decisive actions of the New Orleans Province, and contextual issues that influenced the failure of each institution.

St. Charles College in Grand Coteau, Louisiana

At the end of Reconstruction, the American Assistancy of the Society of Jesus described St. Charles College in Grand Coteau, Louisiana, as "destined to rise into fame." While illustrating the then short history of the institution in the 1876 edition of the *Woodstock Letters*, Jesuits compared St. Charles College to other successful Jesuit institutions, including the titular Woodstock College in Maryland.[1] Despite this herald of success, the college faced many hardships including social upheaval, fire, and war. St. Charles College, the first Jesuit college in the American South, was subject not only to the historical trials and tribulations of the Jesuits but also struggled to adapt to the changing ideological and educational climate of rural Louisiana. Even though the college experienced numerous hardships, the history of St. Charles College presents many issues that lend themselves to the understanding of how institutional identity and mission influence town and gown relationships to hinder survivability.

After fifty-one years of suppression, French Jesuits returned to New Orleans in 1837 by the invitation of Archbishop Antoine Blanc to found a college and aid in the propagation of the Catholic faith. Upon their arrival, the Jesuits attempted to acquire a site for the proposed college. Blanc suggested the parish of Iberville, Louisiana, due to his familiarity with the territory, but the Jesuits rejected his proposal. Various other localities, such as Houma and Mandeville, Louisiana, were visited but could not, on account of lack of funds, be considered. Donaldsonville was also considered, but because of blatant anti-Jesuit outcry from the community, the Jesuits decided against it.[2]

While sites for the new Jesuit college were under consideration, Grand Coteau, Louisiana, was nominated due to its high Catholic population and the successful work of the Sisters of the Sacred Heart in their academy for young women. Founded in 1821, the Academy of the Sacred Heart in Grand Coteau is considered one of the oldest Sacred Heart schools in the world and has educated a host of young women from southern families.[3] The Jesuits concluded that local sugar and cotton planters might support a similar college for young men close to the Sacred Heart Academy. The discovery of Grand Coteau proved most fortunate, as the previous sites of Iberville, which was prone to yearly floods, and Donaldsonville, where the populace had publicly announced their opposition to the Jesuits, had been rejected.[4]

However, after visiting Grand Coteau, the Jesuits expressed doubts about the location as it was difficult to reach. The small town was, and remains, surrounded by swamps and marshlands, which, in addition to making it isolated, made it susceptible to occasional bouts of yellow fever.[5] Taking note of the fathers' hesitance, the Sisters of the Sacred Heart encouraged the Jesuits to establish the college near to their academy, and donated $1,000 for construction costs. This heartening support, along with $10,000 and 800 acres provided through the efforts of Archbishop Blanc, as well as an additional $2,000 left by an influential Grand Coteau resident, Charles Smith (who left money for the establishment of a college in his will), prompted the fathers and brothers to settle on the small town.[6] It was not long before the Jesuits and the Sisters of the Sacred Heart struck up a strong, supportive relationship. To aid the sisters, the Jesuit fathers in Grand Coteau said mass and held retreats for the nuns and their students.[7]

With the support of the Sisters of the Sacred Heart and positive encouragement from local Catholics, the Jesuits set up residence on the acreage designated for their new institute. With Archbishop Blanc's blessing, a ceremony was held at the church next to the construction site, and the college's cornerstone was laid. In an unpublished manuscript, Michael Kenny illustrates the founding ceremonies of the college:

> On the Feast of St. Ignatius, 1837, Most Rev. Bishop Blanc addressed the people in the parish Church in the spiritual educational blessings which the accession of the Jesuits promised to themselves and their children. Following a long procession and a chanting choir to the chosen site, his Excellency, with solemn ceremony laid the cornerstone of St. Charles Borromeo College. He then signed with Father Point the new contract by which the Bishop of New Orleans ceded to the Jesuits St. Charles College and Church besides the full parish properties and revenue . . . with right to rent, cultivate, and build at pleasure in the college and boarding school thereon and assume charge of the Church and parish of St. Charles.[8]

With all contracts signed and cornerstone in place, construction was underway. Before long, an imposing structure soon dominated the landscape, rivaling the adjacent St. Charles Borromeo Church in height. According to Albert Biever, "a four story brick building ante bellum was immediately erected. Heavy Doric columns supported wide gabled verandas. Over the upper veranda was placed in large gilt letters the inscription: 'Deo et Patriae.'"[9] As student numbers increased, the Jesuit fathers and brothers found it necessary to construct an additional three-story building next to the main edifice. Jesuit novices, priests, and brothers occupied the older building, while college students were housed in the new structure.[10]

Not only was the physical plant impressive, but large gifts of land afforded the production of agriculture and livestock. According to land acquisition maps concerning the college property, it appears that the acreage was slowly enlarged through the cobbling together of donated lands. Maps indicate that the property was controlled by the parish but was to be used exclusively by the Jesuits for their college. Other additional pieces of land were given "in payment of tuition by Humbert Perrodin for Charles and Theodore Perrodine," donated to the parish through wills, or deeded by residents of Grand Coteau.[11] Through these various land donations, the college developed a farming system to garner additional capital and provide sustenance for enrolled students. On the south side of the college campus were several fields filled with corn, cotton, and sugar cane. This four-thousand-acre farm produced more than was necessary to sustain the college and its inhabitants.[12] The institution was indeed fully self-sustaining. Along with produce, cows, hogs, and chickens were raised in abundance.[13]

The majority of Grand Coteau's population consisted of Catholics from old French families and immigrants, many of whom had undergone primary education with the Sisters of the Sacred Heart. The town was described as having a peaceful attitude with a low crime rate, and its inhabitants had cheerful dispositions and rich Creole histories.[14] According to Father Albert Biever: "Grand Coteau received its name from the early settlers because of its position on the crest of a sloping hill about sixty feet above sea level. The northern limits of the college estate are watered by Bayou Teche flowing through a picturesque country immortalized by Longfellow. The inhabitants of these sections were known under the name of Creoles. The origin of their name, and history of their ancestors were of no small interest to us."[15] Such an environment, rich in land and heritage, typified by the observance of the Catholic faith, was deemed a proper locale to impart the Jesuit mission of education and allow for the regrowth of the Society of Jesus in Louisiana. From 1836 to 1840, St. Charles College was under the control of French Jesuits serving the Mission of Lyons. In 1840, the college briefly passed to the jurisdiction of the Vice Province of Missouri, but in 1847, Father Jean Baptiste Maisounabe returned the college to French control. In 1852, the State of Louisiana empowered the institution to confer degrees, and twenty years later, the college became the novitiate for the training of southern Jesuits. This clerical department was maintained along with separate college courses for lay students.[16] Such an amalgamation strengthened the identity of the institution as a Jesuit college not only for the instruction of young men but also for the formation of new Jesuit priests and brothers.

An advertisement disseminated throughout the community of Grand Coteau and surrounding areas announced that St. Charles College was situated in a healthy and beautiful environment far removed from the threat of yellow fever; an annual occurrence in the heavily populated city of New Orleans.[17] The advertisement was crowned with a detailed illustration of the existing campus as well as depictions of planned additions to the facilities. Readers were informed that all students who enrolled would be treated to curricula divided by classical and commercial studies. Those students not of age or not prepared for the classical or commercial courses were to be placed in the preparatory department. The advertisement also reported that English, Spanish, French, German, and Italian would be taught in addition to music and drawing. The preparatory department accepted students from nine to fourteen years of age, and the price of yearly boarding was $200. In the advertisement, printed in both French and English, families were notified that during regular semesters all students participating in either the preparatory department or the classical/commercial courses were to remain at the college until the end of term unless leave was granted due to extraneous circumstances.[18]

After St. Charles College was established, it was not long before criticisms arose regarding the very identity of the religious order administering the college. An Opelousas newspaper published articles inciting anti-Jesuit sentiment and called for the expulsion of the Society of Jesus from Grand Coteau and south Louisiana. Threatening letters were sent to the fathers and brothers giving them fifteen days to leave Grand Coteau and abandon their college or they would be "stripped, whipped, and driven out."[19] The lay residents of Grand Coteau took aggressive action to defend the Jesuits should anyone attempt to attack the priests or the college.[20] In his rehashing of this history of St. Charles College, Father Michael Kenny gives the following account: "When the threats of the enemies to their now beloved Jesuits became serious, they armed themselves with guns and let it become widely known that any injury to the fathers or their prospective students would be attempted at the risk of the limbs or lives of the assailants. They actually kept armed watch night and day before the opening [of the college]."[21] With the protection and support of the local community, the Jesuits began to expand their institution, taking in more students and reaching out further in an effort to secure legitimate acceptance of the educational practices performed at the college.

On December 15, 1847, an act of legislation in the city of New Orleans confirmed that an association titled the Catholic Society for Religious and Literary Education was formed by four Jesuits—"John Baptist [Jean Baptiste] Maisonnabe, Francis Abbadie, Hypolite Gache, and Louis Roccefort"—and formally approved by Louisiana governor Isaac Johnson. Johnson's signature sealed the society's documents of incorporation thus aiding to legitimize the attempts of the Jesuits to provide education for the young men of Louisiana. The newly formed constitution indicates that the primary purpose of the southern Jesuits was "forming and operating of colleges, schools, and other literary and scientific institutions in this state [Louisiana], as well as to build and administer in the same churches of the Roman Catholic worship."[22] This constitution explicitly described the Catholic nature of Jesuit institutes and the scope of their administration:

> In the city of New Orleans, State of Louisiana, within the United States of North America, on this the fifteenth day of December of the year One Thousand Eight Hundred & Forty-seven (1847) the seventy second [*sic*] of the Independence of America, there appeared before me, Octave D'Armas, Notary Public residing in the said city of New Orleans and in the presence of the witnesses here after named and undersigned, 1st Mr. John Baptist [Jean Baptiste] Maisonnabe in his own name, as well as that of Messers, Francis Abbidie, Hypolite Gache & Louis Roocefort all three residents of the State, Parish St. Landry, in virtus of the special procuration [*sic*], dated the first of this month, which is hereby annexed for resources.
>
> 2. Mr. Joseph Voller, also residing in this City
> 3. Mr. Roussell of the same city
> 4. Mr. William Lemercier Duquesnay, also of this City

> The above said gentlemen declared that for the purpose of forming and operating colleges, schools, and other literary and scientific institutions in this State, as well as to build and administer in the same churches of the Roman Catholic worship, they agreed all seven to form among themselves and with such as thereafter should join them, a religious association in conformity with the act of legislature of this State which bears the title "An act to provide for the organization of certain cooperation's in this State" approved on the 3rd day of April 1847.[23]

Imbued with the power of the state of Louisiana to organize educational programs, the Jesuits set forth to enhance their college at Grand Coteau and soon obtained a state-authorized charter.

In 1852, according to the New Orleans newspaper the *Daily Picayune*, "the college was incorporated by the State of Louisiana on July 13 . . . and endowed with the full powers and privileges of a university."[24] The college's charter greatly resembles the wording of the *Constitution of the Catholic Society of Religious and Catholic Literary Education* in that the college's main purpose was the dissemination of knowledge that pertained to literature, scientific information, and religious morality. The charter was accepted by the city officials of Grand Coteau and signed by Louisiana secretary of state Charles Gayarré.[25]

With the incorporation of the college, the student population increased, drawing young men from a variety of locations. Most students originated from the southern coastal states, Louisiana in particular; however, several students were brought by the Jesuits from Mexico to study at Grand Coteau. The trip from New Orleans to St. Charles College during the nineteenth century was an arduous one. Students arrived in New Orleans where they would convene at the train station. Supervised by Jesuits from Grand Coteau, the students would board a train for Berwick Bay, a section of the Lower Atchafalaya River. There the students and Jesuits would take a steamboat to New Iberia, Louisiana, and then in horse-drawn carts, the travelers would continue to Grand Coteau via Lafayette, Louisiana. The total travel time was tantamount to several days.[26] According to Albert Biever:

> There were no railroads to Grand Coteau at that period, and the journey often prolonged over four and five days had to be made by water transportation from New Orleans to Port Barre or Washington in St. Landry Parish. . . . At the sound of a bell, a deafening whistle was heard and the "Fleta" left its mooring and swung into mid River [the Mississippi]. The Fleta left the Mississippi and swung into Red River. From the Red River, we launched into the Atchafalaya. Then we left the Fleta and went aboard a miniature little stern wheeler that brought us up Bayou Courtableau to Port Barre. . . . The ve-

> hicles were waiting for us . . . and our wagon pulled by two sturdy mules was in water up to the hubs of the wheels. . . . The worse came when we crossed the frail bridges of the Bayous. . . . At last we reached the foot of Grand Coteau's hill.[27]

Indeed, a criticism that followed St. Charles College throughout its existence was related to geographic access and the distance of the college from larger cities.

In his diary, Father Maisounabe confesses the difficulty of traveling to the college, his considerations to purchase the defunct Jefferson College in Convent, Louisiana, and thoughts on the relocation of St. Charles College students and staff in order to relieve transportation issues. Jefferson College, located halfway between New Orleans and Baton Rouge and situated on the banks of the Mississippi River, offered a tempting solution to the isolation and poor accessibility of St. Charles College. As Maisounabe continued to explore the idea of relocation, his opinions on the matter seem burdened with the thought of the purchase of Jefferson College and the disposal of St. Charles College. Maisounabe did not believe that the two colleges could coexist with the small number of Jesuits present to administer each site. In time, Maisounabe did indeed decide to purchase Jefferson College and foster an institutional move for the amount of 80,000 Spanish piastres; however, due to encumbering financial difficulties, the plan to purchase Jefferson College was abandoned and all hopes were placed upon the continuation of St. Charles College.[28] An exasperated Father Maisounabe makes the following notes in his letters: "College at Gr. Coteau; difficulty of access to it, amazement at the choice of this location. Historical details concerning the project of settling at Iberville, Donaldsonville, the choice of Gr. Coteau; presumed reason for the selection of this spot. Then what strange terms were agreed on! I believe it is the intention of divine Providence to humiliate us in this way and thus preserve us from the danger of riches; just as St. Ignatius obtained for us the grace of persecutions, some other saint of the Society must have obtained for us the grace of being dupes in financial matters and business affairs."[29] Father Maisounabe was not alone in thinking that St. Charles College was poorly located. Other Jesuits agreed with Maisounabe and encouraged the purchase of Jefferson College.

In a letter to Father Francis Abbadie, Anthony Jourdant expressed similar hopes for the purchase of Jefferson College. The struggles of St. Charles served as a distraction for Father Jourdant, even to the point of neglecting Spring Hill College in Mobile, Alabama. The exhaustive efforts of stabilizing the college at Grand Coteau were taking their toll on Jourdant, and he states his preference for Jefferson College over St. Charles: "Spring Hill about to open—had not counted on it and had concentrated on G. C. [Grand Coteau] . . . Gladly would exchange G. C. for Jefferson."[30] Not only was locale a cause for concern, curricula at the Jesuit institution had not adapted sufficiently to meet the needs of changing south Louisianans. The majority of Jesuits teaching at St. Charles College were French, and although several French-speaking persons populated the area, English-speaking Americans were moving into the region to become cotton and sugar planters. As a result, Jesuit superiors focused their efforts on adapting the instructional methods at St. Charles College and at its sister institute, Spring Hill College, to reflect the linguistic needs of southern Americans. The Jesuits, despite their efforts to adapt instructional practices to English-speaking students, did not act fast enough, and college enrollment, which had reached a high of 120, dropped to approximately 60 students.[31] The Jesuits, concerned with the fate of their educational efforts in Louisiana, once more considered closing St. Charles College and relocating to a larger city with a denser population. This time, the Jesuits considered the capital city of Baton Rouge. Upon learning of the Jesuits' desire to close St. Charles College in favor of a new institution, Grand Coteau residents spoke out against the Society of Jesus's departure. Several arguments were put forward in support of sustaining the college. Town officials conveyed to the fathers and brothers that town and vicinity residents dearly appreciated them and did not wish their departure. The Jesuits responded indicating that Grand Coteau was a small town and far too removed from larger cities. This isolation, argued the Jesuits, hindered student enrollments. Town officials once again urged the Jesuits to stay. The order was informed that a new railroad would soon be established to link Grand Coteau to other Louisiana cities and that communication and access lines would improve. The townspeople of Grand Coteau wrote numerous letters to the Jesuits, the New Orleans archbishop, and even the Jesuit father general in Rome urging the Jesuits to stay. One individual went so far as to remind the Society of Jesus that all land issued to the order for their college was actually owned by the parish, and so by closing St. Charles College the Jesuits would forfeit access to the property.[32]

Despite Grand Coteau's best efforts to retain the Jesuits, the decision had been made to close St. Charles College in favor of an institution in Baton Rouge. Indeed, the fathers and brothers were determined to move all resources to the capital city. Perhaps the Society of Jesus felt its higher education fortunes might improve in such a largely populated city and that a fresh start might place them in a more communal environment with the state government; however, these continued aspirations of relocation did not please Grand Coteau residents. As the Jesuits were making final preparations to close St. Charles College, the citizens of Grand Coteau rallied together and held a meeting imploring the Jesuits to reconsider. The following sentences are excerpted from the minutes of the meeting:

> The Chairman, having declared the object of the meeting to be an expression of the public sentiment on the discontinuance of the Saint Charles

> College . . . Be it resolved that we the citizens and inhabitants of Grand Coteau and vicinity have learned with astonishment and regret, the determination of the [Jesuit] Superiors to discontinue the college . . . an institution we have aided to erect with our means, and cherished and such justified by all the contributions in our power. . . . We do most solemnly protest . . . and still hope . . . such a reconsideration be given by the proper authorities as to change their determination and resend their orders. . . . in parting with the President and Professors at the present time, (if part we must) we sincerely regret the necessity that takes them from our midst, and tender them our heartfelt thanks for their attentions and kindness to us and Ours, and wish them health and happiness wherever be their stations hereafter.[33]

The communities of Grand Coteau and Lafayette, Louisiana, communicated to the fathers and brothers that the region's economics had been greatly influenced by the education of so many businessmen and merchants at St. Charles College. Not only did the college benefit local financial welfare, the Jesuits offered spiritual solace to a community historically rooted in Catholicism.[34] Despite local outcry for the college to remain open, the Jesuits had begun the process of closing St. Charles College in favor of Baton Rouge and the newly founded College of Saints Peter and Paul.

The Jesuit-administered College of Saints Peter and Paul opened in Baton Rouge in 1849 despite heavy opposition from the Protestant population, particularly the Methodist church. This new college was intended to replace St. Charles College; however, due to local opposition, yellow fever, low attendance, and predicted hindrance to Spring Hill College via the reception of boarding students from Alabama, the Baton Rouge college did not last long.[35] With the fall of the College of Saints Peter and Paul, the Jesuits decided to reopen St. Charles College much to the pleasure of Grand Coteau residents. Upon their return, the Jesuits sold several acres of the immense college farm in order to remodel existing buildings, refurnish facilities, and purchase new instructional instruments. Renewed student enrollments demonstrated the enthusiasm of locals as 150 students registered for courses.[36]

The excitement felt by Grand Coteau residents over the return of the Jesuits was short lived. In 1861, Louisiana seceded from the Union and the Civil War began. Older students withdrew from colleges across the South to enlist in the Confederate Army. St. Charles College was no exception to this exodus. As Father Kenny explains, "some of the larger boys dreamed of the freedom of camp life, and military glory, and united to join the army even against the will of their parents. They only sought for an occasion or a pretext to escape the burden of college life."[37] Although some of the older students left to enlist, many remained at the college.

Worry turned from the declining student population to conscription policies regarding lay faculty and Jesuit scholastics. Community leaders of Grand Coteau petitioned the Confederate Army to excuse lay and scholastic college staff from conscription due to the indispensable nature of their work and instruction at the college. The college had already suffered the loss of several enlisted students and was now relying on its preparatory department to maintain the college. In fact, St. Charles College remained open throughout the war primarily due to its preparatory department, which made up the bulk of the student population. Confederate authorities agreed to leave the faculty of St. Charles College alone, as it was understood that their departure might force the college's closure. This decision was also partly due to the closure of the Louisiana State Seminary of Education and Military Academy (known today as Louisiana State University) in Pineville, Louisiana. The academy had previously been under the administration of William Tecumseh Sherman, but after his departure due to Louisiana's secession, the seminary was without competent leadership and closed for the remainder of the war. As such, Louisiana officials did not want the Jesuit college to close as it was now the only Louisiana college still in operation west of the Mississippi.[38] Due to the closure of secular colleges on account of the war and the reliance on preparatory education, the Jesuits maintained one of the only functioning educational institutions in Louisiana.

With decreased enrollments and the incorporation of new Confederate dollars, the Jesuits raised tuition in order to remain financially viable. At the onset of the Civil War, the college opened with tuition set at $500. This was later increased to $1,200 due to the reduced purchasing power of Confederate currency.[39] The Jesuits of St. Charles College, realizing the low security in Confederate monies, quickly invested their funds in cotton and a steam grinder used to mill corn. The steam grinder proved most useful in fortifying the loyalty of the community and army troops during the war. The Jesuits allowed citizens of Grand Coteau, as well as Confederate and Union troops, to use the grinder. Also, with the discovery of salt deposits in New Iberia, the Jesuits sent one of their own to collect the precious mineral for the college and local community. After obtaining permission from Union general Benjamin Butler, the Jesuits became transporters of a variety of goods and livestock to the relief of Grand Coteau residents.[40]

During Confederate occupation, St. Charles College, and subsequently Grand Coteau, was afforded protection by the army. This protection safeguarded faculty, staff, and students. After the fall of Vicksburg, Mississippi, Grand Coteau and the surrounding Louisiana parishes were overrun with Union troops on the march to New Orleans. With the egress of Union troops several northern Baptist and Methodist preachers marched through Louisiana toward New Orleans. A flurry of anti-Catholic sentiment arose as Protestant leaders preached to former slaves, instructing them that "the Protestants had liberated them whilst the Catholics kept them in bonds."[41] Many ex-slaves from across the South followed Union soldiers and Protestant missionary movements to the large port city of New Orleans without provisions. As a result, many died of starvation.[42]

Despite the efforts of the Society of Jesus to maintain the efficacy and sustainability of their institution, St. Charles College emerged from the war with heavy debts, which increased during the years of Reconstruction.[43] In 1869, the Jesuit visitor, Father O'Neill, decided that the college should close as it was too difficult to sustain high enrollment numbers given the depleted livelihoods of southern families. Father O'Neill also argued that the rural college strained the already taxed human resources of the New Orleans Mission. The lack of southern Jesuit fathers, brothers, and scholastics was given as the predominate reason for the closure. However, in 1870, the Jesuit father general in Rome, Peter Jan Beckx, overturned O'Neill's decision and declared that the college should remain open as it was needed to serve as a shelter for students and Jesuits from Spring Hill College who had lost their facilities to a fire.[44] In order to retain students, the Spring Hill College Jesuits relocated several young men to St. Charles College. Spring Hill College students adapted well to Grand Coteau. In fact, "they [the Spring Hill College students] brought back life and animation [to the college campus], were seen or heard through the fields and over the creeks, and soon there was hardly left a rabbit unchased."[45] Though the Alabama students enjoyed their sojourn in Louisiana, they longed to return to their college in Mobile.

After Spring Hill College was rebuilt, the students that so infused St. Charles college with merriment were returned to Alabama leaving the Grand Coteau college with a significantly reduced enrollment. As the Jesuits of St. Charles College attempted to increase enrollment, troubles persisted in the form of disease. In 1878, an outbreak of yellow fever in New Orleans forced the residents of Grand Coteau to quarantine the city from outsiders. Guards were stationed around the city to prevent those infected with the disease from entering the town. The college was provided the same protection. Such quarantine, however, kept foreign students from attending St. Charles College and further decreased enrollment.[46] War, disease, low resources, anti-Catholic, and anti-Jesuit sentiment had damaged the college severely, but the Jesuits were not willing to give up, and soon the college was up and running once more. The *Woodstock Letters* of 1885 provide a candid account of the state of affairs at the college: "Formerly very prosperous, it had some time after the late [Civil W]ar undergone a nearly total eclipse, when in the year 1881, the college being in a fair way of again rising to its former pre-eminence among southern educational institutions, it was reorganized and has ever since yielded most consoling results by developing filial devotion to Mary and frequent reception of the Sacraments even among the students who do not belong to the Sodality."[47] With the college on the mend and support coming from the local community, the Jesuits were able to continue the promotion of their method of instruction and religious mission of Catholic education, while attempting, albeit slowly, to adapt and match curricular offerings at secular institutions.

Unfortunately, such adaptation also conformed to the local racial ethos regarding students and men of color. Father Biever, originally from Luxembourg, wrote in his journal about a Jesuit scholastic from South America who traveled with him to study at St. Charles College. In his notes concerning this Jesuit novice, known as Mr. Koch, Biever writes:

> After mass we were ushered into the dining hall of the [college] students and breakfasted with them. All eyes were turned towards us especially towards Mr. Koch. . . . The faces of the students showed surprise and dissatisfaction, and sundry remarks were passed which I did not understand. When dinner bell sounded, the students refused to enter the dining hall, stating that they would never sit at the same table with a Negro. In fact, Mr. Koch was of dark complexion, had kinky hair and possessed other symptoms peculiar to the Negro race. Our European Superiors, not knowing the social conditions of the Southern States where the Negro had just emerged from slavery, thought that Mr. Koch because of his dark complexion and South American origin would prove a most valuable subject. Unfortunately this was not the case. The house doctor was called in for consultation and after close scrutiny declared Mr. Koch to be of the colored race. Poor young man who but yesterday was supremely happy in the hope of that he had reached the goal of all his ambitions had now to pack up and tearfully resume the return trip to Europe. Mr. Koch himself stated that his father was a German physician and that his mother was a colored woman. On his arrival in Europe, he entered the Belgian province of the Society of Jesus for the mission of Calcutta where he was ordained priest and named secretary to His Grace Archbishop Gothals. His biography which has appeared recently shows him to have been a man of great holiness and learning.[48]

Such racial tension limited the number of students that could be instructed at St. Charles College and defined what was racially acceptable for any Jesuit who wished to learn or teach in the American South. Such a limitation further stretched the resources of the institution, and with the 1900 hurricane that decimated Galveston, Texas, Jesuit instructors, who were greatly needed at St. Charles College, did not arrive to relieve overworked Jesuits in southern Louisiana.[49]

In the years that followed, the college stabilized as student enrollments slowly increased. But this stability did not last long. In 1900, fire ripped through the main college building igniting books and destroying equipment as students and priests watched the seminal building of their campus collapse in flames. After the fire destroyed the main building of St. Charles College, a report was printed in the *Varia* section of the *Woodstock Letters* that described the destruction of the columned edifice and the overall safety of the staff and students. The report also explained that the fathers and brothers were in the process of conducting a day institute for the remaining students in adjacent campus buildings. With the reconstruction of the main college building, it was reported that approximately fifty students were enrolled;[50] however, a second fire ravaged the campus of St. Charles College in 1907. A drought had caused wooden roof shingles to become particularly flammable and vulnerable to chimney sparks. Once again, flames engulfed the main campus building. Locals helped rescue books and educational apparatus; however, what the fire did not destroy, a rainstorm finished, and those saved items were damaged as the fire was quenched by the ensuing storm.[51] The college minister's diary elaborates:

> July 8, 1907: A very sad day for G. C. While at dinner and at first course . . . cries of fire from outsiders were heard. The shingle roof near the kitchen was ablaze, no doubt from a spark from chimney. . . . The tolling of the Church bell brought together a fabulous crowd of people (black and white) who toiled like Trojans to save whatever could be saved from the doomed historic building. . . . All those who could not help in any way, owing to sex or age, were on their knees praying under the guidance of Father Bovan, About two o'clock a heavy rain fell which interfered greatly with fire workers, who up to this had been frantically trying to save the Church close by and succeeded. . . . The heat from the fire was terrific and several were prostrated and others fainted from over exertion. . . . Offers from all for hospitality and meals were greatly appreciated by Ours but none of the venerable fathers could be urged to take advantage of them.[52]

After the second destruction of the main building, the New Orleans Mission superiors resolved to rebuild the college on a larger and more modern scale in hopes of reviving the institution. Many of the students were sent to Spring Hill College until St. Charles College was rebuilt.[53]

With the reconstruction of St. Charles College, students reenrolled and a plethora of new students enlisted for studies. Support surged as the institution grew and rounded its seventieth anniversary. A telegram sent from Louisiana governor Jared Young Sanders to Father Henry Maring at St. Charles College offered the following congratulations on a successful commencement and seventy years of educational work at Grand Coteau: "Congratulations and best wishes for today's auspicious event, another link in the Golden Chain of Jesuit progress and enlightenment for present and future generations."[54] Later, upon the college's seventy-fifth anniversary, alumni banded together to form an association to support the institution and agreed that the new alumni organization should meet every year on commencement and aid in plans for college and curricular expansion.[55]

A report in the *Varia* section of the *Woodstock Letters* in 1913 indicates that St. Charles College had expanded its campus to include a physical and chemical laboratory in order to better lay the foundations for scientific and technical waves of education rippling through the South. Also, the Jesuits advertised the college's connection with a wireless telegraph station that tied the institution to other regional cities. The report described a proposed seismographic observatory and explained vast improvements to the campus, including new walkways, improved facilities, and a swimming pool.[56] Good fortune seemed to increase for St. Charles College. Despite these improvements, curricular problems persisted and governmental concerns of educational legitimacy would soon have to be addressed.

By 1916, the state of Louisiana acknowledged that several graduates from St. Charles College had become teachers and that many more wished to do the same; however, at this time in Louisiana's history, policies had been established regarding the educational requirements for all who wished to teach. The following letter, sent to Reverend Michael A. Grace, president of St. Charles College, from the Department of Education in Baton Rouge explained the situation as it applied to the Jesuit college:

> Dear Sir:
>
> I wish to acknowledge receipt of your letter of the 18th inst. as well as that of Father Brooks giving information about the courses of study of St. Charles College.
>
> Graduates of the Classical Course of your institution who earn a Bachelor of Arts Degree upon the completion of four years' course will be exempted from examinations for teachers' certificates. The graduates of the Non-Classical Course upon whom you confer the B.S. Degree cannot be granted teachers' certificates under the provisions of the law which requires a full four years' college course over and above their high school work.
>
> Trusting that you understand thoroughly the conditions under which college graduates are exempted from examinations for teachers' certificates, and with best wishes for the continued prosperity of your college, I am,
>
> Very sincerely yours,
J. P. Conniff
Chairman.[57]

Along with such policy changes regarding teacher qualifications, curricula in southern colleges and universities had adapted through the years following the

Civil War to meet scientific and agricultural needs. The Jesuits had deferred adapting their curriculum and relied on classical educational models utilized by the Society of Jesus via the *Ratio Studiorum*. This delay would cost them dearly as enrollment dropped at St. Charles College in response to instructional stagnation. In an effort to once more reinvigorate the institution, the Jesuits began to slowly adapt the college's academic and commercial curricula. These curricular changes and adaptations are stated in the *Varia* section of the 1917 edition of the *Woodstock Letters*. In the following passage, the religious nature of agricultural instruction in non-Catholic institutions and its effects on student development are presented as a cause for concern:

> There is on foot a plan to introduce in our college a Scientific Agricultural Course, as soon as ways and means have been devised. There is no doubt that this course will prove a valuable addition to our curriculum. Most of our boys' parents are wealthy planters and farm owners and the boys themselves look forward to the time when they in turn will follow in their fathers' footsteps. But in this age of improvement one studies farming on scientific lines and on leaving us the boys generally go up for a course of Agriculture in some non-Catholic college or university. Who does not see the world of good that such a course works in a Catholic college? We could keep those boys in the right paths and avert evil influence bound to be brought upon them in non-sectarian colleges and universities.[58]

Clearly, the Jesuits meant to impart moral lessons alongside agricultural instruction as a continued method to demarcate the religious identity and mission of their college from the perceived dangers of secular colleges and universities.

In addition to expanded scientific and agricultural curricula, the Jesuits added military instruction in the form of Reserve Officers' Training Corps (ROTC). The 1919–1920 academic catalog of St. Charles College indicates that the purpose of having an ROTC cadet unit was to provide military and civil training to qualify college students "as reserve officers in the military forces of the United States."[59] Cadet training was meant to instill hygienic habits, to increase a sense of patriotic duty and active citizenship, and to promote the "utilization of elements of military training and instruction for the development of physique, discipline, manliness, teamwork and leadership."[60] According to the ROTC guidelines, students at St. Charles College had to be both physically fit and United States citizens in order to participate in the corps. Seeing a benefit in connecting St. Charles College to the popular ROTC program, the Jesuits made it compulsory for all US students over the age of 14 to participate in military instruction and don the requisite uniform.[61] ROTC cadets at St. Charles College were issued field equipment and one military uniform per year free of charge, which included a "hat and hat cord, coat, shirts, breeches, leggings and shoes."[62] In addition, 10 percent of the college's cadet unit was afforded the opportunity to participate in an ROTC summer camp sponsored by the US Military. The camp lasted six weeks, and all traveling expenses, meals, camp uniform, as well as room and board expenses were covered by the government.[63] Encouraged by the support of the War Department, the Jesuits reported the college cadets' successes:

> In the Inter-Reserve Officers' Training Corps Victory Loan campaign, the St. Charles College R.O.T.C. unit won fourth place among all the R.O.T.C. units of the United States, and first place among those units that comprise the Tenth Military District, R.O.T.C., of Louisiana, Texas, Arkansas and Oklahoma. It was the only unit from among the couple of hundred that was established in States south of Tennessee that was mentioned by the United States War Department on the honor roll for especially patriotic work performed during the recent Victory Loan Drive. Also, with the exception of one other college unit, that of St. Charles was the only one west of Chicago, Ill., that was included in the roll.[64]

Despite the accomplishments of the St. Charles College ROTC unit, enrollment continued to dwindle as the local population could no longer supply enough students to meet the financial needs of the college. Resulting from curricular intransigence, many students chose to forego enrollment at St. Charles College in lieu of state colleges and universities. As financial disparity became more evident, the Jesuits noted with some degree of enthusiasm that oil companies had taken an interest in the vicinity of St. Charles College. The excitement was heightened by corporate negotiations concerning the possibility of drilling for oil on the college property. Finding oil on the campus grounds, as stated by the fathers, "would change very materially, the conditions, not only of the surrounding country, but of the college, and should the precious liquid be brought to the surface on our own property, it would afford a soothing remedy for the monetary wounds that harass those responsible for the finances of the college."[65] However, misfortune struck once again. Oil, in any immense quantity, was not discovered and so the chance for capital via petroleum was not acquired.

In the early twentieth century, spiritual retreats (held twice yearly) for the community of Grand Coteau and surrounding Louisiana populace began to take place at St. Charles College. These retreats were held in order to increase local support for the college and promote lay Catholic presence on the campus.[66] Secular clergy were invited to attend and assist with the retreats, and it was found that priests from other parishes had been very supportive of the Jesuit presence and educational missions in Grand Coteau. As one Jesuit described the attitudes of the regional secular clergy, "an admirable feature of our success here is the friendliness and hearty co-operation of the Secular Clergy. The secularly clergy in the nearby parishes supported the religious fervor, spiritual retreats, and educational endeavors the Jesuit fathers pursued and promoted at St. Charles College. Their support was not only verbal but also extended to recruitment efforts by encouraging parish families to send their sons to St. Charles College."[67] Such encouragement was too late to provide any major assistance to the declining institution. In 1921, the Jesuit visitor Norbert de Boynes arrived, reviewed the college, and presented his recommendations for the restructuring of higher education in the New Orleans Province. St. Charles College was given a poor evaluation. It was decided that the Grand Coteau college should close and the campus disposed of. However, the Jesuit novitiate in Macon, Georgia, had recently burned. As such, it was decided that the old St. Charles College buildings would become the cumulative site for New Orleans Province scholastic training and remains so to this day.[68]

Father de Boynes's visitation was the final blow to St. Charles College as an academic institution for lay students. De Boynes deemed it necessary that all Jesuit colleges in the South, with the exception of Loyola University New Orleans and Spring Hill College, should shut down so that the educational efforts of the southern Jesuits could focus on two institutions instead of a string of small, poorly staffed colleges.[69] Following father visitor's recommendations, St. Charles College closed for good in 1922. The secular clergy in Lafayette, Louisiana, were consulted about the closure, and despite their wish for the college to continue, they complied with the decision.[70] Even though lay education had been removed from St. Charles College, the Jesuit fathers and brothers still provided spiritual direction as well as the use of the former college campus to aid the community. This aid was apparent during the Mississippi River flood of 1927, when the college buildings were utilized by the Red Cross to provide relief for the people of Louisiana.[71]

St. Charles College was the first attempt of the Society of Jesus to construct and maintain a Jesuit educational institution in the American South. The college saw the effects of war, was occupied by both Union and Confederate soldiers, experienced anti-Jesuit sentiment, and was closed more than once due to fire. In its eighty-five-year history the institution educated young men from Louisiana, from across the South, and from various countries. The college also served as the training ground for many Jesuits who worked along the Gulf Coast educating lay students and performing mission work for the New Orleans Province. With its closure, St. Charles College left a legacy of Catholic education that can still be viewed through the multitude of Catholic images and statues that cover the campus today, not to mention the campus identity as a spiritual retreat, Jesuit seminary, and locale for one of the two New Orleans Province cemeteries, where numerous priests and brothers have been buried since the antebellum period. The third edifice of St. Charles College still stands in Grand Coteau, Louisiana, not far from the Academy of the Sacred Heart.

The history and ultimate failure of St. Charles College is a prime example of how the combination of institutional identity and mission affect town and gown relationships to influence survivability. Granted, the Jesuit-administered institution did face a plethora of hardships, including destruction, war, and wavering student enrollments; however, some of these events were related to and triggered by the college's identity, mission, and societal interactions.

Jesuit institutional identity at St. Charles College was physically expressed through Catholic images, statues of saints, crosses, and inscribed religious phrases that proclaimed the Catholic nature of the institution. For example, in a photograph of the first campus of St. Charles College, the main academic building was adorned with the Latin phrase *Deo et Patriae*, meaning "God and country." Not only was the Catholic identity of the institution clearly visible, so was the religious nature of the Jesuit administration. During the existence of St. Charles College, all Jesuits wore cassocks and vestments marking them as clergy and members of the Society of Jesus. Such clear demarcation of the identity and religious mission of the college had an affect on neighboring communities. From the public outcry against the antebellum closure of the college, it is clear that the immediate community was supportive of the Jesuits' educational presence, but other adjacent communities were not and voiced their opposition. The existing coeducational nature of lay students and Jesuit scholastics contributed to the religious identity of the college. The training of students and "Jesuits-to-be" in tandem may have contributed to further anti-Jesuit sentiment from neighboring communities as it may have been perceived that lay students might choose the life of the cloth instead of returning home after the completion of studies. Such anti-Catholic, and specifically anti-Jesuit sentiment, may have led to a restriction of resources, including potential students whose tuition dollars could have financially helped the institution.

Aside from issues of regional opposition, the local Catholic community did what it could to keep the college stocked with students. Also, the neighboring Sisters of the Sacred Heart enjoyed a healthy relationship with the Grand Coteau Jesuits. Certainly, the identity and mission of the Society of Jesus at St. Charles College flourished alongside the Catholic identity of the residents of Grand Coteau in addition to the Sisters of the Sacred Heart. As a result, local residents and nuns aided the college financially and harbored a connection between religious institutions that was noted in the community. Such a relationship between religious orders must have created a palpable educational mission based on Catholic ideologies in a localized community where the predominant religious denomination of preference was Catholicism. Additional factors that affected institutional mission were instructional methods and slow curricular adaptation. The curricular regime at St. Charles College was one based on liberal arts imbued with theology. Even with a formalized curricular structure, the original college administration and instructional staff of French Jesuits were reported as problematic due to their inability to fluently speak English. In time, the college became associated with a language barrier that acted as a hindrance to the educational mission of the college. This language barrier caused enrollment numbers to drop, and eventually the Society of Jesus replaced the French fathers with Jesuits fluent in English.

Despite linguistic barriers, the Jesuits made a point to constantly inform the public of the institution's educational purpose: to holistically educate young men with curricula imbued with theology. Several advertisements were created that explained religious aspects pertaining to curriculum and instruction at St. Charles College. Also, the college charter indicated that the institution was rooted in the educational dissemination of religious morality. This projected mission may have increased regional negative sentiments toward the institution and hindered enrollment numbers, thereby affecting capital gain. However, local Catholic families supported the religious mission of the college and sent their sons to be educated by the Jesuit fathers and brothers.

Along with the analysis of institutional identity and mission, the relationship between the college and surrounding community is imperative to understand, as it is a central issue that influences institutional survival. We can extract from the St. Charles College case that the local community was supportive of the college. Not only did the residents of Grand Coteau supply land and resources, they also protected the college when outside communities threatened its existence. The case also indicates that the communal relationship was strong between the Jesuits, Sisters of the Sacred Heart, and the secular clergy of Louisiana. Such associations may have further fostered the town and gown relationship, as the presence of both Catholic orders meant the education of young women and young men. Also, the relationship between the Society of Jesus and priests outside of the Jesuit order potentially meant additional support and encouragement by the clergy who governed the Holy See of Louisiana. In addition, throughout the Civil War, the college provided a source of sustenance via the intercession of the Jesuits to supply resources and protect the younger sons of the community through the continued operation of the institution's preparatory department. Prior to the war, when the Jesuits wished to abandon St. Charles Colleges in favor of the College of Saints Peter and Paul in Baton Rouge, the community clung to the fathers and brothers, requesting them to stay. When the Baton Rouge college failed, the community welcomed the return of the Jesuits and the reopening of the St. Charles College without any sign of hesitation.

So, if there was enough local encouragement from the adjacent community and the identity and mission of the college were relatively supported, why did the college close? The possible answer lies outside of Grand Coteau. External communities did not support the college and forced the Jesuits to import students from other states and countries to increase enrollment. In addition, geographic location played a role in the downfall of the institution. As has been presented, Grand Coteau was difficult to reach. The Jesuits often felt that an institution located in a major city (the College of Saints Peter and Paul in Baton Rouge, Louisiana) or one that was more accessible via river transportation (Jefferson College in Convent, Louisiana) would promote the survival of Jesuit education in Louisiana. However, attempts to relocate were difficult and met with failure. In addition, the Jesuits were reticent to quickly adapt the curricular structure of St. Charles College. By keeping the institution focused on liberal arts curricula until early twentieth-century accommodations were implemented for agricultural education, expanded science instruction, and military training, the college failed to remain competitive with regional secular institutions. Finally, the internal directives of the Society of Jesus served as the terminal blow to the college. As the case presents, the college was not well supported regionally and strained the human resources of the New Orleans Province. With the visitation of Norbert de Boynes, the decision was made to sacrifice St. Charles College so that Loyola University and Spring Hill College could benefit from the additional Jesuit priests and brothers. Keeping these points in mind, it can be understood that foundational principles of institutional identity and mission coalesce to affect town and gown relationships. Such factors led to low student enrollments and periods of difficult financial gain, thus influencing the ultimate survival of St. Charles College.

St. Mary's University in Galveston, Texas

From the founding of Galveston, Texas, the religion of choice, adopted by law, was Catholicism.[72] As such, the clergy of Galveston sought to construct a Catholic college. In 1854, the call for an institution of higher education was answered with the establishment of St. Mary's University for boys and young men. A two-story building was erected adjacent to the Church of the Sacred Heart with funds obtained by the Oblate fathers. With the approval of Texas legislators, St. Mary's University became the first state-charted institution for higher education in Texas.[73] However, according to a souvenir volume from the university's silver jubilee, it was reported that "few educational institutions have had a more precarious existence than St. Mary's University."[74] When the Society of Jesus came to Galveston by request of Bishop Gallagher in the late nineteenth-century, they found a community of Catholics in a poorly organized parish, where according to the Jesuits, there was much work to be done. The parish was in disarray and the church poorly attended. In the coming years, the city seemed pleased with the work of the Jesuits at reorganizing the parish and increasing church attendance. As a result of the Jesuits' progressive parish work, St. Mary's University was entrusted to the Society of Jesus to administer in 1884.[75]

The bishop of Galveston, Right Reverend Nicholas Aloysius Gallagher, concluded the arrangements for the Society of Jesus to take control of the university, and on the Feast of St. Ignatius, the bishop, local clergy, and Jesuit fathers dined to celebrate the transition.[76] The *Woodstock Letters* describes the transition of the university into the hands of the Jesuits: "Rev. Fr. Butler, then Superior of the Mission, finally accepted St. Mary's University at the urgent request of Right Rev. Bishop Gallagher. This institution had been successively in the hands of various religious bodies all of whom quickly resigned their charge. The Jesuits were looked upon as a last resource. If they should fail there was no hope for Catholic education in Galveston; and the loss of Galveston would be the loss of Texas."[77] The Society of Jesus believed that Galveston was the key to ensuring their religious and educational work throughout Texas. Jesuits also believed, as many southerners did, that Galveston would become one of the most prominent port cities in the United States.

Prior to the Jesuit administration, the St. Mary's University had been governed by the Fathers of Minor Conventuals and later the Brothers of the Holy Cross. After the Brothers of the Holy Cross were recalled by their superiors to Indiana, the Sisters of Divine Providence took control, and the college buildings were expanded to accommodate a growing student body.[78] Once before, in 1860, it was thought that the Jesuits would assume control of the university, but due to the order's low numbers in the South, this did not take place.[79] With the 1884 offer, the Jesuits accepted and now had control of an expansive parish, church, and adjoining university that was situated at the east end of Galveston on Avenue 1 and 14th Street, approximately twelve blocks from the shoreline.[80] In time, this location would prove detrimental to the university.

The parish consisted of approximately 1,600 Catholics, with the church and university centrally located in the city. According to Father John B. Quinlan in his predictions regarding the progress and future of the university and parish, "even greater success, I trust, is in store for us here in the near future, for Galveston is the key to the grand and developing State of Texas, where there will be found many souls ready to embrace the sweet yoke of Christ."[81] To the surprise of the Jesuits, the alignment of their newly acquired institution's educational mission to the Society of Jesus's instructional principles was simple enough. The college charter so aligned with the Jesuit philosophy of education that no amendment was made. Set forth in 1856, the charter of St. Mary's University states "that the objects and purposes of said corporation are hereby declared to be, the instruction of male youths, in all those branches of literature, science and the arts which are now, or may hereafter be taught in the higher classes of Seminaries in the United States of America, and . . . power to confer academic degrees, as generally conferred by universities in the United States."[82] With the identity of the institution reconfigured to the Society of Jesus and educational missions set forth, other problems, such as low enrollment and institutional competition, could be addressed.

In 1884, the college opened with fifty students. Despite this low enrollment, the Jesuits made the most of the student population, and by the close of the year, the students of St. Mary's University performed a well-rehearsed and well-received drama to over 1,500 Galveston residents.[83] When the Jesuits began the next term's instruction, the student body numbered approximately one hundred; however, the educational merits of the new students were far lower than the fathers and brothers had expected. In the years that followed, the Jesuits steadily increased instructional expectations to the standards matching other existing American Jesuit institutions.[84]

A particular difficulty facing St. Mary's University was the presence of other local Catholic schools. Since the Jesuit model of academic organization relied on younger students to make up a large percentage of the student population, it was difficult to stock the preparatory department and thus, in time, stock the college courses.[85] To better suit the preferences of local Catholic families and to increase attendance, the university was transformed from a boarding college to a day institute. With this change the Jesuits found that they could rely on the city to support the university financially, and Galveston families responded positively.[86] Using financial gifts from community members, the Jesuits modernized the institution's educational equipment and erected a new building in addition to the existing facilties.[87] On July 4, 1887, shipments of brick arrived for a new church designed by Brother Cornelius Otten. The new Church of the Sacred Heart arose next to the college building with similar architecture, although much more grand than the previous church and physically connected to the college buildings.[88]

As the university continued to grow, the Jesuits played host to a variety of guests, both local and from abroad. In addition, the Jesuits expanded the curricula, adding military training to the regime of courses. In 1893, a cadet corps was organized for the students of St. Mary's University.[89] The corps was stocked with the sons of local Texans and promoted by Bishop Gallagher. Gallagher was an ardent supporter of the cadets; he blessed the corps' banners and presented them to the students as a sign of his favor. [90] In 1893, however, the Jesuits were forced to relinquish the student corps' rifles as a result of a citywide work strike. City authorities kept the rifles and ammunition until the strike dissipated.[91] With the return of the rifles, the number of students requesting admission into the university cadet corps increased. The enlarged cadet corps performed at city and university ceremonies and was a prominent fixture at the welcoming of a papal official to Texas. In 1896, the papal delegate to the United States, Cardinal Francesco Satolli, visited St. Mary's University. To honor Satolli, the mayor of Galveston permitted the college cadets to fire a welcoming salute of six shots. It was discovered, however, that no blank rounds could be obtained. To protect local citizenry and property, it was decided to gather the cadets at the center of the campus yard, uniformly aim their rifles at the ground, and fire on command. The cardinal was so pleased by the salute that he cried out, "Good, go it again!" More live rounds were fired, and, according to the St. Mary's University silver jubilee publication: "The campus looked like a plowed field next day."[92] Satolli, pleased with the reception and the work of the Society of Jesus in Galveston, praised the Jesuit's educational efforts and the academic abilities of their students.

As a result of church and community support, enrollment swelled and the institution was soon in need of further physical expansion. As such, a new wing was constructed to add class space.[93] Beyond the expansion of the physical campus, the Jesuits became aware of additional educational needs that went beyond undergraduate instruction. In 1896, the college provided postgraduate courses for those who wished to enroll and opened classes to the public. Prominent town leaders, men, and women attended these classes, which were held on Monday nights.[94] By 1898, the Jesuit institution in Galveston was showing obvious signs of curricular and physical growth. Enrollment had increased beyond one hundred students, and plans were underway to construct even more additions to the existing university campus. The church, with its stained-glass windows from Munich, adjoined the college campus and was opened to both students and the public.[95] Regarding the progression of the college and support from the community, the university's souvenir volume reports the following sentiment: "And so as year followed year for the space of a quarter century has St. Mary's Collegiate department gone on in her work of imparting higher education to the Catholic community of Galveston. And though perhaps as a college she has not met that brilliant success that attracts the public eye, she has never ceased to do good, never lost heart in the good cause once begun."[96] Several Jesuits in their memoirs and historic accounts of the Galveston parish and college echoed such progress. None recorded the actions of the institution with such alacrity as Father Albert Biever.

After a stint at Spring Hill College, Father Biever was moved to Galveston where he was appointed vice president of St. Mary's University, professor of rhetoric, and confessor in the church. As Biever states, "the College, or St. Mary's University, as it was called in those days, prospered also. We had one hundred and fifty students on the roll. All the classes were in operation."[97] In addition to servicing the educational and spiritual needs of the institution, Biever gave public lectures to help solicit St. Mary's University. These public lectures are recorded as "helping the college not a little."[98] In September of 1900, Biever was called away from Galveston to give a spiritual retreat in New Orleans. His exit was timely and may have saved his life, as on September 8, 1900, a hurricane made landfall at Galveston and decimated the lives and livelihoods of the city residents.[99] According to Biever, "on leaving Galveston, Mr. Ott a devoted friend of mine accompanied me to the train. As we parted he said 'Come back soon.' Jokingly I said I am afraid for one of these days you will be washed away. No danger, answered Mr. Ott, we have survived the storms of seventy-five years and we will survive those of seventy-five more years. After that we will leave the worry to others. I was unwittingly a prophet for a few days afterwards, the storm did come and well nigh wiped out the city of Galveston."[100] The 1900 Galveston census indicated that approximately 38,000 people lived within the city limits, but with the arrival of the cataclysmic storm, the population dropped below 20,000.[101]

On September 6, the barometer reading began to fall and continued to fall for two days as winds began to increase. Despite all indication that a massive hurricane was looming offshore, the city did nothing to evacuate its residents. The citizens of Galveston believed that the city was not located in a hurricane path nor was any tidal wall ever constructed to prevent flooding as city officials believed that the geographic "shelving" formation of the beach served as a natural storm surge deterrent. The citizens of Galveston soon came to regret their failure to develop preventative measures against the effects of a hurricane on the morning of September 8, when the devastating storm made landfall.[102] In a 1900 letter from Father John Hogan to the New Orleans Mission superiors, we learn the following: "the boys were dismissed at noon, some never to return. At 2 o'clock people began to come in from all the houses along the gulf, men, women and children, some in boats, some in vehicles that were axle deep in the water, as they came they were located in the club room—the storm went on increasing and the water rising, at 5 o'clock it was up to your waist in the yard, and finding its way into the club room, and the three or four hundred people within had to wade through the water with the children in their arms across to the college."[103] Such an account does not fully convey the scope of the tragedy that would determine the future of St. Mary's University and the city of Galveston.

As the storm raged, a multitude of people risked the wind and rain, leaving behind their flooded homes, to take shelter in the Church of the Sacred Heart. When the church windows began to succumb to the high winds, the Jesuits made the decision to move the refugees to the College Club building. The following recounts the decision to relocate the refuges from the church to the college: "[The loud] crash was caused by the fall of a costly Munich stained-glass window from a height of about twenty feet above the [church] altar. It is clearly unwise to remain longer in the sacred edifice. We hustle in a few remaining stragglers, and then abandon the church to its fate. Is it not God's own house, and is not the storm God's own storm? He can save, and He can destroy; let His will be done."[104] As the hurricane bore down on the city, water poured into the College Club room. The Jesuits and refugees made a hasty retreat to the main college building only to experience another flooding two hours later. The refugees, now comprising well over two hundred persons, climbed to the second level of the building to escape the rising water. In the hours that followed, the number of refugees steadily increased to four hundred while the water steadily rose in the college building. As the water made its way into the second floor, the Jesuits and refugees crammed into the newly constructed west wing of the building that sat slightly higher than the rest of the college. They huddled together as bits of the roof were stripped away, allowing wind and rain to enter the cramped quarters.[105] As the water rose in the university buildings, books, desks, tables, clocks, pictures, and all educational material were carried away into the Gulf of Mexico.[106] As the hurricane raged the church collapsed, and the university was severely damaged. The people in the college building would have died if left in the church, but their removal to the university provided only momentary relief as the water filled the final floor of the two-story institution.[107]

Father Hogan, in his account of the 1900 hurricane, indicates that there was only one last place for the Jesuits and Galveston refugees to go: "into eternity." The Jesuit fathers led the refugees in prayer before what seemed to be an inevitable end. Inside the college the water surged again, filling the highest room where all were located. Classrooms that had been used earlier that day for instruction were now completely submerged. Water also covered the city, destroying homes and killing thousands. However, before completely overtaking the Jesuits and refugees, the waters began to recede. Those inside realized their lives had been spared. Even so, everything outside of the university building lay in ruin. In the city's east end where the university was located, 746 homes had been destroyed. St. Mary's University had not felt the pull of the tidal current as the massive church stood directly in front of it, facing the beach. The ruined church, its front steeples all that remained, had protected the university from the same fate as so many other structures. Following the storm, the Jesuits converted the once-flooded classrooms into an emergency hospital for the sick and dying, and they remained in this capacity for three weeks.[108] According to Father James O'Brien, the hospital wing illustrated the entire travesty of the storm: "In one corner of the university, the whole effect of the tragedy is enacted; the hungry, the homeless, the ill, and above all these earthly miseries, the kneeling before the throne of God in submission and prayer."[109]

The Galveston hurricane of 1900 produced winds that topped 120 miles per hour and a tidal surge of twenty-five feet. As a result, the city had been torn apart. Despite the "carnival of death," as one priest described the scene, no Jesuit had perished in the storm or the resulting aftermath; however, bodies filled the streets and had to be disposed of via sea burial or cremation. After the massive loss of life and property, the destruction of the Jesuit church, and damage to the university, the city began to rebuild while the Jesuits considered the reconstruction of their educational institution. The cost to rebuild the university and church was estimated at $125,000.[110] With the reconstruction of Galveston underway, the Jesuits were not sure if it was entirely possible to resurrect St. Mary's University. In a letter from Father Hogan to the New Orleans Mission, he states: "it is not certain that our College will be reopened."[111] In time, however, the zeal of the Jesuits returned when they realized that the local community wished to retain the Catholic college. In fact, locals were willing to provide support as well as young men for enrollment.

Despite the hurricane and subsequent tidal flood, the Jesuits decided to chance a reopening of the university. On October 8, 1900, approximately one month after the storm, St. Mary's University opened with thirteen students. This number later increased to thirty, all of whom were Galveston residents and survivors of the disaster.[112] The Jesuits in Texas made their case known to the entire American Assistancy of the Society of Jesus, shown in the *Woodstock Letters*: "What the future has in store for us here, no one seems to know. Our college opened with some 30 boys, and, as the ground which many of our parishioners dwelt, was swept away in the sea by the great storm, the attendance in our temporary church has been proportionally lessened."[113] Even with a significantly decreased enrollment, the Jesuits intended to carry on with their educational and religious work. Since the Church of the Sacred Heart lay in ruins, the Jesuits opened the large hall in their main college building and converted it into a chapel for survivors. The altar from the destroyed church was rescued and placed in the hall, along with a new set of the Stations of the Cross donated by the College of the Immaculate Conception in New Orleans.[114] By 1902, enrollment at St. Mary's University had increased to seventy-five, and ground was broken for a new church on Easter of that year.[115] The *Woodstock Letters* indicate that in 1904, the university was improving as the new church reached completion.[116]

It was hoped that St. Mary's University, as one of the only educational institutions to survive the Galveston disaster, would thrive. Despite the rather quick campus renovation and the slow but steady increase in student numbers, the Jesuit institution never regained its pre-hurricane enrollments. This low enrollment was probably due to the multitude of families who perished in the flood or moved away for fear of a similar disaster.[117] The college catalogue of 1906 indicates that the Jesuit fathers and brothers were attempting to expand the curriculum in hopes of attracting additional students. The catalogue lists curricular offerings on the preparatory level and the college level with courses in philosophy, religion, mathematics, science, chemistry, logic, metaphysics, theology, psychology, ethics, political economy, mechanics, astronomy, and physics. Languages were also offered, including Spanish, French, and Latin, in addition to the classical curriculum of history, elocution, poetry, composition, drama, and geography. Not only was curricular expansion highlighted in the catalogue, extra emphasis was placed on the religious nature of St. Mary's University and the fact that the institution's existence relied on tuition dollars, as there was no private endowment or state support. College course tuition per term is listed at five dollars, preparatory course tuition at three dollars, the use of chemicals for lab sciences at ten dollars, and the printing of a diploma upon graduation, an additional ten dollars.[118] Upon the completion of repairs to the damaged university and the rebuilding of the parish church (physically linked to the main university building and symbolically linked by the letters *AMDG* above the central stained-glass window), college catalogues were issued to local residents and efforts were increased to spread the identity and mission of the institution to the still largely Catholic city of Galveston.

In 1909, St. Mary's University alumni held a silver jubilee celebration that marked the twenty-fifth anniversary of the Jesuits' arrival in Galveston. It was announced that, with the exception of the local Ursuline Academy, St. Mary's University was the second oldest educational institution in Galveston and the oldest university in Texas.[119] That same year a souvenir booklet was printed and provided an account of the history of St. Mary's University. The price of the souvenir volume was twenty-five cents. The booklet is covered with Jesuit symbols and includes the order's motto, *Ad Majorem Dei Gloriam*.[120] When the souvenir volume was published, forty-one local businesses, including banks, insurance firms, clothing stores, ice cream parlors, and dry goods stores, solicited in the publication along with a large advertisement for the Sacred Heart Academy administered by the Dominican Sisters and an equally large panel dedicated to St. Mary's Infirmary and Training School for Nurses conducted by the Sisters of Charity. The Jesuits of St. Charles College in Grand Coteau also advertised the reopening of St. Charles College, the "oldest Catholic College in Louisiana," following its post fire reconstruction. Also, the Jesuits of Spring Hill College took out an advertisement heralding its revised curriculum and new buildings.[121]

Supporters of St. Mary's University listed in the souvenir volume included a number of Galveston citizens as well as C. R. Gallardo, Marquise of Guadalupe; Father Elguero, lawyer and former vice president of the Mexican Catholic party; and E. Tamariz, former minister of agriculture for Mexico. These men had fled their country due to civil unrest, resided in Galveston, and supported the educational work of the Jesuits.[122] In an effort to further promote the Jesuits, a ladies' altar society was formed and contributed to the renewal of the church and overall support of the fathers and brothers.[123] Certainly, the university was well supported by many residents of Galveston. One former student recounted in the *Silver Jubilee Memorial* that his grandfather had insisted that he attend the Jesuit institution due to its Catholic identity and high level of individual instruction.[124]

As the Galveston Jesuits continued to promote and adapt their Texas institution, the ideals of the Society of Jesus changed in regard to the strength of educational missions in the New Orleans Province. Following Father Visitor Norbert de Boynes's recommendations, St. Mary's University was closed in 1922. The secular clergy and residents of Galveston were consulted about the closure and raised opposition to the decision;[125] however, the recommendations of Father Visitor de Boynes carried the strength of the superior general of the Society of Jesus in Rome, heralding the end of reconstruction efforts at St. Mary's University and formally shutting down the institution.[126] In reviewing provincial correspondence, which only Jesuits are given permission to read, Father Thomas Clancy discovered the seminal reasons behind the removal of the Jesuits from Galveston. The recommendation of Father Visitor Norbert de Boynes indicated that St. Mary's University was to close because the society wished to redouble their educational efforts in New Orleans and Mobile, where there was a higher Catholic population and the order was already well established.[127]

With the closure of St. Mary's University, the attempts of the New Orleans Province to expand their higher education mission throughout the Southwest came to an end. Originally, the Jesuits had proclaimed that the administration of the Galveston university was an opportunity to expand Catholicism and educational practices throughout Texas, rooting all further higher education attempts in St. Mary's University. After the destruction of the church and damages sustained to university facilities by the 1900 hurricane, it is surprising that the Jesuits did not give up and retreat; instead, they attempted in all earnestness to revive the institution and succeeded in placing it on the path to recovery. As the New Orleans Province realigned its efforts based on de Boynes's recommendations, any chances of maintaining a Jesuit university in Texas disappeared, and St. Mary's University, which had survived so much, closed its doors. Fifty-five years later, however, a visiting Jesuit priest noted the dismay of Galveston residents concerning the absence of the Society of Jesus.

In 1977, when an anonymous Jesuit priest traveled to Galveston to research the history of the Society of Jesus in Texas, he sent a postcard to Father Ed Bergan at the St. Charles College Novitiate picturing the Church of the Sacred Heart, stating that as he was "trying to get some authenticated history. . . . I have been really getting an earful as I speak to people and say that I am a Jesuit."[128] Whether this "earful" was on account of the Jesuit egress from Galveston or the numerous accounts told to the anonymous priest concerning the Society of Jesus and their work in the city, one cannot be sure; however, it seemed of importance to communicate to Father Bergan that there was a significant response on the part of Galveston citizens regarding the order despite its absence of five and half decades.

The example of St. Mary's University provides insight into the survival of an institution when not only the campus is destroyed but the surrounding community also suffers a similar fate—in this instance, the effects of the hurricane of 1900. It is clear that the institutional identity and mission of the university led to slow and steady growth, including increased student enrollment and support from the local Catholic community. Indeed, the community seemed to have been in agreement with the identity and mission of the institution, as no animosity was recorded arising against the university or the Jesuits. However, when the local Catholic population was depleted as a result of the 1900 hurricane, the university felt the effects of decreased student enrollments. Historically, the identity and mission of St. Mary's University contributed to its growth but when a supportive social environment was removed it became difficult to maintain the institution.

Prior to the 1900 hurricane, the close proximity and physical connection of the church to the college fostered a public identity that labeled the university as Catholic; however, the abundance of Catholic institutions in Galveston led the Jesuits to adapt the boarding policies of the college and convert it to a day institution, thus creating an identity of accessibility without the student encumbrance of having to reside within the campus buildings. Such a move may have strengthened local relationships between town and gown, but it possibly hindered potential student connections outside of Galveston, as any foreign student would not have been able to reside at the university, thus keeping student populations relatively low. Such an attempt to create a "day college" was unusual as Jesuit colleges and universities in the American South typically reserved a large portion of campus space for boarding students. Even so, this attempt illustrates the Jesuits' desire to adapt and foster local accessibility to the institution and further enhance the educational mission of the university.

According to the Jesuits, the original college charter, though not authored by the Society of Jesus, was well aligned to the Jesuit educational mission. In fact, very few changes were required. As time passed, the curricular mission of the college changed to include modern sciences. This may have been prompted by the impact of the 1900 hurricane, which resulted in a decreased student enrollment. The change in curricular mission may have been an attempt to increase student enrollment through varied course offerings. At the same time, curricular standards in the American South were changing and Jesuit institutions were attempting to add courses and provide more industrialized curricula while asserting the instructional mission of Catholic higher education. Certainly, curricular transitions had worked in the past as St. Mary's University had incorporated public graduate courses, much to the delight of the community. After the 1900 hurricane, however, curricular transitions were greatly needed to increase student enrollment—a change that may have come too late for St. Mary's University, as student numbers were not high enough nor was the Jesuit presence strong enough to resist closure orders from Father Norbert de Boynes.

From this history of St. Mary's University we can see that the town and gown relationship was strong and supportive. It is impossible to know what relationships were like between secular religious and other religious orders managing neighboring Galveston schools as documentation on the subject has yet to be uncovered; however, there are many instances in which the Galveston bishop and papal delegates supported the university and lauded its success. Even so, the town and gown relationship was tested during the 1900 hurricane. The Jesuits used the main university building as a refuge for many Galveston residents during the storm and subsequent flooding. After the storm, the university was converted into a temporary hospital for the wounded and additional space was used as a Catholic chapel for survivors. When the community began to revive from the devastation, the Jesuits reopened their institution and those students who could attend did so. As the city rebuilt, the community financially supported the university as best it could, provided an ever increasing numbers of students, and aided in promoting the institution in a silver jubilee booklet, where a variety of local business owners purchased advertisements in order to both solicit their wares but also to support St. Mary's University. Despite such support, the university, as was the case with St. Charles College, was pulling Jesuits away from the central educational foci of the New Orleans Province: Loyola University New Orleans and Spring Hill College.

Ultimately, St. Mary's University was closed on the order of Father Visitor Norbert de Boynes. De Boynes declared that it was time to strengthen the identity and mission of Jesuit education in the New Orleans Province by focusing all resources on two institutions located in cities with a much higher Catholic population than that of Galveston, Texas. If the 1900 hurricane had not reduced the population of Galveston so dramatically, then perhaps the university would have grown to a size that warranted its survival; however, this was not the case as the educational structure of the New Orleans Province was redesigned, inclining the Jesuits of Galveston to relocate to New Orleans or Mobile and permanently close St. Mary's University.

St. Mary's University did not necessarily experience negative external effects of institutional identity and mission from the local community of Galveston. However, regional issues regarding the adapted day college structure may have hindered student enrollment. Certainly the devastating hurricane caused a long-lasting strain despite the efforts to revive the institution in the years following the storm. Through the history of St. Mary's University and its closure, we can identify several issues that influenced its survival and typifies the effects of institutional identity and mission on the town and gown relationship. Such factors illustrate the influential nature of institutional identity and mission on regional support, the reenrollment of students, and the revival of an institution following a major disaster. Low support from a devastated community caused the institution to revive slowly and resulted in its closure when the New Orleans Province realigned its structure of higher education.

College of the Sacred Heart in Augusta, Georgia

In the years following the Civil War and Reconstruction, Bishop William Hickley Gross of Savannah, Georgia, surveyed the city of Augusta, noted the low lay Catholic population, and regarded negative attitudes toward Catholics as a cause for concern. Gross deemed that a stringent Catholic college would improve these negative sentiments and perhaps increase the number of Catholics in Georgia. In 1873, Gross offered the Augusta parish to the Society of Jesus in the hopes that the Jesuits would eventually establish a college. The Jesuits responded positively to the invitation and sent a small group of priests and brothers to Georgia.[129] Concerning the offer by Bishop Gross, in 1874 the Catholic clergy of Georgia expressed concerns that opening a Jesuit college would put a strain on other regional Catholic educational institutions. A letter was sent to the New Orleans Mission of the Society of Jesus on March 1, 1874, which indicated that the Jesuits should not build a college until a Jesuit seminary was constructed in Georgia for the training of instructors for such a college. This order was followed and a novitiate was established in Macon, Georgia.[130] In a letter from Bishop Gross to the New Orleans Mission, he expresses the need for a Jesuit college in Augusta:

> The need of a college here can be seen from the large number of young Catholics who are clerks, bookkeepers . . . and who in another city would not think of leaving college for several years. Many Catholics cannot understand the advantage of a full college education. This is very natural, for many parents had no more than a business education, and they think and say, "What was good enough for us is good enough for our children." This accounts for the falling off in numbers after the Third Academic. . . . We have therefore a threefold end to accomplish: in the first place to raise the ambition of many whose talents warrant them to aim higher than a clerkship or a bookkeeper's desk; secondly, to make those desiring to be engineers . . . realize that a

> liberal education is the very best foundation for their specialty: thirdly, to make non-Catholics especially, appreciate the fact that our diploma is of as much intrinsic worth as that of one of the State Universities.[131]

Michael Kenny reported that with the arrival of the Jesuits, "they [the Jesuits] won the hearts of Augusta's stout Catholics."[132] After the purchase of a 360 by 240 feet lot on McKinney and Ellis Streets, a church was constructed and dedicated by Bishop Gross on November 30, 1874. The new church, dedicated to the Sacred Heart of Jesus, had been constructed with the plan to adapt its physical structure into that of a college building when a larger church could be erected.[133]

After the construction of a new church in 1900, under the same name of Sacred Heart, the old church was converted into the first building for the new College of the Sacred Heart. The original church structure was renovated to house college classrooms upstairs with a gymnasium on the first floor. In addition, a second building was constructed near the old church to house additional classrooms. The superior general of the Society of Jesus, Luis Martín, gave permission for the college to open in 1900 with the stipulation that no parish funds should be used to finance the new institution. The Augusta Jesuits would cover the cost of construction and tuition dollars would be used for operation expenses.[134] Soon adjacent properties were purchased and the campus grounds were expanded.[135]

On September 1, 1900, the Jesuits opened their College of the Sacred Heart with seventy students. This number increased gradually to eighty-three. Because the Jesuits needed to "home grow" their own college students, the institution began with only a preparatory department. When the students came of age, higher-level courses equivalent to college courses were offered with the ultimate goal being the A.B. degree. Despite this desire to cultivate their own students, the Jesuits were concerned that local boys would not want to remain so long in instruction and thus not complete their college degree. Also, there was concern over the religious faith of the students and their families, as many were not Catholics. In the first years of the college, Father John O'Shanahan reported that "so far, we have encountered no serious difficulty; our boys are on the whole studious, and the parents are fully satisfied. . . . We do not expect to go far beyond 100 boys, and foresee that it will prove difficult here to get them to complete the course. We can only do our best."[136] Making students understand the importance of obtaining a college degree proved most difficult. For many, the curriculum was too lengthy and did not amount to practical, "job-related" training.

In spite of retention issues, the college made itself known throughout the community via public plays and musical exhibitions. The community responded well to these student-produced dramas that varied in theme from religious to patriotic.[137] In 1901, a college brass band was organized and performed at various civic events.[138] In addition to public performances, the Jesuits made a point to communicate the identity of their new college and the mission behind their educational methods. As stated in the 1903–1904 College of the Sacred Heart catalogue:

> Education as understood by the Fathers of the Society of Jesus in its completest sense, is the full and harmonious development of all those faculties that are distinctive of man. It is not, therefore, mere instruction or the communication of knowledge. In fact, the acquisition of knowledge, though it necessarily accompanies any right System of Education, is a secondary result of education. Learning is an instrument of education, not its end. The end is culture, and mental and moral development. . . . The Jesuit system of education, then, aims at developing, side by side, the moral and intellectual faculties of the student. . . . Moreover, morality is to be taught continuously, it must be the underlying base, the vital force supporting and animating the whole organic structure of education. It must be the atmosphere the student breathes. . . . In a word, the purpose of Jesuit teaching is to lay a solid substructure in the whole mind and character for any superstructure of science, professional and special, also for the building up of moral life, civil and religious.[139]

With the presentation of such publicly disseminated material, the college began to increase in enrollment. Augusta citizens realized that Jesuit curricula, focused on the education of the whole person, presented an instructional design that would fully and holistically educate their sons. However, success was not to last as Protestant unrest regarding regional Catholic education increased and a torrential flood damaged the College of the Sacred Heart.

By 1905, the College of the Sacred Heart had garnered support and pupils from local Catholics and non-Catholics. In fact, between 40 and 50 percent of the student population was Protestant. Some of these Protestant students had transferred from the local county-supported academy. But even though the college was growing, it still experienced difficulties. One initial problem was that Protestants largely populated Augusta. The *Woodstock Letters* reports that for every Catholic, there were seven Protestants. Wealthy Protestant families, interested in liberal arts education, sent their sons to be educated by the Jesuit fathers and brothers. Local Catholics, however, were comparably poorer than Augusta Protestants and leery of a liberal arts degree, as it did not "guarantee" a job post graduation. As such, college enrollment ratios shifted as the number of Protestant students increased and the number of Catholics decreased. In addition to declining Catholic support, the American Protective Association (APA), an organization founded toward the end of the nineteenth century to combat the rise of Catholicism in America, maintained a strong presence in the city. Leaders of the APA held prominent positions in city offices, and the organization had, in previous years, successfully closed two schools managed by the Sisters of Mercy. Fully aware of the College of the Sacred Heart, the APA of Augusta printed encyclicals promoting the need for a college in Augusta without mentioning the existing Jesuit institution. When the solicitation reached the public, one Catholic individual approached the editor of the encyclical and asked the editor to accompany him on a tour of the Jesuit college. The editor accepted and upon completing the tour, reported that he was indeed impressed with the college. On the following day, a new publication was released acknowledging the presence of the College of the Sacred Heart and its complete readiness to provide higher education for the students of the city.[140]

Despite the tentative success of the college, signs of foreboding appeared on the morning of August 26, 1908. On that day, the Jesuit fathers and brothers watched in shock as a large drove of horses galloped wildly through the street in front of their college. The Jesuits believed that the horses had been spooked while a farmer was in the process of moving them to higher ground due to the amount of rainfall that had recently inundated the city. What the priests did not know was that the heavy rainfall had affected the local river, which had swollen beyond its banks and was making swift progress toward the city. On the following morning, August 27, water gushed from sewers and filled gutters to overflowing. The morning paper had not been delivered to the Jesuit residence, nor had the baker arrived with his shipment of bread.[141] The Jesuits had not been alerted to any emergency situation, so they sent one of their own to investigate. Shortly the priest returned with disturbing news. The streets running parallel to the college only a block away were completely submerged by muddy water. By 9:00 A.M., water had reached the street directly in front of the college, and just before noon the college grounds began to flood. With no students present as the term had yet to begin, the Jesuits decided to quickly eat lunch, cook all food stocks, and prepare for the worst; however, mid-meal, water began to stream into the rectory, and the fires in the kitchen were extinguished, filling the lower floor with steam. By nightfall, the lower floors of the college were submerged. The Jesuits were kept awake on the upper floor by the gurgling of swift currents as water flowed through the college building. Fires broke out that night across the city, and by the next day, all plumbing pressure was lost, leaving no potable water. By the week's end, the water had receded; however, the city lay in ruins, and many bridges that connected various parts of the city had been washed away, leaving lines of communication damaged.[142]

The college, like so much of the city, had sustained extensive damage. The lower floors had been filled with water and mud. Several large holes caused by swift currents had formed around the foundations of the buildings. The worst damage, however, was the loss of students. The college had been scheduled to open on

September 1. After much labor, it opened on September 8 but to only half of the expected enrollment. The Jesuits were hopeful that those families with financial means would contribute to the institution's future success; as such, this experience did not shake the Jesuits. Indeed, they were confident in their abilities to renew the college. Two of the priests employed at the college had survived the Galveston hurricane at St. Mary's University, and still another had survived both fires that had destroyed St. Charles College in Grand Coteau, Louisiana.[143]

As long as the Jesuits knew they could count on their financial patrons and the capital investment of wealthy Protestant families who agreed with the liberal education provided by the the Society of Jesus, the fathers and brothers felt they could continue their educational work. The Jesuits understood that a majority of the college's enrollment came from the local Protestant population. As such, the Jesuits addressed the populace concerning their openness to Protestant students. An essay, published to explain the non-Catholic student enrollment dependence issue, states that "though its maximum regular of students has never exceeded 120, [enrollment] may nevertheless be said to be a success when we take into account the relatively small number of Catholics compared with the entire population of Augusta now over 41,000. Though the bulk of the population is non-Catholic and abundantly furnished with non-Catholic educational institutions, our college has always been patronized by the children of non-Catholic parents of the better class."[144]

Documents show that the reputation of the Jesuits as excellent educators drew a number of Protestant students from wealthy families. By 1907, due primarily to heavy Protestant enrollments, the student population had reached 138, thus weakening the local Richmond Academy. The academy's administration, in an effort to reverse declining enrollments, transferred control of the school to the Georgia Board of Education, remaking the academy as a formal state-supported high school with free tuition to all students. The revision of Richmond Academy damaged enrollment at the Jesuit college, and by 1914, the number of students attending the College of the Sacred Heart had dropped to 45.[145] This decreased enrollment caused much apprehension, but the Jesuits seemed more concerned with the Catholic to Protestant student ratio than retention. Reports indicate that "very nearly half this [student] number are Protestant. One of the many difficulties we have to contend with is to get the students to complete the course. Many of them would gladly receive the A.B. degree, but at the cost of less labor; and as we have no commercial course, and hence give no degree in science, our graduates are necessarily few."[146] As Catholic student enrollment continued to decline and Protestant students withdrew before completing the college course, curricular changes had to be considered, and the mission of the institution as a form of higher education had to be reconsidered.

By 1913, the college had degenerated to the status of a high school with a lower preparatory department. Seeing that students were no longer enrolling in college-level courses, the Jesuits sought to capitalize on high school–level students. The college catalogue of 1912–1913 describes the institution as comprising two parts: preparatory and high school. No college level is listed. The high school level offered a curricular regime including the classic languages of Greek and Latin, natural sciences, mathematics, geometry, poetry, history, rhetoric, mechanics, and geography. The catalogue indicates that although religious elements infused the course work, the institution was not meant primarily for Catholic students.[147] In addition, the Jesuits realized their dependence on Protestant pupils and made it clear in publications that the religious beliefs of all attending non-Catholic students would not be infringed upon. As such, the Jesuit identity of the college was maintained despite the increased education of Protestant students.

Despite the Jesuits' attempts to re-advertise the former college-turned-high school as an institution with respect for varying religious beliefs and a clear focus on lower preparatory and high school curricula, enrollment numbers continued to dwindle. Ultimately, the Jesuits had to consider the possibility of closing the College of the Sacred Heart. In an account discussing the need to close the Augusta college, Father John Salter remarks that many students, especially those of Catholic families, were choosing other academies over the Jesuit institution. Salter indicates that the secular institution in Augusta was one "whose course, perhaps, better meets the needs and the wishes of the greater part of our Catholic population."[148] Indeed, the curriculum at the former Richmond Academy was more pragmatic, less focused on languages and the classics, promoted "job-related" skills, and was, as a state institution, far less expensive than the College of the Sacred Heart. In addition to a lack of curricular adaptation, the relationship between the Jesuit college and its social environment, in particular the relationship between the Jesuits and the city's Protestant population, began to suffer from politically led anti-Catholic sentiment and a misapprehension of Jesuit identity.

Prior to the formation of the College of the Sacred Heart, the Jesuits had organized a church-sponsored cadet corps to create greater confraternity between young Catholic men and the church as well as to inspire a sense of decorum concerning gentlemanly behavior. Originally, the Sacred Heart Cadets were named the Total Abstinence Society; however, the name was not an alluring recruitment tool. The titular change to the Sacred Heart Cadets emphasized a masculine, military ideology that young men admired. According to an unpublished history of the Sacred Heart Cadets, they were one of the first cadet regiments in Georgia. After aligning the corps with the newly created College of the Sacred Heart, the Jesuits employed an experienced military officer to oversee cadet training.[149] With a skilled military instructor at the helm, a student cadet constitution and by-laws were written. The cadet by-laws required all members to "conduct themselves in a gentlemanly and soldier like manner."[150] Cadets were to perform weekly drills, compose themselves in "uniform rank" and maintain the discipline of the corps.[151] Ultimately, it was assumed that the addition of the cadet corps to the college curricula would entice students to enroll in the college and reverse declining enrollments. The College of the Sacred Heart's cadet corps did draw attention. However, this attention was from a local, anti-Catholic political activist who had utilized the writings of Maria Monk to create a legislative bill that would allow the unwarranted search of any Catholic convent or agency in Georgia.[152]

In 1915, US senator, Thomas Watson, an agrarian populist and promoter of the recently established anti-Catholic Veazey Bill, attacked the College of the Sacred Heart with claims that "the drill team was actually being trained for militant Catholic action."[153] Fueled by anti-Catholic literature such as *The Awful Disclosures of Maria Monk* and backed by the Veazey Bill, Watson appointed committees to visit Catholic orphanages, convents, schools, and colleges to ensure that no student or resident was "illegally deprived of his or her liberty."[154] Due in part to Watson and the Veazey Bill, Protestants in Georgia became increasingly wary of Catholics. In response to the tenuous situation in Georgia, Bishop Benjamin Keiley, a proponent of the College of the Sacred Heart, encouraged Catholics in the state to oppose "grossly malicious" accusations hurled against the church and reason with local Protestants to decrease anti-Catholic sentiment.[155] As a result of the bishop's zeal, the Catholic Layman's Association (CLA) was formed to further halt Watson's efforts and dispel anti-Catholic propaganda.[156] The Jesuits, however, were beginning to lose hope for amicable relations between Catholics and Protestants in Georgia. According to the *Woodstock Letters*: "We [the Jesuits fathers and brothers] cannot hope very well for non-Catholics, as religious prejudice is so strong, and state schools have improved wonderfully in the last ten years. We are having a fight for our plainest civil rights just now. To combat prejudice we are organizing a 'Catholic Laymen's Federation [Association].' A convention was held in Macon, on Sunday, September 24, at which all parishes and societies in the state were present. We expect much good from this move."[157] In light of Watson's attempt to defame the Augusta Jesuits, one can image that his efforts might not have garnered total regional Protestant support as the college enrolled several Protestant students. What long-lasting good might have been derived from the CLA cannot be speculated; however, the creation of a supportive Catholic association in Georgia might have strengthened regional Catholic support for the Jesuits and the College of the Sacred Heart by explicitly communicating the educational goals of the Society of Jesus. Even so, no records have been uncovered that illustrate the effect of the association on the Jesuit college.

In addition to anti-Catholicism, many Georgians simply misunderstood Catholicism, its symbols, and the Jesuit role to educate, not dominate, the region's youth. An example of local populations' misapprehension occurred in 1921, when the Jesuit novitiate in Macon, Georgia, caught fire. The fire brigade indicated the burning building as the "Irish High School." The fireman had misinterpreted the "IHS" above the main entrance of the novitiate to mean "Irish High School" instead of its emblematic representation of the name of Jesus. Following the fire, a local hotel manager offered several rooms to the Jesuits, and citizens loaned automobiles for the use of the priests. The priests and brothers, despite their acceptance of such accommodations, decided, out of fear of anti-Catholic sentiment, to don suits instead of cassocks as they resided at the hotel in order to maintain a low profile.[158]

Such misunderstanding and anti-Catholic sentiment were the impetus for the formation of the CLA. Though, in time, the CLA was successful in dispelling overt attacks on Catholic schools and institutions, it was not until 1966 that the Veazey Bill was finally repealed.[159] Even so, the efforts of the CLA were too late for the College of the Sacred Heart as Protestant enrollment had already begun to drop prior to Watson's attacks. As well, rural Catholic students, dismayed by the high tuition cost of attending the College of the Sacred Heart and its curricular structure based solely on liberal arts, sought instead practical education at regional, state-supported academies and universities. If any good was wrought by the CLA it was too late for the Jesuits. Catholic student enrollments at the College of the Sacred Heart steadily declined prior to the formation of any such supportive religious organization, whereas Protestant enrollments increased only until Thomas Watson induced a social climate of Catholic suspicion.

As a result of low Catholic and Protestant support, the Jesuits, in 1915, had on their hands a poorly attended high school with close to $10,000 in debts. In the face of overwhelming opposition, the Society of Jesus decided to close the College of the Sacred Heart, and Bishop Keiley gave his consent; however, Father Patrick Ryan of the New Orleans Province tried to reopen the college by securing funds from the small Catholic population in Augusta. Even though Ryan secured enough to cover all debts and reopen the college, the Jesuit superior general in Rome, Wlodimir Ledóchowski, had had enough of the failed attempts of the Jesuits in Georgia and in 1917 informed Ryan that he did not "want to hear anymore about Augusta," and the college was closed for good.[160]

The Jesuit College of the Sacred Heart was created at the behest of a bishop eager to see a strong Catholic college service the educational needs of Augusta, Georgia. The college did acquire a public and student following, and despite a destructive flood was able to remain open. In light of the change in pubic opinions regarding the Catholic presence in Georgia, misunderstandings relating to the

Society of Jesus's identity and mission, increased anti-Catholic sentiment, and low Catholic interest in liberal arts education caused the College of the Sacred Heart to eventually fail. After the conflagration and destruction of the Jesuit novitiate in Macon, its removal to Louisiana, and the departure of the fathers and brothers from Augusta, the presence of the Society of Jesus in Georgia came to an end. Today, the Church of the Sacred Heart still stands in Augusta as a cultural center, though not governed by the Jesuits:[161] it is a lingering testament to the former presence of the Society of Jesus in Georgia and their attempt to promote education for Catholics and Protestants.

The College of the Sacred Heart was a Jesuit institution in a highly Protestant community typified by anti-Catholic leanings. As a result, the social context affected the survivability of the institution. The case of the College of the Sacred Heart is a telling account of what can happen when town and gown relationships become negative. Student enrollments at the Jesuit college were never exceptionally high, and the ratio of Catholic to Protestant students was disproportional. The greatest concern for the Jesuits in this case was the inability to successfully communicate the mission of the college in order to promote student success through the A.B. degree. Such prompting was difficult and led to the reformation and redirection of the college.

It is also evident that the institutional identity of the College of the Sacred Heart was a cause for concern. The Jesuit college was affected by increasing anti-Catholic sentiment in the surrounding city and state. Thus, student enrollments decreased and the college eventually functioned as a high school without college-level courses. Though the Catholic community provided some support until the reformation of Richmond Academy and its subsequent free tuition, the Jesuits had to find ways to reach out to Protestant elite in order to maintain sufficient enrollment numbers. As has been explained, the Catholic community of Augusta desired practical education and did not care to enroll their sons in a college, albeit Catholic, that provided only liberal arts curricula. In addition, wage-earning Catholics probably could not afford tuition at the College of the Sacred Heart. In light of these elements, the Jesuits had no choice but to promote their educational structure for wealthy Protestant youth whose families could afford traditional liberal arts instruction. The identity of the College of the Sacred Heart was often conveyed through publications (catalogues, advertisements) in an attempt to promote public understanding and increased support.

The college's mission was promoted and advertised throughout Augusta, Georgia;

however, it had to be adapted to appeal to the Protestant population and deflect anti-Catholic sentiment. In the course catalogues of the College of the Sacred Heart, words such as "religious" and "moral" are present; however, the word "Catholic" cannot be found. Such promotion supports the notion that Catholic identity was at times confusing to the populace or was considered negative. Perhaps by not overtly disclosing the Catholic nature of the college, the Jesuits felt that they might have been able to secure larger numbers of Protestant students. After the Augusta flood, enrollment numbers dropped exponentially. Augusta Catholics disregarded the liberal arts curricula at the College of the Sacred Heart and resorted to the city's public academy, where a more pragmatic curriculum was offered. Also, wealthy Protestant families, after the flood, lost homes and livelihoods. It could be argued that the loss of property and resources, as a result of the flood, directly influenced Protestant student enrollments at the Jesuit institution. Even so, issues of institutional identity and mission continued to cause problems for the crippled college.

Institutional identity and mission were difficult to navigate and adapt for the Augusta Jesuits. So, too, was the relationship between the city and the college. The town and gown relationship was often tenuous. In this case it is also noteworthy that the Jesuits attempted to forge stronger links with the city by producing plays and musical performances. These attempts had some effect, but ultimately the bonds that appeared to be the most important were financial, such as those with elite protestant families who could afford to send their sons to the Jesuit college and were more interested in formal education rather than job training. With the recession of floodwaters, many Catholic families could no longer afford to send their students to the College of the Sacred Heart as entire livelihoods had been erased. When the local Richmond Academy was converted to a free public school, the Jesuits realized that their college, as an institution of higher education, was lost and slowly converted the curriculum to that of a high school in order to promote survival. As well, the anti-Catholic attacks of Thomas Watson negatively influenced town and gown relationships. As a result of Watson and the Veazey Bill, Protestants who once supported the Jesuits, began to shift away from the College of the Sacred Heart.

Indeed, the Catholic identity and mission of the College of the Sacred Heart was difficult for the citizens of Augusta to grasp and even more difficult to adapt. This college's curricular structure weakened relationships between the Jesuits and the Catholic populace of Augusta, thereby forcing the Jesuits to turn to the Protestant community for support. In time, however, communal support did not match the needs of the Jesuit college. In essence, the Augusta community reacted poorly to factors relating to institutional identity and mission. This poor relationship between the College of the Sacred Heart and Augusta residents caused the college to diminish to that of a high school and ultimately the college closed due to an overwhelming lack of local support.

Reviewing Institutional Failure

The cases of St. Charles College, St. Mary's University, and the College of the Sacred Heart present a myriad of details that shed light on the evolution and failure of Jesuit higher education in the American South. Also, each case illustrates problems confronted by the Society of Jesus in regard to the social acceptance of Jesuit institutional identity and mission. These factors caused problems for Jesuits in regions of the South opposed to Catholic education. When examining and comparing all three cases, certain similarities arise. One such similarity is the predominance of communal support as it relates to student enrollment and financial gain. In two cases (St. Charles College and the College of the Sacred Heart), external social relationships were strained by anti-Catholic sentiment, limiting the pool of students that could enroll. Also, in the case of St. Mary's University, the need to convert the college and cease boarding requirements in order to remain competitive with other local Catholic institutions limited accessibility to foreign or out-of-state residents, thus barring students from beyond Galveston, Texas.

Regarding the institutional identity and mission of all three institutions, it is evident that the Jesuits of each institution were intent on conveying who they were and what factors defined their educational methods. Catalogues and advertisements were used to communicate the nature of Jesuit higher education and to recruit students. In addition, the Catholic identity of each college or university was evident, as advertisement photographs illustrate. Catholic symbols and imagery adorn the college buildings, and in all cases, the Jesuit-run Catholic church was situated near, if not connected to, all three institutions. However, in the case of the College of the Sacred Heart, institutional identity became skewed as the Jesuits attempted to enroll more Protestant students. The disappearance of the word "Catholic" from college advertisements could be viewed as an attempt to avoid anti-Catholic sentiment. By promoting the moral and character development aspects of the curricula, the Jesuits enhanced their institution through increased Protestant enrollment. Such an attempt displays the desperate need for student numbers in light of low Catholic enrollments. Even with such advertisement attempts, the College of the Sacred Heart closed due to low social support as a result of poor town and gown relationships.

The identity and mission expressed in each institutional history promoted a positive or negative social relationship that resulted in either increased or diminished support. The cases of St. Charles College and St. Mary's University demonstrate that certain communities, whose identity is congruent with a Catholic college or university, formed strong bonds with respective institutions and supported the educational mission of the Society of Jesus. In other instances, anti-Catholic or anti-Jesuit sentiment hindered the growth of southern Jesuit higher education.

Following years of poor support and the attempt to restructure higher education in the New Orleans Province, all three of the aforementioned institutions shut down. Father General Ledóchowski ordered the closure of the Augusta college as a result of poor enrollment and lack of local support and the Jesuits complied. Father Visitor Norbert de Boynes ordered the closure of St. Charles College and St. Mary's University in an attempt to strengthen the southern educational presence of the Society of Jesus via retrenchment. Again, the Jesuits obeyed.

This chapter, with the inclusion of cases focusing on St. Charles College, St. Mary's University, and the College of the Sacred Heart, has focused on the presentation and analysis of institutional failure. These three Jesuit institutions all suffered closure for a variety of reasons that can be traced, in ways, back to institutional identity, mission, and town and gown relationships. In the next chapter, cases of institutional closure and program amalgamation are presented for continued analysis. With the presentation of micro-histories pertaining to the College of the Immaculate Conception and Loyola College, both located in New Orleans, Louisiana, similar factors of identity, mission, and societal relationships will be examined to add to the analysis of institutional survivability.

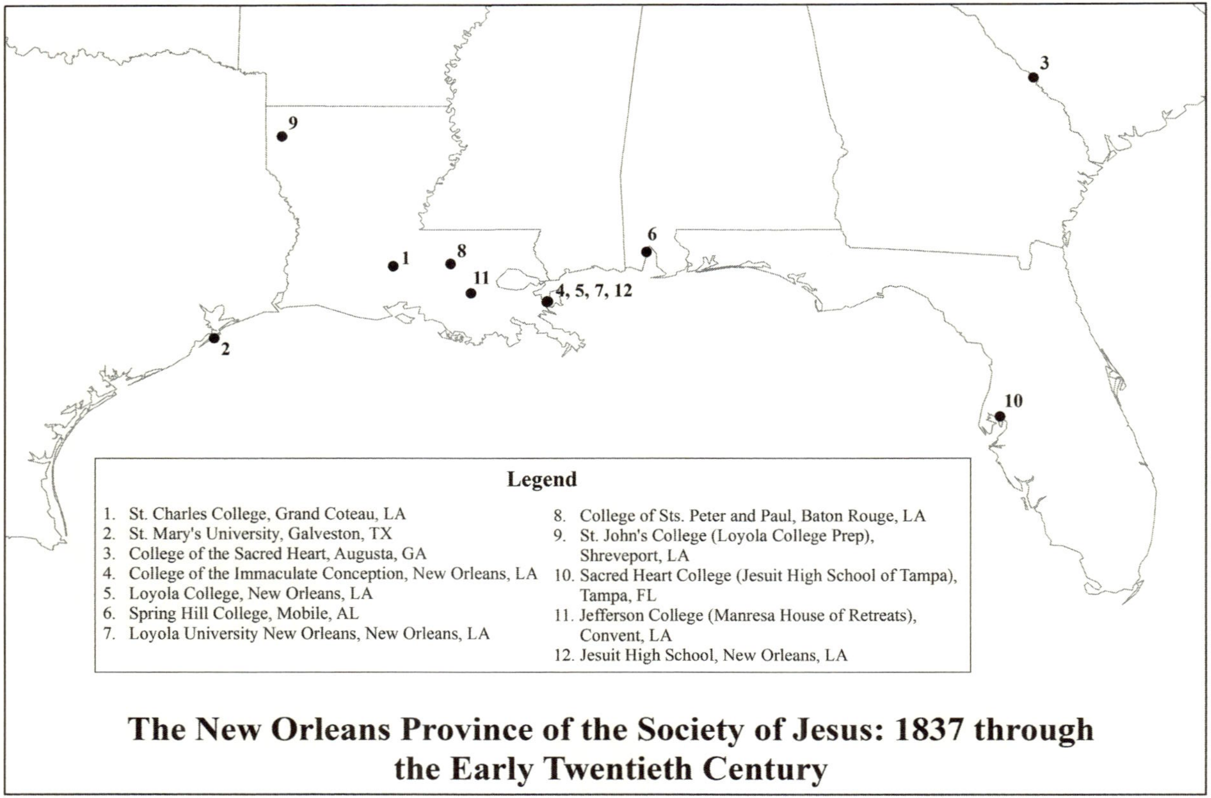

1. Map of the New Orleans Province of the Society of Jesus, 1837 through the early twentieth century

2. Rebuilt St. Charles College, Grand Coteau, Louisiana, c. 1920s. Photograph courtesy of the Archives of the New Orleans Province, Society of Jesus, Loyola University New Orleans, Monroe Library

3. St. Mary's University, Galveston, Texas, prior to the 1900 hurricane. Photograph courtesy of Archives of the New Orleans Province, Society of Jesus, Loyola University New Orleans, Monroe Library

4. The College of the Sacred Heart, Augusta, Georgia. *Catalogue of the Officers and Students of the College of the Sacred Heart, Augusta, GA. 1914–1915* (Augusta: Chronicle Job Print, 1915), n.p. Photograph courtesy of Archives of the New Orleans Province, Society of Jesus, Loyola University New Orleans, Monroe Library

5. The College of the Immaculate Conception, New Orleans, Louisiana, 1904. Photograph courtesy of Archives of the New Orleans Province, Society of Jesus, Loyola University New Orleans, Monroe Library

7. Loyola University New Orleans, Louisiana, 1930; by Franck—Bertacci Photographers; Photograph courtesy of Archives of the New Orleans Province, Society of Jesus, Loyola University New Orleans, Monroe Library

6. Loyola College, New Orleans, Louisiana, 1904. Photograph courtesy of Archives of the New Orleans Province, Society of Jesus, Loyola University New Orleans, Monroe Library

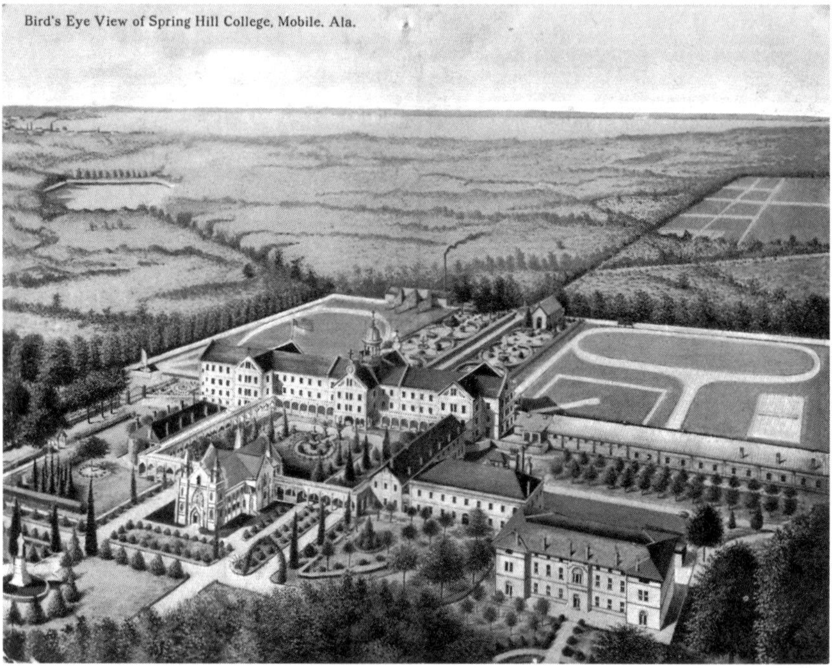

8. Postcard of Spring Hill College, Mobile, Alabama, date unknown. Photograph courtesy of Archives of the New Orleans Province, Society of Jesus, Loyola University New Orleans, Monroe Library

4
Closure and Amalgamation

> This departure [from old college methods to new], made imperative by our plans for the development of a great University, will eventually work unto the benefit of all.
>
> —Father Albert Biever

As a college or university evolves, so too does its curricular structure. Changes in societal expectations, legitimacy standards, or developmental issues related to ideological conceptions of "high school" and "college" curriculum impose pressure on administrators and faculty to adapt their educational institution if they want it to survive. As has been shown, the traditional Jesuit college consisted of a preparatory department as well as the college division. As American standards changed in regard to this age-old European structure, preparatory departments were separated from colleges to become high schools or were dissolved entirely, leaving the college department to function as a formalized institution separate from preparatory and secondary curricula. This was not always a successful venture in securing survival. In some cases, academic departments were removed and merged with another institution prior to the closure of a college. Such was the case with the College of the Immaculate Conception (1849–1912) and Loyola College (1904–1912) in New Orleans, Louisiana. In this chapter, both of these Jesuit colleges are presented as examples of program amalgamation and institutional closure. Although located in the same city, neither shared the same immediate geographic area, and the impetus for founding each institution was particularly different. As the institutional identities and missions of both the College of the Immaculate Conception and Loyola College influenced relationships with surrounding geographic regions, the Society of Jesus began to plan a new Jesuit university that forced the merging of academic departments from both colleges, thus signaling their demise.

College of the Immaculate Conception in New Orleans, Louisiana

Imagine if you will, receiving a letter emblazoned with a collegiate seal bearing Mary the mother of Jesus at the forefront of the crest. Clouds surround Mary, her head is haloed with stars, and light streams from her hands. Scripted above the seal is the following appeal: "Mary, conceived without sin, pray for us, who have recourse to thee." This was the common letterhead and seal of the College of the

Immaculate Conception in New Orleans, Louisiana.[1] But before there was a seal, there was the foundation of a Jesuit residence in New Orleans and later a college for the education of young men.

According to the diary of Father Jean Baptiste Maisounabe, communications regarding a Jesuit residence and college in New Orleans had already been established with Archbishop Antoine Blanc during the first years of the Jesuit return to New Orleans. This project was delayed, however, due to inadequate funds.[2] Eventually, through the efforts of Father Maisounabe, property was purchased on the corner of Common and Baronne Streets. The purpose of the purchase was to build a Catholic church and rectory for the Society of Jesus, as well as a college for the instruction of young Catholic men in the city. Despite petitions to the Catholic populace for financial assistance, none was given;[3] however, in November 1848, the Society of Jesus borrowed the sum of $2,000 for the construction of a small college next to their Barrone Street church from the Ursuline Sisters. The Ursulines, who had been brought to New Orleans by the Jesuits in the eighteenth century, maintained a strong alliance with the Society of Jesus. Over the course of fifty-six years, the Ursulines loaned the Jesuits an additional $28,000. In total, the sisters loaned the Society of Jesus $30,000 completely without interest. All of the money went toward the betterment of the New Orleans college and the Jesuit residence.[4]

Seated on a portion of the property once given by Sieur de Bienville to the Society of Jesus for their New Orleans plantation and later confiscated through the colonial Jesuit expulsion, the new college was founded in 1849. With the visitation of Father John Cambiaso, it was decided that the college should expand and that the architectural style of the college should match that of the Jesuit church, which was Moresque, a form of Moorish architecture. Cambiaso was enthusiastic about the development of the college and added an additional plot of land valued at $10,000 to the Maisounabe purchase on Common Street.[5] The Jesuits were not only pleased to return to an original piece of land once owned by the society, they were also excited about the arrival of several foreign Jesuits to aid in the progress of the College of the Immaculate Conception. These new Jesuit fathers, originally from European countries, marveled at New Orleans with its features so like the homelands they had left behind for the service of God. As Albert Biever, a German immigrant and Jesuit priest, indicates in his journal:

> On arriving at New Orleans, the first Jesuit we met was good Brother Ignatius . . . who guarded the college door and who of all those who came to New Orleans in 1849 remained through all the changing years and witnessed the gradual growth and improvement of the Church and College of the Immaculate Conception. . . . The College buildings were modest, but the church . . . was superb. Baronne Street was still paved with cobblestones,

> and the street was lined with stables. . . . We were allowed to stay in New Orleans some days. . . . We were surprised to notice the remarkable likeness between New Orleans and the cities of Europe, and were more surprised when we heard French spoken almost everywhere. Even in the Church of the Immaculate Conception on Baronne Street, we had the privilege of hearing a fine French sermon . . . and the singing of the choir at the High Mass was entrancing. Who could have believed that a country that I had pictured to myself as half civilized, was able to produce music the like of which we had not heard in any church in Europe.[6]

Such a reminder of their homelands encouraged many foreign Jesuits to entrench themselves in educational work and aid in the development of the New Orleans college, which enjoyed ever-increasing student enrollments regimented by a rigorous daily schedule.

The "order of the day" was indeed arduous. Students were admitted to the inner college courtyard at 7:30 A.M. All students were required to be seated in the church for morning mass no later than 8:30 a.m., and in classrooms from 9:00 A.M. until 12:00 P.M. By noon, all students had experienced one fifteen-minute recess. At lunch, students were free to join their families at home should they so choose. After the lunch break, classes resumed at 1:30 P.M. with no further interruptions until 4 P.M. Including any club, organization, or activity time, students spent on average six hours inside the walls of the college. This schedule was maintained throughout the nineteenth century, and attendance ranged from two hundred to three hundred students in the earlier years of the college. However, with the growth of New Orleans populations and shortened school hours, enrollment numbers increased.[7]

As the institution grew, the Jesuits issued full encyclicals to the public regarding the nature of the college and its curricular legitimacy in the eyes of the state of Louisiana, as well as the curriculum based on the *Ratio Studiorum*. According to the 1910–11 college catalogue, "the College of the Immaculate Conception, conducted by the Fathers of the Society of Jesus, was founded in December 1847; and in March 1856 was endowed by the Legislature of the State of Louisiana, with the full powers and privileges of a University. The plan of studies embraces the Doctrines and Evidences of the Catholic Religion, Logic, Metaphysics, Ethics, Astronomy, Natural Philosophy, Chemistry, Mathematics, Rhetoric, Composition, Elocution, History, Geography, Arithmetic, Penmanship, Book-keeping, Stenography, Typewriting, the Latin, Greek, English, French, German and Spanish Languages."[8] In fact, the legislation utilized by the Society of Jesus to confer degrees was formulated under a corporation known as the Catholic Society for Religious and Literary Education, the same corporation established in 1847 to aid the Society of Jesus in constructing southern colleges. Even so, at the end of the nineteenth century, the College of the Immaculate Conception began to stretch its curricular offerings and expand into the realm of graduate coursework.

Surviving the Civil War unscathed due primarily to the early surrender of New Orleans, the Jesuits promoted public classes and lectures for adults and college graduates. In 1886, the College of the Immaculate Conception advertised a formal graduate and professional curriculum for those students who graduated from the Jesuit institution or any other institution of equal standing. The courses were offered sparsely and mainly comprised sociology, political economy, international law, and general physics. Upon completing a course cycle of seven years, graduate students were eligible to receive a Master of Arts degree.[9] As student enrollment increased through preparatory, college, and graduate courses, the need for a larger facility became apparent. Under the leadership of Father Theobald Butler, the College of the Immaculate Conception was expanded and remodeled in the 1880s to more closely resemble the Jesuit church, including a new three-story main building.[10] These expansions sufficed until 1900, when the student population swelled to the point that an even larger structure was required. When this structure was completed, the architecture again mirrored that of the Jesuit church.

As the College of the Immaculate Conception continued to grow, the geographic and contextual characteristics of New Orleans had an immense impact on the Jesuits, none as strong as yellow fever. In 1897, yellow fever descended on the city, causing numerous fatalities. The College of the Immaculate Conception felt the effects of the epidemic as a student succumbed to the disease during the outbreak. As the death toll increased, the New Orleans Board of Health decreed that all educational institutions must close. The College of the Immaculate Conception complied, and to the dismay of the Jesuits, approximately three hundred students were released until further notice. Not only did the disease close the institution, priests were sent forth into the community to aid the sick and perform last rites for dying Catholics. This exposed the Jesuit faculty to the same disease that had killed so many.[11]

Yellow fever was an annual occurrence in the city. However, relegated to the warmer months of the year, the fever never fully stopped Jesuit educational efforts despite temporary college closures. Indeed, residents of New Orleans had taken note of the Jesuits' persistence and began to share in the celebrations and successes of the College of the Immaculate Conception. As new campus structures were completed in 1901, the city prepared for a visit from President William McKinley. The college too had reason to prepare, as its military cadet division had been requested by city officials to act as a special honorary guard to the president. Upon McKinley's visit, the cadets escorted him to the historic Cabildo Building in New Orleans's Jackson Square. That year the student population had grown to a record high for the college with 470 students.[12] As the college population grew, so too did the cadet corps. The corps became increasingly popular with the city and was invited to march in a variety of public events, parades, and Mardi Gras festivals. In 1909, the cadet battalion of the College of the Immaculate Conception was featured yet again in a presidential gala. From his balcony at the St. Charles Hotel, President William Howard Taft reviewed the college cadets as they led a city parade held in his honor. Taft was visiting the city of New Orleans to speak in favor of national river improvements at the Lakes-to-the-Gulf Waterways Convention. After lunch with New Orleans archbishop James H. Blenk, Taft traveled to the College of the Immaculate Conception and addressed the cadets, students, and faculty from a balcony draped in the American flag. Taft spoke directly to the students and cadets saying, "My boys, I am glad to be with you. I congratulate you on being where you are."[13] The president's visit to the college was noted by the public and did much to enhance the popularity of the institution.

The college cadet battalion, known as the Jesuit College Cadet Corps, wore regulation West Point fatigues but was under no obligation to be called upon for military service by the state or federal government.[14] The use of a military model may have served three purposes: to solidify a form of discipline, to provide a curricular service similar to regimented training at other southern colleges and universities, and to increase the perceived patriotic zeal of the college. In fact, the college cadet regime became so popular that military dress became the institutional norm. This, in and of itself, increased patriotic perception. As one Jesuit priest stated: "Our cadets are the pride of the city, exciting much applause and commendation. . . . The daily spectacle of 450 uniformed student cadets on the streets of the Queen city of the South, and the sight of the star-spangled banner floating daily, by military rule, in the most conspicuous part of the city, goes far toward forcing on non-believers the conviction that Catholics are Uncle Sam's best friends."[15]

Indeed, the college had become extremely well known throughout New Orleans communities. In light of the ever-increasing number of graduates, a Jesuit alumni association was formed and elected Paul Capdeveill, mayor of New Orleans, as the organization's president.[16] As the college continued to forge connections with the surrounding city, the students were asked to participate in additional public events heralding the identity of the Jesuit college. At the centennial celebration of the Louisiana Purchase in 1903, the college's cadet corps was invited to march in yet another grand parade. One of the centennial event speakers was the Jesuit Father E. de La Morinier, who spoke about the intertwined history of Louisiana and the Catholic Church. According to the *Woodstock Letters*, the event's attendees were a mix of Catholics, Protestants, Jews, and nonbelievers who received de La Morinier's speech with enthusiasm despite objections to the proposed speaker by nonsectarian residents of New Orleans. Also, many Catholic organizations, such as the Catholic Knights of America and the Society of St. Vincent de Paul, began to use rooms in the college for spiritual retreats directed by the Jesuit fathers.[17]

As the years passed, changes occurred in the legitimacy standards for accrediting colleges and high schools that forced the Jesuits to adapt curricular standards at the College of the Immaculate Conception. The three-year collegiate course of study, previously used at all Jesuit institutions, was lengthened to a four-year curriculum to match the changing trends in American higher education.[18] For those enrolled in commercial courses, a certificate of proficiency was issued upon successful program completion; however, with the addition of Latin or Greek, those same commercial course students could receive a B.S. degree.[19] All college graduates who completed the classical curriculum received an A.B. degree, and those who pursued postgraduate study and completed an approved list of courses received an A.M. degree.[20] Even with these curricula adaptations, the Catholic identity and mission of the college was unwavering. The college catalogues expressed the religious nature of the institution:

> The College authorities are convinced that, without Religion, there can be no education in the true sense of the word, that is to say, no complete and harmonious development of the intellect and heart of man. They hold, furthermore, that religious truth, being definite and certain, like any and every other truth, is as susceptible of teaching as the science of language, or the theory of numbers. Hence, the Catechism of Christian Doctrine is a textbook in every class, and lectures on it are given twice a week. In all the classes the day's work begins and ends with prayer. The Catholic Religion alone is taught, but non-Catholics will also be welcome and their religious opinions studiously respected. Catholic students go to confession on the Saturday previous to the third Sunday of each month, and on the following day, in the Church annexed to the College, hear Mass and receive Holy Communion.[21]

In response to the outpouring of materials publicly describing the identity and mission of the College of the Immaculate Conception, enrollment numbers increased. The Catholic population had strong ties with the college and regarded it as a success for the city.

The college was frequently visited by prestigious alumni and military figures who gave orations and lectures to the student body heralding their connection with the Society of Jesus and commended the great work of the Jesuits in New Orleans and throughout the United States. One such guest was Admiral Winfield Scott Schley, who informed the student body "that he attributed any success he might have had in his career to the solid training as a boy at [the Jesuit administered] St. John's Institute, Frederick[, Maryland]."[22] Local donor support for the College of the Immaculate Conception was, at times strong, though lay-community support for the original college construction had been nonexistent. Donations made up the bulk of construction money during years of rebuilding and campus expansion. The McClosky brothers of New Orleans contributed $15,000 for a new building to be erected adjacent to the Baronne Street church, with the stipulation that the architecture was to match the church exactly. Also, the widow of Thomas J. Semmes, an alumnus of the college, ex-officer in the Confederate Armies, and former Louisiana politician, donated $10,000 for the construction of a college chapel, which was dubbed the Thomas J. Semmes Memorial Chapel.[23] Locals attended the dedication of the Semmes Memorial Chapel en masse, including the New Orleans auxiliary bishop Gustave Augustin Rouxel, representatives from the secular and ordered clergy of New Orleans, the McClosky brothers, and Lawrence Fabacher, a great supporter of the Society of Jesus and member of the Jackson Beer Brewery Fabacher family.[24]

Not only was the college philanthropically supported, it was also academically promoted. Faculty presented public lectures to anyone who would attend. In fact, in 1905, the *Woodstock Letters* reported that the College of the Immaculate Conception played host to lectures on the nature and spread of yellow fever.[25] As the academic side of the College of the Immaculate Conception flourished, so too did its alumni. In 1906, the college's Alumni Association was reported as steadily growing and counted among its members a large number of the leading Catholic gentlemen of New Orleans. That same year, Major Joseph Dickman from Washington examined the college cadet corps. Dickman had previously reviewed the cadets at Louisiana State University in Baton Rouge and reported that he was highly impressed with the cadets at the College of the Immaculate Conception. Later that year, the Jesuit college cadets accepted an invitation to participate in the Rex Mardi Gras parade.[26] However, as the academic rigor of the institution increased, staff members were reallocated to attend to intellectual programs and any extracurricular programs that conflicted with academic courses were deleted. As a result, "the Cadets Corps which . . . [had] been a feature at the College of the Immaculate Conception, New Orleans, [was] disbanded. It was found that the time given to drilling could be spent more advantageously in study."[27] This end to the popular cadet corps did not seem to have an effect on enrollment. Numbers continued to increase, and New Orleans residents continued to support the institution.

As the city grew and curricular legitimacies changed as a result of regional demands for practical, industrial, and job-related training, the need to further alter the system of Jesuit higher education in the New Orleans Province became apparent. Thus, in 1912, the college department of the College of the Immaculate Conception on Baronne Street was transferred to the newly created Loyola University on St. Charles Avenue, leaving the old College of the Immaculate Conception as an accredited high school.[28] Following this realignment, the high school division of the former Loyola College was transferred to the Baronne Street campus while the new Loyola University absorbed its college division.[29]

The remaining high school division of the College of the Immaculate Conception was expanded to include courses in physics and chemistry in order to compete with public high schools. The Jesuits reported in the *Woodstock Letters* that the separation of the high school and college was advantageous, parents and community members approved, and there was an increase of students at both the high school and new Jesuit university.[30] When the decision was made to separate the high school and college departments, the following letter was sent to all students and parents:

> Dear Sir:
>
> The President and Faculty of LOYOLA UNIVERSITY beg to inform you that after mature deliberation . . . it has been decided to discontinue the Academic Department which hitherto has prepared for the College.
>
> This departure, made imperative by our plans for the development of a great University, will eventually work unto the benefit of all.
>
> Whilst we fully appreciate the disappointment this change may cause to our boys and to their parents, we also believe that the lofty motives that underline our conduct will renew and increase the active interest, patronage and generosity of the friends of the Society of Jesus, and the noble cause it represents. The College of the Immaculate Conception on Barrone Street, will adjust courses of studies so as to prepare its students for the entrance requirements of Loyola [University].
>
> Bespeaking then for the University, the same loyalty and support which the College has shared, we remain,
>
> Yours very cordially,
> THE PRESIDENT AND FACULTY[31]

In conjunction with the above letter, the 1911–12 catalogue for the College of the Immaculate Conception announced the institution's transition from a college to that of an American high school:

> In the fall of 1911, on the completion of the college building, Marquette Hall, of Loyola University, the Faculty transferred thither the College classes, retaining the High School, and on account of its location, being within a distance of only a few paces from all important street cars in the city, while two

> of the principle car lines pass in front of the Baronne street entrance. GENERAL PLAN. – The High School Department is primarily a school preparatory for admission to Loyola University, and leads naturally to the College course at Marquette Hall. At the same time the course offers as full and complete a training as can be had in any of the best High Schools in the country; and while a long and varied experience has shown that no Academy or High School can supply what is essentially the work of a college in preparing for the higher studies of a University, the entire training and the graded courses of studies pursued in the High School Department offer to every student as thorough and complete an education as can be obtained within the short term of a high school course.[32]

The course of high school training was still described in the 1911–12 catalogue as based on Catholic doctrine. Students were admitted to the high school upon proof of good character and primary school attendance. Students were required to participate in a course of study that included Latin, English, Greek, algebra, geometry, physical geography, biology, chemistry, physics, and elocution. All of these courses were mandatory if a student wished to receive a certificate of high school completion. According to the catalogue, "all these studies are compulsory, and necessary as a condition for obtaining the certificate, the Faculty being convinced that the system of allowing young boys [to] select their own course of study is an experiment often tried and long ago found wanting."[33] This reliance on mandatory courses reflected the Jesuit model of education and maintained a curricular system that justified certification upon course completion according to state high school legitimacy standards.

In 1926, with the establishment of a new facility on South Carrollton Avenue, the remaining high school division of the former College of the Immaculate Conception was transferred to create Jesuit High School.[34] An increasing student population prompted the move, and the new high school campus was designed to accommodate approximately 1,000 students. John William Shaw, archbishop of New Orleans and Judge John St. Paul of the Louisiana Supreme Court both gave speeches praising the new high school and the efforts of the Society of Jesus in the city. Henry Prevost, a wealthy New Orleans resident, made a donation to the high school in memory of his son who died while attending the College of the Immaculate Conception. Prevost's monetary gift endowed a scholarship that provided several students with "a chance to earn a place in the world through education."[35] Regarding the curricular structure of the new high school, it was reported in the *Woodstock Letters* that "the high school course is strictly a college preparatory course, in accordance with the ideals of the time honored Jesuit curriculum."[36] This instructional regime aligned with changing American ideals of "high school" and "college" curriculum. Thus, Jesuit High School more closely resembled legitimized standards of education in the early twentieth century.

In 1946, the Jesuit fathers received a letter from Fred W. Rickert, the president of Rickert Rice Mills, Inc. Rickert's letter describes a donation of $250 to the National Jesuit Fund, an educational endowment intended to further Jesuit education in the United States, along with his reasons behind the donation. Rickert explains:

> I am an alumnus of the Jesuit Fathers' schools, having been educated in New Orleans in the College of the Immaculate Conception. . . . During the time I was in the Jesuit school I received my education and finished in 1895, and learned to respect and regard the Jesuits as the finest educators I have ever had the experience to meet. . . . It was my pleasure to have not only a recollection but the knowledge of what a real education is, not particularly in the elementary part of the school but in the higher branches. Above all, the religious training and the principles taught by the Jesuits in their religious training, have no doubt built a large part of the character of the men of this country because one who does not develop character under a strictly Jesuit training in a Jesuit school, certainly will be an impossible subject anywhere else.[37]

This supportive act reflects a variety of financial gifts from graduates and illustrates the continued support of alumni from the College of the Immaculate Conception long after its closure. Today, Jesuit High School on Carrolton Avenue supports a full alumni office with staff dedicated to keeping all graduates connected with the school.

With the demise of the College of the Immaculate Conception, the city saw the rise of two new institutions geared toward a more Americanized standard of education: Loyola University New Orleans and Jesuit High School. These institutions continue to service students while promoting the educational identity and mission of the Society of Jesus through symbols, curricula, and Jesuit leadership. In fact, the Semmes Memorial Chapel formerly located at the old Baronne Street campus was disassembled piece-by-piece and reconstructed at Jesuit High School, thus establishing a distinct and impressive connection with the first Jesuit college in New Orleans. As for the old College of the Immaculate Conception, the majority of the campus was demolished to make way for a high-rise structure known today as the Pere Marquette Building. This high-rise structure, named after Pere Jacques Marquette, the seventeenth-century Jesuit explorer of the Mississippi River, was built atop the foundation of the former college and sits next to the still extant Church of the Immaculate Conception. One remaining building, McClosky Hall, serves as a lasting reminder of the College of the Immaculate Conception. This building, emblazoned with the seal of the Society of Jesus surrounded by the Jesuit motto, *Ad Majorem De Gloria*, has the phrase, *Fides Quaerens Intellectum* engraved above the front door. This Latin axiom is translated to mean "faith seeking understanding," and is a fitting slogan for the higher educational identity and mission of the Society of Jesus in the American South.

The history of the College of the Immaculate Conception provides a very different scenario from the previous Jesuit college cases. Unlike several of its peer institutions, the College of the Immaculate Conception was well supported by the populace of New Orleans and suffered no physical damages from war, fire, or other natural disasters. Drawing on the large Catholic population of New Orleans, the Jesuits were able to increase enrollment far beyond that of any other New Orleans Province college. How was it that this Catholic college, unlike other institutions of the Society of Jesus in the South, achieved such success only to close anyway? Were there influential factors pertaining to institutional identity, mission, and town and gown relationships, or were there other, external reasons? A careful review of this case will bring pertinent answers to light.

The Jesuits of the College of the Immaculate Conception certainly made the institution's identity and mission clear to the public. Whether it was through specifically worded advertisements, college catalogues that detailed the Catholic nature of the college and its curricula, or the matching architecture between the church and college, the public knew exactly what the college stood for and who administered it. From the early construction of the institution until its final physical form great pains were taken to ensure the architectural similarity between the church and college. In fact, many Catholic symbols echoed from one structure to the other and conveyed a sense of institutional uniformity between the two facilities. Even the seal of the college represented the institution's patron saint Mary, a clear demarcation of Catholic affiliation.

The mission of the college was presented to the public and well received, as evidenced by the fact that the student population only decreased when yellow fever was present in New Orleans. Otherwise, enrollment constantly increased and prompted several expansions to the college campus. As time passed and educational norms changed, the College of the Immaculate Conception matched those changes but continued to focus on liberal education. With the addition of physics and other sciences, the college progressed and enhanced its course offerings to include commercial courses, graduate studies, and public lectures to meet the educational needs of New Orleans residents who desired professional forms of instruction. The Jesuits even added military training to the college in order to match the disciplinary and structural regimes of public colleges in Louisiana such as Louisiana State University. The student cadet corps in full military regalia led several parades in New Orleans that further spread the identity of the institution.

The town and gown relationship between the College of the Immaculate Conception and the residents of New Orleans began poorly but strengthened over time. When the college opened, the people of New Orleans provided no financial support; however, through the positive relationship between the Ursulines and the Society of Jesus, the Jesuits were able to acquire the capital needed to begin their college. In time, the city responded more positively to the Jesuits. Donations were made, and eventually a strong alumni base was developed. As such, several graduates expressed their appreciation of Jesuit education and gave financially to the college. Other lay-Catholic organizations utilized the college and developed a healthy bond with the institution. Considering such strong ties between town and gown, it is important to ask why the College of the Immaculate Conception closed. Why did the Jesuits make the decision to divide the high school and college curricula and relocate the college-level courses to Loyola University? Why not remain in the same location next to the Church of the Immaculate Conception?

The ultimate issues that affected the closure of the College of the Immaculate Conception lie in the modernization of American educational standards and the order's desire for the Jesuit mission of higher education in the American South to survive via adaptability. As the Jesuit educational system in the New Orleans Province began to retrench into Mobile, Alabama, and New Orleans, Louisiana, the need arose to construct substantial facilities that could better house increasing student numbers and match new educational standards. When the College of the Immaculate Conception closed, the high school division was eventually moved to a larger facility and the curricular structure adapted to more closely match other public high schools. Also, with the removal of the college department to the new Loyola University, the college curriculum was amalgamated and adapted to meet changing higher education standards. The old facility and its limited space could not house the revised educational program and increased student enrollment, while the newly created Jesuit High School and Loyola University could. Therefore, the college closed and was absorbed into a new system with separate physical and curricular structures, adding to a more modernized system of southern Jesuit higher education.

Loyola College in New Orleans, Louisiana

With much pomp and circumstance, the World's Industrial Cotton Centennial Exposition opened in 1884. Amid the fanfare and celebration, people swarmed the exhibits to witness mechanical marvels, agricultural achievements, new methods of transportation, geological samples, and a host of displays brought from around the world to the New Orleans exposition. In addition to modern science, the display of educational merit was also a high priority. The American Bureau of Education capitalized on this feature of the exposition. In a letter to the secretary of the Department of the Interior John Eaton, the commissioner of the bureau described the prospects for education at the exposition: "It was early manifested that the exhibit would present a rare opportunity for the promotion of the advancement of education. The desire on the part of the management to improve this opportunity to the utmost was expressed in the most explicit and emphatic terms by the director-general Hon. E. A. Burke, when he declared that they sought not only that the exhibit should be thoroughly national and international and in all its aspects educational, but that education itself, its systems, institutions, principles, methods, and results should be shown as far as possible by its literature and appliances, by models, by graphics, by actual class work, and by papers and discussions from the ablest educators."[38] No doubt the commissioner of the Bureau of Education was intent on utilizing the whole event to draw attention to American education. Exhibits and lectures displayed aspects germane to classical studies, industrial education, and the merger of art and science.[39] Such curricular ideals exemplified the industrial theme of the exposition.

The New Orleans exposition was a lucid example of the changes influencing the United States at the end of the nineteenth century. Indeed, education seemed to be at the forefront of the exposition. In the reports of Herbert Fairall to the governor of Iowa, Buren R. Sherman, Fairall states that "the Educational exhibit was one of the most complete and attractive features of the Exposition. The Department of Education occupied the greater portion of the immense gallery of the Government and States Building, and comprised the display of foreign educational systems and institutions; that of the United States Government and those of several States and Territories, supplemented in many instances with exhibits of private academies schools."[40] Understandably, educational exhibits were meant to illustrate and compare the educational fortitude and progress of national, international, and private education. In fact, educational exhibits from religious schools and colleges were present. Catholic orders such as the Christian Brothers, an order originating with John Baptiste de La Salle, whose members are devoted to education, were present to display the achievements of literary and technical instruction at their colleges and schools.[41] Though the exposition was ultimately deemed a financial failure,[42] the event was so large and its effect on the growth of New Orleans so great that it attracted the attention of the Society of Jesus.

The Jesuit involvement in the New Orleans cotton exposition was not restricted to taking stock of educational materials or marveling at impressive steam-powered machinery. The Jesuits had their own exhibit: a pipe organ that was considered one of the largest and finest in the United States. According to a booklet published in 1928 to celebrate the history of the New Orleans Church of the Immaculate

Conception, William Pilcher and Sons of New Orleans built the organ at the request of the Society of Jesus for their church on Baronne Street. Its maiden performance was in the music hall of the World's Industrial Cotton Centennial Exposition before it was installed in the Jesuit church.[43] Its genesis notes filled the auditorium, entertained the public, and represented the presence of the Society of Jesus at the exhibition. But where were the Jesuit educational exhibits? Where were the examples of student and faculty efforts from the New Orleans Mission colleges? Nowhere in the *Special Report by the Bureau of Education: Educational Exhibits and Conventions at the Worlds Industrial and Cotton Centennial Exposition* is the Society of Jesus described as having any educational presentations or otherwise except for the pipe organ.

Despite the Jesuits' lack of educational participation, the exposition did have an effect on the formation of another Jesuit college. As a result of the New Orleans exposition, the city expanded outward toward the festivities, and the regional increase in population attracted the Jesuits. This expansion was the impetus for the Society of Jesus to purchase and develop a large tract of land near the exposition, situated above Napoleon Avenue.[44] As the population increased around this newly purchased tract of land, John O'Shanahan, then superior of the New Orleans Mission, became aware of the number of wealthy Catholics migrating to this uptown section of New Orleans.[45] In an account of the purchase of the uptown property, Father O'Shanahan explains that his reasons behind the acquisition were fourfold. First, the acquisition would allow for the establishment of a new Jesuit parish near the Carrollton area of New Orleans. Second, it would allow for the possibility of a future Catholic college. Third, religious retreats for laypersons could be offered in this new parish, and finally, the construction of a college on this uptown property might afford some respite for the faculty at the College of the Immaculate Conception by drawing students away from the downtown institution.[46] O'Shanahan urged the archbishop of New Orleans, Francis Janssen, to write to a prefect in Rome for permission to purchase the required land.[47]

A reply was sent to Archbishop Janssen in the form of a Beneplacitum for the establishment of a new parish under the Society of Jesus, which approved the purchase of land that would aid in the incorporation of the Jesuit parish, a church, house of retreats for clergy, and, most importantly, a college for the education of young men.[48] Albert Biever's diary provides a translation of the Latin Beneplacitum from Cardinal Prefect John Simeopni that established the uptown New Orleans parish and college:

> As the most Reverend Francis Janssens, Archbishop of New Orleans in the States of North America, appealed to this Sacred Congregation of the Propagation of the Faith for the purpose of obtaining and giving to the fathers of

> the Society of Jesus the permission to have a parish near the city of New Orleans, to exercise therein the care of soul[s], and to establish a house of retreats for the clergy, and moreover to erect a college for the education of the youth, this Sacred Congregation of the Propagation of the Faith grants to the Most Reverend Archbishop the favor expressed in the above petition.
>
> Given at Rome this December 6th 1890
> John Cardinal Simeopni, Prefect[49]

Upon the acceptance of the Beneplacitum, Archbishop Janssen offered the western region of New Orleans to the Jesuits. The acquired land, measuring 447 feet on St. Charles Avenue opposite Audubon Park and running 12,196 feet in lessening width to the Illinois rail tracks, was purchased for $22,500.[50] Once the land was purchased, a church was erected in 1892.[51] The purchase, however, was difficult. The *Varia* section of the *Woodstock Letters* indicates that "the person who owned the proposed site was utterly opposed to Catholics in general and to Jesuits in particular; so a close friend of Ours [the Society of Jesus] undertook to purchase the desired spot. He spoke to a Protestant friend, and the result was the sale of what was known as Jesuits Place."[52] The purchased land included all of the territory now occupied by Loyola University New Orleans, much of Tulane University, and the neighborhood known as Audubon Place.[53]

The need for a Catholic college in this uptown portion of New Orleans was justified in the *Daily Picayune*: "Considering the territorial extent of the city of New Orleans and its large population, it has become evident to the Jesuit Fathers that one Jesuit school or college is inadequate to meet the demands of the times. The college on Barrone and Common Streets, is overcrowded, having at the close of the session 1903–04 over 400 pupils. The school uptown will not be a branch of the College of the Immaculate Conception, but will be independent and distant from it . . . there will be no preparatory department. . . . Later on the Jesuits will erect a modern, spacious stone edifice."[54] As plans were described in local papers, the Jesuits set forth to begin their college in modest lodgings until such time that capital could be acquired to expand the facilities.

In 1904, the Reverend William Power, superior of the New Orleans Mission believed that the time for educational work had dawned. He appointed Father Albert Biever, Father Augustine E. Fields, Father William Salentine, and Father Lawrence White to found and staff a new institution, Loyola College, next to the wooden church of the Most Holy Name. Two lay brothers, Edward McCarten and Emanuel Arrizabalaga, joined the endeavor to attend to the material needs of the institution. Such work was often strenuous as indicated by Father Biever: "Pioneer work is always difficult. The aspirations of the college faculty were high, but the material resources were extremely limited."[55] From the purchased land originally used for the Cotton Centennial Exposition, portions were sold to raise funds for Loyola College. A section was sold to John Morlas for $8,000 and a section to Tulane University for $1,500, leaving the Jesuits with fifteen acres on which to construct their uptown college.[56]

The need for a building to house the college was filled by the purchase of a wooden house from a New Orleans judge and supporter of the Jesuits. The former home of New Orleans Court of Appeals Judge Frank McGloin became the first building of the college.[57] The house was purchased on January 26, 1902, for $7,075,[58] moved to the Jesuit tract of land, and painted white like the wooden church of the Most Holy Name.[59] Desks and educational materials were obtained, and the building was furnished with the necessities to house students until a larger building could be constructed. Published advertisements extolled the religious nature of the college and its ability to provide private tutoring sessions to all who enrolled. The college opened on September 6, 1904, with nine students. Enrollment applications came from as far away as Georgia; however, the new college would not possess a preparatory department like its sister institutions. This decision limited the number of students who could apply. Despite the low enrollment, hopes were high for Loyola College; as reported in the *Woodstock Letters*, "if the uptown sister of the Immaculate Conception thrives as well as the college on Baronne Street, there will be every cause to feel satisfaction that Loyola College has been started."[60]

The college opened with a curricular structure practically identical to the downtown college, except for the preparatory department. In fact, so closely aligned were the two institutions that members of the faculty were often interchanged between Loyola College and the College of the Immaculate Conception. The main difference between the two institutions was that they served different sections of New Orleans.[61] In order to continue the expansion of Loyola College, an additional portion of the originally purchased uptown tract of land had to be sold off. In the same year that the college opened, an advertisement ran in the *Daily Picayune*: "An unusual opportunity for investment and speculation. Grand sub-Division of the rear portion of the 'Jesuit Tract,' in the rear of St. Charles Ave., extending from Freret St. to Claiborn Ave., and comprising about 300 splendid building lots in the most promising and rapidly growing section of the sixth district. At public auction, Tuesday, May 24th, at 12 o'clock M., at the real estate exchange, No. 311 Baronne Street."[62] The land was sold to neighboring Sophie Newcomb College for $150,000. Later, Newcomb College and Tulane University would exchange properties, and the land passed to the ownership of Tulane's board of directors.[63] The revenue drawn from the sale of land was used to establish a financial endowment to promote the growing needs of the small Jesuit college.

As Loyola College progressed, the Jesuits disseminated advertisements to Catholic and Protestant New Orleans families in order to increase enrollment. The advertisement detailed the identity and mission of the institution and reported the following: "Your attention is respectfully invited to the new school opened by the Jesuits in the garden district of the city, on St. Charles Avenue near Audubon Park. . . . [Educational] methods based on long and accurate observation and sound psychology, and embodied in the famous 'Ratio Studiorum,' will be followed as closely as the times permit in Loyola College. . . . Besides the religious and moral training of pupils . . . great stress will be laid on the development of the manners of a perfect gentleman. . . . Non-Catholics will be admitted and their religious opinions scrupulously respected, nor shall they be debarred from any College honors or distinctions because of their religious tenets."[64] It was the intent of the Jesuits that intellectual, physical, and spiritual development would be amply provided for via the instructional methods of the *Ratio Studiorum*;[65] however, the Jesuits communicated that the religious tenets of the Catholic faith would not be imposed upon students of differing faiths.

This change to the traditional Catholic program of Jesuit education reflected the need of the New Orleans Jesuits to extend their grasp and attract greater numbers of students, regardless of religious preference. Even so, the Jesuits intended to maintain their heritage and history of education in the South. As indicated in the journals of Father Biever, "at the approach of spring, Loyola had its first Arbor Day[, and] . . . tiny oak trees were obtained from St. Charles College Grand Coteau, La."[66] Father Biever goes on to explain that "the trees planted today by the 28 pioneer students, are the descendents of the first sturdy oaks planted by Jesuit Fathers nearly a century ago at St. Charles College, La. May you young Gentlemen grow strong and sturdy even as these oak saplings do and show to the world the deep rooted principles of religious faith and justice that are planted in your hearts in the institution."[67] Not only was the history of the Jesuits imparted to students as well as citizens of New Orleans, religious images were also installed to more widely circulate the identity of the institution. Such an example was the seal of Loyola College. The seal was circular in nature with the Latin phrase *Collegium Loyolaeum Neo Aurelian—MCMIV* (Loyola College New Orleans—1904) cyclically framing a large shield. Half of the shield is covered in diagonal stripes, while the other half is emblazoned with portions of the Loyola and Ognez family crest. The center of the shield contains the Jesuit IHS, and atop the shield rests the Louisiana pelican feeding her nest of chicks.[68] Such historic markers and collegiate symbols communicated the breadth and history of Jesuit educational traditions and imparted this identity to the public.

As alluded to previously, the initial plan for this new college on St. Charles Avenue was to only accept high school graduates and other college students who wished to attend;[69] however, out of necessity, the Jesuits of Loyola College eventually allowed high school students to enroll in order to increase the college's student population and thereby garner additional capital through tuition dollars.[70] The tuition at this "uptown" Jesuit institution was ten dollars per month, as opposed to the six-dollar tuition of the "downtown" College of the Immaculate Conception. Father Patrick Ryan supposed that this discrepancy was due to the varied economic status of families located in the different districts of New Orleans.[71] Even so, a demarcation was evident in the student body. Wealthy families in uptown New Orleans enjoyed the presence of a college in their geographic area and enrolled their sons. Likewise, sons of families with lower incomes who lived in or around downtown New Orleans attended the College of the Immaculate Conception.

The 1905–1906 Loyola College catalogue provides an interesting glimpse into the existence of this institution. First, enrollment was selective so as to maintain manageable student numbers and enhance the quality of individual instruction. Students where enrolled based on geographic city residency, aptitude, and behavior.[72] In essence, Loyola College became an educational institution for uptown New Orleans residents only despite the original plan to siphon students from the downtown College of the Immaculate Conception. This emphasis on city-region selectivity so far had not existed at the other Jesuit institutions in the American South. Second, as the Loyola College catalogue states, "the plan of studies at Loyola is the same as that followed in other colleges of the Society of Jesus." The catalogue goes on to explain the religious and moral training that students would receive. Finally, and most telling, are the mentions of further construction plans for the college. At this time, the college was situated in a few wooden structures; however, the Jesuits had plans to enlarge the physical campus via the erection of new brick buildings.[73] Such construction would require additional capital. To aid in fundraising, a lay Catholic association for educational support was formed.

In the 1905 academic catalogue, the Jesuits of Loyola College took special care to acknowledge the aid of the Marquette Association for Higher Education. This association was created to secure funds for the Jesuit institution in uptown New Orleans[74] through fundraising, donations, and solicitations. Also, to increase public awareness of Loyola College's financial needs, the dates and times of every association meeting were advertised in city papers.[75] It was the belief of the Marquette Association that the word "failure" did not exist in the vocabulary of the Society of Jesus and that New Orleans, as well as the rest of the South, should support the continued success of Loyola College. To garner funds for the uptown college, members of the Marquette Association contacted prominent Catholic commercial and industrial businessmen. These businessmen were aware of the Jesuits' financial and religious struggles to sustain education in the American South.[76] Members of the Marquette Association plied their public connections and solicited through a variety of city publications. Such publications included the following statement: "If the Catholics of New Orleans will give their support to the proposed college, they will receive the blessings of God and will perform an act that will forever stand to the credit of the earnest Catholicity of the city."[77] The efforts of the Marquette Association prompted many city residents to endow Loyola College with monetary gifts ranging in the thousands.[78]

With funding on the rise and enrollment increasing, Loyola College conferred its first academic degrees in 1908. Three candidates successfully completed the prescribed course of study and were now prepared, according to the Jesuit administrators and faculty, for the work force or continued study in graduate or professional programs.[79] As Loyola College had no state charter, it conferred degrees under the same corporation document as the College of the Immaculate Conception: the Catholic Society for Religious and Literary Education.[80] The Jesuits of Loyola College believed this association document to be supported by the state of Louisiana as a legitimate basis for the confirmation of degrees; however, this was not the case. News circulated to neighboring institutions that the college faced an immense difficulty regarding institutional legitimacy due to the lack of a formal state charter and published curricular material.

In 1910, the Jesuits were notified that Tulane University was refusing Loyola College diplomas as sufficient academic evidence to enroll in graduate programs. Father Ryan, after learning of the situation, sent a letter to Dean Walter Miller of Tulane University reminding him that Tulane had received boys into medical and law courses with only the presentation of a high school diploma. Ryan posed this question to the dean: "How in reason then can you refuse to accept the college diploma of Loyola College which represents four years of college work in addition to high school work?" Following this correspondence, the graduates of Loyola College were admitted into Tulane's graduate programs. The reason presented to Father Ryan for the refusal to admit Loyola College graduates lay in Tulane's inability to gauge what courses Loyola graduates had taken during their years of Jesuit education. Tulane requested a course catalogue from Loyola College; however, the Jesuits were not printing catalogues for that year and instead sent a catalogue from Spring Hill College, as the course structure at Loyola College and Spring Hill College were identical at the time. As this catalogue seemed to assuage the academic suspicions of Tulane University's administration, both Loyola College and Spring Hill College students were informed that they could apply for and be accepted into Tulane's graduate programs henceforth.[81]

With this hurdle cleared, the time had come to address other issues regarding legitimacy. Standards for American higher education were changing, and with limited resources, the Jesuits intended to reorganize their system of higher education in the South. As Father Ryan indicates, "the school year of 1910–11 was a . . . transition for it marked the last of the small college and was a forerunner of the university."[82] Father Thomas Clancy describes the events that outlined the dismantling of Loyola College to make way for a bifurcated system of Jesuit education in the New Orleans Province, one in which high school departments and college-level curricula would be separated. As Clancy states, "it was in the beginning of the twentieth century that Loyola [College] . . . was started, first as a six year, school just like the College on Baronne Street. But it was decided in the second decade of the twentieth century to make Loyola the College Department and to transfer the High School Department to Jesuit High School which was finally located on Carrolton Avenue."[83] With this change came a new wave in the development of Jesuit higher education in the New Orleans Province. As curricular and physical changes were implemented, the New Orleans Jesuits announced their educational adaptations via the *Woodstock Letters*.

The *Woodstock Letters* explain that Loyola College was founded in 1904 as a highly selective institution priding itself on low student enrollment for optimal student-teacher interaction; however, the college was closed to allow for a reorganization of Jesuit education in the province. Thus, on the same site as Loyola College, Loyola University was born. Loyola University would, in time, possess departments of arts and sciences, dentistry, pharmacy, medicine, and law; a school of commerce and finance, a school of civil engineering, a school of architecture, and a school of auto mechanics.[84]

Loyola College was, in and of itself, a transformational step for the New Orleans Province of the Society of Jesus. Although the original plan for accepting only high school graduates at Loyola College did not come to fruition, the seed was planted for an academic realignment that more closely matched American educational standards. The closure of Loyola College marked the end of the old six-year system of Jesuit education and the birth of a new stratified system through Loyola University and Jesuit High School. Such a change placed southern Jesuit higher education in line with the academic needs and wants of modernizing communities while satisfying the legitimacy requirements of changing educational ideologies.

When examining the Loyola College case through the concepts of institutional identity, mission, and town and gown relationships, a picture emerges that closely resembles the College of the Immaculate Conception yet contains important differences. Loyola College was relatively well supported by the public, and the institutional identity and mission of the college were clearly advertised; however, Loyola College never achieved the high enrollment numbers of the College of the Immaculate Conception. What reasons made it difficult to increase the number of students attending Loyola College, and were these factors related to the need to close the college? The answers become apparent when the case is analyzed via the conceptual framework of this study.

First, the identity of Loyola College was a cause for concern. Although supported by the Catholic population of New Orleans, a majority of New Orleans's Catholic boys and young men were enrolled in the College of the Immaculate Conception, which possessed a similar religious and curricular identity as Loyola College despite geographic location. The major difference between the two institutions was locale. Loyola College, on St. Charles Avenue, was surrounded by a region of New Orleans populated by wealthy citizens, unlike the more impoverished downtown region, which hosted the College of the Immaculate Conception. Acknowledging the wealth of St. Charles Avenue residents, the "uptown" Loyola College raised its fees to garner additional capital. Also, Loyola College reverted to the old Jesuit model of enrolling high school in addition to college-level students to offset inadequate enrollments. Because the institution did not stay true to its original mission of being a modern college that only accepted high school graduates, Loyola College was in a position to be closed once a new university was established that aligned with modern higher education curricular trends. This wavering mission ultimately caused the institution to shut down in lieu of a new university that would service students with an American higher education curriculum without a preparatory department.

Second, the direct purpose of Loyola College was to service the Carrollton region of New Orleans and provide a modicum of relief for the Jesuits at the College of the Immaculate Conception by attracting some students away from the downtown college. Although no existing data has been found to support the possibility that Loyola College educated students formerly enrolled at the Barrone Street college, it can be surmised from the high regional selectivity of the college, low student enrollments, and steadily increasing enrollments at the College of the Immaculate Conception that this transfer of students did not occur. In servicing the Carrollton area, Loyola College, in tandem with the wooden Church of the Most Holy Name, provided an educational institution for the expanded region of New Orleans. In essence, Loyola College established a foundation for further developments in Jesuit higher education by creating a physical presence in "uptown" New Orleans on St. Charles Avenue.

Third, the town and gown relationship between Loyola College and New Orleans was enhanced via the development of the Marquette Association for Higher Education; however, this development was accomplished too late to be of any lasting worth to Loyola College. By the time the Marquette Association had begun fundraising, the Jesuits of the New Orleans Province had devised plans for a new Jesuit university. With the public announcement that the Jesuits were in preparation to launch a new university, the efforts of the Marquette Association were redirected in order to raise financial capital and increase support for the new higher education initiative. Although Loyola College was supported by the community and possessed an institutional identity and mission that were well received, it was constructed during a period of educational transition for the New Orleans Province. As such, it suffered the same fate as other southern Jesuit institutions. The college was closed to make way for a more Americanized form of higher education as the Jesuits were in the process of redesigning their network of colleges and universities across the province, leaving the old curricular system behind and sacrificing Loyola College for the new Loyola University.

Considering Closure and Amalgamation

In the cases of the College of the Immaculate Conception and Loyola College, there are a variety of similarities yet subtle differences that infuse each case, creating an interesting analysis of intertwining events that affected the closure of each institution. These events demonstrate the influential nature of institutional identity and mission as it affects societal relationships and thus college closure and curricular amalgamation. Despite the shared city aspect and similar institutional identities and missions, the College of the Immaculate Conception and Loyola College had unique histories and roles in the revision of southern Jesuit higher education.

Both the College of the Immaculate Conception and Loyola College were established to aid in the education and development of Catholic boys and young men in New Orleans; however, whereas the College of the Immaculate Conception was originally meant to serve the entire city, Loyola College was created to aid the Carrollton area, and if possible, attract some students away from the Baronne Street campus. Ultimately, the Society of Jesus decided to close each institution in an effort to more closely align Jesuit higher education in the American South to twentieth-century standards of curricular legitimacy. The curricular similarities between the two colleges allowed for a relatively straightforward departmental amalgamation of college-level courses into the new Loyola University. Also, the visible identity and propagated mission of the two Jesuit institutions led to an enhanced public understanding of Jesuit education that ultimately enhanced Loyola University.

The major difference between the two institutions, despite preparatory education, was the religious openness of Loyola College. The public promotion of Loyola College made it clear that non-Catholic students were accepted and that their beliefs would be respected. This was never indicated in the publications of the College of the Immaculate Conception even though a variety of students with various religious affiliations attended the downtown college. Nevertheless, the population differences between the "uptown" Loyola College and the "downtown" College of the Immaculate Conception may have prompted this subtle adaptation. It is possible that the uptown region of New Orleans (the Carrollton area) was not as highly populated by Catholic families as downtown New Orleans might have been.

Even so, town and gown relationships were strong at both institutions, although potentially stronger at the College of the Immaculate Conception given the length of its history in New Orleans as compared to Loyola College. With the aid of the Marquette Association for Higher Education, ties between the public and Loyola College were strengthened, albeit a bit too late, as Loyola College was established during an era of Jesuit educational reform. This era of reform, as shown in the cases presented thus far, was typified by the adaptation of curricular missions. It is also important to note the sacrifice of colleges and universities in order to strengthen the Jesuit educational identity and mission of the New Orleans Province by retrenching Jesuit efforts into the cities of Mobile and New Orleans, where Catholic populations were larger and support was stronger. These college sacrifices and retrenchment efforts will be discussed further in chapter 5.

The public identity of each institution was commonly understood as Catholic and Jesuit. Indeed, the architectural similarity between the two colleges and their adjacent churches linked the identities of church and college in the public eye. Such visual representation of the Catholic origins of both institutions affected societal interactions by solidifying the understanding that church and college were connected institutionally as well as ideologically. Also, both institutions had college seals adorned with Catholic icons representing patron saints and Catholic symbols. This did not hinder either institution. In fact, it may have strengthened bonds between the Catholic population of New Orleans, the College of the Immaculate Conception, and Loyola College. Certainly, the shared Jesuit identity of both institutions was meant to enhance the reciprocity of faculty, as was presented in the Loyola College case through the transfer of Jesuit instructors from the College of the Immaculate Conception to Loyola College and vice versa.

Regarding educational mission, both the College of the Immaculate Conception and Loyola College presented and followed their mission of religious, Catholic-based education rooted in moral holistic development. This mission sustained both institutions and was slightly adapted over time to include varying courses in the sciences, as well as a cadet corps at the College of the Immaculate Conception. However, as has been previously argued, the educational standards in America and the South were shifting, and the New Orleans Province of the Society of Jesus understood the need to adapt colleges and curricula if the Jesuit educational presence was to be maintained in the American South. In the end, it was the change in American higher education and high school curricula that caused these institutions to close in favor of constructing a new Jesuit university and high school.

Two additional examples of structural adaptation occurred at the Jesuit administered St. John's College in Shreveport, Louisiana, and at Sacred Heart College in Tampa, Florida. The Jesuits had planned to develop both St. John's College and Sacred Heart College into fully functioning Jesuit institutions with preparatory and collegiate departments; however, according to the provincial catalogues, no students ever enrolled in college-level classes at either institution.[85] Even though curricular structures were defended as true liberal arts regimes based on the *Ratio Studiorum*, neither institution grew beyond that of a high school. When St. John's College opened for the 1913 academic year, the vice president's diary indicates that the institution was referred to as a "college." But by 1928, the same diary notes that the institution had become, in name and function, a high school.[86] In 1941, the college changed its name to St. John's High School and later to Jesuit High School. Today, the school is known as Loyola College Prep.[87] If anything, this shift from a "college" in title only to that of an accredited high school indicates the awareness of the Jesuits to changing educational ideologies. As such, in order to keep St. John's College alive, the Jesuits enhanced the perception of the institution as a high school and dropped the empty college department, thus aligning the institution with new academic standards and providing a formalized Jesuit high school for Shreveport.

Sacred Heart College in Tampa, Florida, was adapted in much the same way as St. John's College in order to promote its survival. The first high school diplomas were issued from the preparatory department in 1912.[88] With the success of the preparatory department, the Jesuits of Sacred Heart College had every intention of establishing a formalized college and even applied for a state charter. A document, marked 1914, from Sacred Heart College's records indicates that the "question is to apply for a charter and give the college an American name. . . . After much discussion it was agreed by the majority to call it Tampa College, [and] apply for the university degrees to the state Legislature."[89] Even with the new Tampa College title in place, Father Visitor Norbert de Boynes's edicts concerning the reformation of education in the province were carried out and the Tampa Jesuits began to restructure the institution before any college-level students enrolled. In 1921, a letter was sent from de Boynes to Tampa College and was read by the rector of the Jesuit community. The letter indicated that the Florida institution was not to offer any college courses.[90] Father de Boynes, however, did not order the closure of the Jesuit college in Tampa. Why was this? The most probable reason is that no students were enrolled in the college division and that the "college" was performing more like a "high school." As such, it can be argued that Father Visitor de Boynes viewed the institution as a functioning high school and allowed it to remain open.

With the closure of the College of the Immaculate Conception, Loyola College, and adaptations to other Jesuit institutions, one era of Jesuit education passed away, giving rise to a new university that would strive to match changing higher educational trends. With a long history as the "downtown" Jesuit college, the College of the Immaculate Conception had garnered public support, developed positive relationships with city officials, and had acquired a host of loyal alumni. Also, the Jesuits of Loyola College had developed the Marquette Association for soliciting and fundraising purposes. Ultimately, these two colleges closed not because they promoted an identity or mission that created a negative town and gown relationship but because the New Orleans Province decided to create a large Catholic university in New Orleans that, via an adapted curriculum, would address the public need for a modern institution of higher education. In the following chapter, the case of this new university, Loyola University New Orleans, and the case of Spring Hill College in Mobile, Alabama, will be presented for analysis. With the presentation of Loyola University and Spring Hill College, both of which are still in existence, this study will attempt to present the evolution of Jesuit higher education in the New Orleans Province as a system affected by and responsive to aspects of institutional identity, mission, and societal relationships.

5
Institutional Survival

> The apostolate of the Society [of Jesus] must needs be greatly influenced by the conditions of Catholicity in the South. It had to adapt itself to such conditions and it has done so.
>
> —Father Norbert de Boynes

Having considering the previous micro-histories, we will now investigate two Jesuit institutions that have survived to the present day: Loyola University New Orleans and Spring Hill College in Mobile, Alabama. Even though both Loyola University and Spring Hill College have passed into the twenty-first century, both institutions faced hardships and legitimacy issues that influenced their relationships with surrounding social environments. The historic analysis of these two institutions concludes in the 1930s. The justification for these early case conclusions lies in the fact that by the 1930s Loyola University and Spring Hill College had conformed to new curricular standards and educational trends regarding higher education accreditation. Certainly both institutions have faced struggles throughout the twentieth and twenty-first centuries, however, with the reformation of curricular structures and college campuses in the New Orleans Province, Loyola University and Spring Hill College emerged as the remaining and adaptive examples of Jesuit higher education in the American South. Within these last two institutional histories, we see examples of curricular modification to address social educational needs, trends, and accreditation standards. In addition to these adaptations, both Loyola University and Spring Hill College managed to maintain their institutional identities and missions while maintaining supportive town and gown relationships. As both Jesuit institutions evolved it was the ability to adapt and sustain positive social relationships that led to their survival. Each institution today represents the religious and educational history of the Society of Jesus in the American South.

Spring Hill College in Mobile, Alabama

In 1825, Father Michael Portier, a French immigrant, was consecrated as Bishop of Oleno and charged by the Holy See to govern the Vicariate Apostolic Territory of Florida, a Catholic region that ran the length of the Gulf Coast. Bishop Portier decided that Mobile, Alabama, would be the religious seat of his territory due to its large Catholic population. Once established, Portier moved quickly to develop the region.[1] In 1833, Bishop Protier established the Visitation Monastery and Academy for religious instruction, and, in 1835, he oversaw the construction of a Cathedral for Mobile. But before any of this was complete, Portier had established a Catholic college for the territory. Spring Hill College, then six miles west of Mobile, was constructed atop a hill on a one-mile square tract of land with a natural spring, thus the name Spring Hill College. The US Congress had ceded this tract of land to Mobile.[2] The Congregation de fide Propaganda (Propagation of the Faith) supplied funds for Bishop Portier to purchase the aforementioned tract and to establish a set of simple wooden college buildings for the education of local Catholic boys. With this financial assistance, 122 acres were purchased from the city of Mobile on April 17, 1830. Soon an additional 380 acres were purchased.[3] This elevated site was selected due to its proximity to the Pascagoula Highway, which provided a link between Washington, DC, and New Orleans.[4]

With land acquired and construction underway, there was an immediate need to acquire additional funds to complete the college buildings. Watching from his exile in Rome, the uncle of Napoleon Bonaparte, Cardinal Joseph Fresch (archbishop of Lyons), contributed 30,000 francs toward the construction of Spring Hill College. Fresch had known Bishop Portier in the Lyons Seminary and was keenly interested in Portier's work in America.[5] Upon the completion of the first set of wooden structures, Spring Hill College opened in 1830 and was heralded as the first institution of higher education in Alabama. On January 9, 1836, the Alabama legislature granted Spring Hill College a state charter, thereby confirming the institute's ability to confer degrees.[6] Later, in 1849, Pope Gregory XVI bestowed the college with the right to confer degrees in divinity and canon law.[7]

From 1839 to 1841, the Fathers of Mercy administered the college, and, from 1841 to 1846, the Eudist Fathers directed the institution. After the egress of the Eudists, Bishop Portier assumed the college presidency but sent a priest to Europe to search for another religious order to direct the college. The directive was given to ask anyone except the Society of Jesus. The reason for this exception is not expressly known; however, when no other religious group accepted the college, the Jesuits were contacted and agreed to take command of the institution.[8] A report concerning the Jesuit acceptance of Spring Hill College states that "in the light obtained from the many failures already experienced in the administration of the College, Bishop Portier saw on the one hand the necessity of giving the institution a more regular, stable and enduring government, whilst on the other hand the increasing needs of his diocese no longer permitted him to devote a sufficient number of his priests for the management of the college."[9] The Jesuits confirmed that they would indeed take over the administration of the institution and lighten the bishop's responsibilities.

In 1847, Father Francis Gautrelet and several Jesuit companions traveled to New Orleans and concluded negotiations with the Mobile bishop. The resulting contract between Portier and the Society of Jesus gave the Jesuits full control of Spring Hill College.[10] Portier, though originally hesitant to release the college to the Society of Jesus, was pleased with the Jesuits' acceptance of the institution and remained a friend to Father Gautrelet. The college opened under Jesuit administration on September 1, 1848, with seventeen boarding students. The tuition for day students was set at 50 Spanish piastres per term and 130 piastres for boarding students.[11] Following the installment of Father Gautrelet as president of Spring Hill College, enrollment increased to eighty-six. This increased population included regional Catholic, Protestant, and Jewish students. Under the supervision of the Mission of Lyon, Father Gautrelet managed Spring Hill College in conjunction with St. Charles College in Grand Coteau, Louisiana, to further develop both institutions along similar curricular and instructional principles.[12]

When Father Jean Baptiste Maisounabe arrived in Mobile to aid in the transfer of Spring Hill College from Bishop Portier to the Society of Jesus, he found that Father Gautrelet had already attended to it. Maisounabe, relieved of purchasing negotiations, turned his attention to the dearth of Jesuits who could speak English fluently in order to teach additional language courses required for the Jesuit curriculum. The need for polyglots was not only for the instruction of lay students but also for the teaching of novices already on their way to becoming Jesuits. Several of the first students at Spring Hill College had enrolled with the hopes of becoming priests, and so Maisounabe had a care not only for opening the college but also for the education of those who wished to follow the religious life.[13]

Despite the need to educate future priests, the Jesuits were often concerned about the behavior and attitudes of lay students, many of whom came from wealthy families and had little regard for hard work or academic rigor. According to the *Woodstock Letters*, the Jesuits reported that these student attitudes were a "consequence of their [the students'] belief that they can succeed in life and get rich without work; the weakness of parents, who tolerate and encourage everything; . . . disciplinarians in those ante-bellum times had difficulties and discouragements, of which their successors now a days have no idea."[14] Following the Civil War, however, these attitudes changed as family lives altered, and the need to work instead of relying on inherited wealth became apparent in student personalities.[15]

Negative student attitudes, however, were the least of the Jesuits' concerns. In February 1853, scarlet fever broke out in Mobile, and two students died of the disease. Others became afflicted, and the decision was made to temporarily close the college until April of the same year.[16] When the institution reopened, the Jesuit community of Spring Hill College noted an outburst of anti-Catholicism from local members of the Know-Nothing Party. By the mid-1850s, vocal opposition resulted in physical violence. According to Father Conrad Widman:

> During the Know nothing troubles, Father [Francis] Nachon, one of the quietest and kindest of men, one Sunday drove as usual to Dog River factory to say Mass for the few Catholics working there. On the way he was suddenly attacked by two ruffians, who dragged him from his buggy and beat him unmercifully, threatening him with the same treatment if he should return the next Sunday. He rose, all covered with blood, went to the place, and said Mass as if nothing had happened. The affair was soon known in Mobile and aroused the greatest indignation amongst all classes. The Father continued his visits as before, without anyone to trouble him.[17]

Following the Nachon incident, no similar acts of violence seem to have taken place.

Unshaken, the Jesuits pressed forward and bolstered the Catholic nature of Spring Hill College. In fact, a new institutional name was promoted. Documents reveal that an attempt may have been made to change the institution's name from Spring Hill College to St. Joseph's College Spring Hill. A letter from Michael Portier illustrates how the name of the college evolved:

> Ever desirous of supporting, to the best of our means, the wants of our Catholic population in Mobile, we could not but feel, that the continually extending limits of our prosperous City, and the rapidly increasing number of its inhabitants, demand another Catholic Church, especially for the convenience of those that are at a greater distance from the Cathedral and the Church of St. Vincent of Paul; we have therefore committed to the Fathers of the Society of Jesus of St. Joseph's College Spring Hill the care of erecting a Church in the vicinity of the Hospital; and we authorize them herewith to appeal to the charity of our generous Public, by way of subscriptions and collections, for the necessary means of executing their plan. We hope and wish sincerely that their zeal and devotedness will meet with the desired success.
>
> Mobile on the 31st of May 1857.
> Michael, Bishop of Mobile.[18]

The letter not only depicts the religious evolution of the college's name, St. Joseph's College Spring Hill, but also acknowledges the growing faith in the Society of Jesus of Mobile to govern their own church separate from the college. However, as with so many institutions, the lengthy name, albeit reflective of the college's patron saint, was abandoned in favor of the original title. As such, the institution became Spring Hill College once more and remains so to this day.

With the college name reestablished, publications were sent out to the local community describing the nature of instruction at the Catholic college. In the upper classes, the professors specialized in science, mathematics, and history. Philosophy was taught in Latin. Father Albert Biever adds a telling description of the learned students of Spring Hill College. Biever states that "even in my own days the examiners were surprised to hear the Collegiate students speak Latin so fluently and so readily. Visitors to the college were surprised as to the ease in which students could recite and translate the Greek edition of the Acts of the Apostles."[19] As the local community enrolled additional students in the college, the curriculum and physical plant were expanded.

During the 1859 academic year, the west wing of the main college building was erected, and the regular curriculum progressed with the addition of commercial courses. In the commercial courses, pragmatic curricula such as simple engineering and woodworking were taught instead of Latin and Greek. Concerns over the new commercial courses arose among the Jesuits, as there was trouble organizing the classic liberal arts courses according to the *Ratio Studiorum*. According to Biever, "whatever advantages maybe derived from the new system, I doubt whether the men trained in this system have the mental formation and intellectual grasp of the momentous questions that men of today have to meet. These old educators and deep students were very versatile and progressive, and though there may be more show and glare in our present methods of education, they certainly are not as solid and effective."[20] Regarding the concerns of effective instruction, teaching languages seemed to be a problem for the fathers and brothers, as English was not their native tongue. Those Jesuit instructors who could converse with students in English were encouraged to do so, and those who could speak French or Spanish were put in charge of students whose primary language was the same. According to Biever's diary, "the Modern languages such as French, German, [and] Spanish [were taught]. . . . As soon as the boys were sufficiently advanced, the teacher conversed with these students in the tongue they were trying to acquire. English of course was taught by experts in this language. . . . Father de Carriere being very conversant with Spanish became automatically the spiritual Father of the Cuban and Mexican boys. As such, he accompanied them to Cuba and brought them back from Havana in time for the opening of classes."[21] As the college was still in its early years of Jesuit control, the firm establishment of organization, continuity, and the religious identity and mission of the Society of Jesus was paramount. Jesuit instructors were expected not only to teach but to also serve as confessors. According to the correspondence of Father Superior Aloysius Curioz, "it is proper that each professor have charge of his own [student penances]. This is the practice in our colleges."[22] Such religious rites were paired with a curriculum that was slowly adapted to local practices.

In the years preceding the Civil War, Father Gautrelet attempted to "Americanize" the college in order to adapt the curriculum to the needs and customs of southern Americans. This was particularly difficult for the Jesuits at Spring Hill College, as most were French and spoke their native tongue far better than the English of southern Alabama.[23] Not only was the introduction of the English language important to the Jesuit fathers, but the holistic development of their students, including nutrition, was also taken into consideration. Father Maisounabe communicated to his colleagues at Spring Hill College, with some amount of levity: "The daily fare for students should also be good and varied as possible; a good cook is what really makes a college, they say in this country."[24] Food aside, Gautrelet's attempt to modernize the college must have paid off as antebellum enrollments reached 180 students, stretching the limits of the facilities, the instructors, and college resources.[25] In an 1859 letter from Father Curioz, the effects of the increased enrollment are noted along with the need to balance the attention given to both St. Charles College and Spring Hill College. Curioz states that "several of our young men [Jesuits] are somewhat fatigued. Very soon Springhill will have no place. There they are now with 220 students, and there is no indication that this is going to stop. It will soon be time for the direction to be towards Grand Coteau. It is possible that this may become a la mode when the railroad begins operation."[26] This increase in enrollment did nothing to relieve the stress of the Jesuits.

Despite over-enrollment, graduates of Spring Hill College were attracting attention across the American South. Alumni included senators, governors, judges, lawyers, bishops, priests, and university professors at other southern institutions. It was reported that there was not a state in the South that had not sent a student to study at the Jesuit college in Alabama.[27] As the college gained fame, the enrollment leapt higher. Father Curioz finally called a halt to the "open door" nature of the institution and indicated that "there [was] no more room at Spring Hill. They [then had] 250 students."[28] With enrollment capped, Father Superior Curioz pushed the college's administrators and faculty to further modernize the college, adapt courses and methods of teaching, and to forgo old models of education in favor of new, American models of instruction. Even though Father Curioz intended to increase enrollment requirements and instructional rigor, he did not intend to expand the institution's already existing military curriculum.

Prior to the Jesuit arrival at Spring Hill College, Bishop Portier had selected Father Pierre Mauvernay, a former officer in Napoleon Bonaparte's army to serve at the Mobile college. Mauvernay formed a cadet corps that was often featured in Independence Day parades and other national celebrations throughout Mobile According to Michael Kenny, "armed at first with wooden guns and later with the implements that their company title of 'Spring Hill Lancers' implies . . . they helped to make the College an integral part of public life and so to promote its [Spring Hill College's] progress."[29] Not only did the Spring Hill College Lancers, later known as the Spring Hill College Cadets, perform for national festivities, they performed for religious events. For example, the cadets led large campus processions for the Blessed Sacrament. They not only led the procession but also fired salutes before the sacrament was placed in chapels and other repositories.[30] After the administration of the college was transferred to the Society of Jesus, the cadet corps was retained.

Just before the Civil War, local interest in the Spring Hill College Cadets increased. As a result the Jesuits enhanced the already uniformed student regiment by hiring a lay military instructor, Mr. R. S. Sands.[31] With tension in the air regarding secession and talk of war from the local populace, Father Superior Curioz expressed his concern about military training at Spring Hill College:

> [The] idea of introducing the . . . military, the uniforms, etc, is for me, dangerous. Almost everywhere it had been introduced they have found reason to repent of it. . . . I am altogether abhorred to the introduction of such a custom. . . . As regards your military company I do not change my opinion. They began at Spring Hill before consulting me. I hear that hardly an hour passes but they talk of their great difficulties, a company according to rule with rifles, uniforms, etc. Already many parents complain of this expense. . . . And they will have many other inconveniences if a bad spirit develops. You will do well to wait. It is possible that experience will prove reason to be on my side.[32]

Indeed, a "bad spirit" developed, and with the secession of Alabama from the United States, the Jesuits found themselves playing host to more military men than students.

The college continued to advance throughout the antebellum period; however, by the start of the 1861 academic year, trouble was in sight. When news of the Confederate election of Jefferson Davis and the secession of Virginia from the Union reached Spring Hill College, the students were excited but the faculty were concerned. College enrollment plummeted as the Civil War began, and several Jesuits took leave of their teaching duties to serve as chaplains in the Confederate Army. During the war, attempts were made to enlist lay members of the faculty as well as older students, but these were soon put to rest when Father Gautrelet paid a visit to the president of the Confederacy, Jefferson Davis, and had all army solicitation and consignment at Spring Hill College stopped. Despite Gautrelet's efforts, the war affected the student population, but the institution remained open due to its large preparatory department stocked with students too young to enlist.[33]

As enrollment dropped, so did the spirits of the Jesuits and students who remained in the preparatory department. With the fall of New Orleans, the Jesuits at Spring Hill College found themselves cut off from much needed supplies normally shipped from the Louisiana port city. All communication between the southern Jesuits and the Society of Jesus in Europe ceased, and when the sacramental wine was exhausted, the Jesuits fermented wild grapes, otherwise known as scuppernongs, to produce wine for communion. With fears running high and student numbers low, the Jesuits' contemplated the future of their Mobile college. However, in 1864, the college opened with an increased number of students primarily due to local families' fears that their sons would be drafted for military service unless enrolled in a college or school. Despite their parents' best efforts, many students ran away from the Jesuit college to enlist in the Confederate Army.[34] Those students who remained had a difficult time adapting to uncomfortable conditions and the presence of Union soldiers camping on the college lawns. As the war raged on, one Jesuit recorded that "the very soul of this system of education was the spirit of religion and [Confederate] patriotism. During the Civil War when the Yankee army was occupying the high plateau near Spring Hill College, the military army would come at the eve and play Northern airs beneath the windows of the dormitories. The larger boys would smart under the humiliation."[35] Spring Hill College students took great pride in their southern heritage and resented the presence of Northern troops residing on the college grounds.

Despite the presence of either Confederate or Union troops, Father Conrad M. Widman indicated in the *Woodstock Letters* that "all through the war, the college was protected with equal kindness and efficacy by the federal and confederate authorities. After the war, it gradually resumed its former prosperity, and though the southern boys, owing to the financial decline of the country, became fewer, they were replaced by students from Cuba, Central America, and Mexico."[36] Following the end of the Civil War, Spring Hill College resumed classes as it had done every semester during the war. Though the college survived the war, disaster struck in the form of a devastating fire.

On the night of December 26, 1868, the campus fire alarm sounded. As the Jesuits ran out of the rectory, they discovered that the second story of the main college building was engulfed in flames. In the course of a few hours, the central college building, adjacent class buildings, and church were reduced to ashes. All students, lay workers, instructors, priests, and brothers were saved, but the college buildings were destroyed. Some students returned home, whereas the bulk of the students were transferred to St. Charles College in Grand Coteau, Louisiana, where they finished out the academic year. Though the students were removed to St. Charles College, they did not find their stay in Louisiana unpleasant. The Mobile students were fond of chasing the Louisiana wildlife including birds and rabbits. According to one Jesuit father in regard to the experiences of Spring Hill College students at Grand Coteau: "This sort of recreation the students had not enjoyed at Spring Hill to the same extent or with equal success, so they highly appreciated it... but all this together with the other luxuries to be had at St. Charles', that land of milk and honey, though sufficient to give content, did not extinguish the student's longing after '*old* Spring Hill.'"[37]

Despite the students' longing to return to Spring Hill College, the Jesuits had to consider if it was at all possible to reopen the college. As they deliberated over the possible closure of the institution, the second bishop of Mobile, Reverend John Quinlan, arrived on the scene, spoke with the fathers, and promptly announced that he would not stand by and watch Spring Hill College fail. Quinlan renounced all debts owed to the diocese by the Society of Jesus and donated a large sum for rebuilding the college. With Quinlan's assistance and an additional $30,000 garnered from the insurance claim, Spring Hill College rose from the ashes. The new central college building was larger than the first, although it resembled the former structure architecturally. The college reopened to boarding students on December 8, 1869, with a celebration mass attended by faculty, students, and Mobile residents.[38] Reconstruction costs exceeded $90,000, which left the institution with a $50,000 debt. Despite the debt, the college opened with 125 students from across the American South as well as South America. Through an increase of yearly tuition to $400 and further donations from the community, Spring Hill College was free of its $50,000 debt in ten years.[39]

In 1889, it was reported in the *Woodstock Letters* that the Jesuits of Spring Hill College were expecting a record enrollment. Despite the Jesuits' expectations, enrollment did not increase as yellow fever broke out in New Orleans. Since many Spring Hill College students were either from New Orleans or arrived at the port city to travel by train to the Alabama institution, the quarantine of New Orleans due to fever could detrimentally affect the college. Quarantine was indeed established in New Orleans and all transportation ceased, leaving the students stranded. The students could do nothing but remain in New Orleans and wait until the quarantine was lifted. The Mobile Jesuits, bereft of a large percentage of their student body, considered closing the institution; however, it was decided to begin the term as scheduled with twenty-eight students and wait for the remaining students to arrive. Consequently, several stranded students who were barred from traveling to Mobile, enrolled in other institutions. By the start of December 1889, the quarantine was lifted, and the student population rose by approximately fifty. The fall term had been difficult due to the late arrival of so many students. As such, it was deemed necessary to extend the term through the Christmas holidays to make up for days missed. Despite the annual occurrence of yellow fever in New Orleans and its frequent arrival in Mobile, Spring Hill College remained untouched by the disease as a result of its distance from the larger city and its supply of fresh spring water. This fact was highly advertised in the years to come and contributed to the overall celebrated status of the institution among local community members.[40]

Upon the reopening of the college, new Jesuits were enlisted to aid in instruction and administration. In his journal, Father Albert Biever provides a candid account of his teaching at Spring Hill College, the student population, and adherence to Jesuit instructional methodologies:

> My first task was to teach the Third Commercial. This class corresponded to the Third Grammar in the classical course and was looked upon as a preparatory class for the Commercial course. Twenty-four boys followed this class. Only three Americans were among my students. The balance were all Cubans and Mexicans. . . . Father F. X. O'Connor, S.J. the Vice-President and Prefect of Studies at the meeting of the teachers commended my method which after all was drawn from the "Ratio Studiorum." This little praise encouraged me greatly. I was young, only nineteen years, and inexperienced. At the end of the school year I was appointed teacher of the Third Grammar.[41]

As a result of improved instruction, expanded curricula, and a reliance on Mobile students as well as international students, enrollment returned to pre-Civil War numbers. In 1901, the *Varia* section of the *Woodstock Letters* indicates that the enrollment at Spring Hill College had increased to 155 and that a gift from Major P. C. Hannon of Mobile, a marble statue of St. Joseph, had been placed on the grounds.[42] In addition, the local community and alumni had begun to show support for the college en masse.

A significant example of this support occurred in May of 1902. At this time, 650 New Orleans residents representing the Jesuit Educational Alumni Association of the College of the Immaculate Conception visited Mobile to celebrate Jesuit education, the success of Spring Hill College, and the progress of the South since the Civil War. The number of Mobile residents and New Orleans visitors attending the college celebration was estimated at 3,000, including notable Spring Hill College alumni representing both Mobile and New Orleans.[43] An account of the event is provided in the *Woodstock Letters*: "The general trend of the sentiments expressed was directed to the central idea of the magnificent gathering of alumni—the idea that no education can surpass that given by the Jesuits, because they combine solid instruction with the inculcation of principles of honor, virtue, and religion; that a Jesuit alumnus is essentially, and by reason of his education a 'virnobilis,' a gentleman; that the Jesuit alumni have occupied, now hold, and will ever shine in the best walks of life; and that the alumnus comradeship is always a pleasing thought."[44] With alumni support, the college continued to expand and draw students from across the Atlantic Ocean. In 1903, Spring Hill College enrolled three students from Spain. As well, the institution had extended its property holdings by purchasing two tracts of land adjacent to the campus. In addition, a new boiler house had been constructed to increase heating and hot water. The hot water was a much-enjoyed improvement by all who resided on the campus. It was also reported in the 1903 edition of the *Woodstock Letters* that doctorates in divinity, music, and fine arts were bestowed at the annual commencement.[45]

As the college entered the twentieth century, a wave of modernization was imposed. Old roads were laid with new cobblestones, drainage was improved, walkways were added, new residence halls were completed, and the campus dining hall was rebuilt to accommodate the increased number of students. As dust from construction and refurbishment settled, Alabama senator John Tyler Morgan visited the campus in 1903 to a fanfare of "Dixie" played by the student brass band. Morgan surveyed the college, and with alacrity, he turned to the Jesuit faculty and declared that Spring Hill College should become "Spring Hill University."[46] This proclamation of respect and veneration was met with great celebration. The name of "college" may have been retained, but the institution's legitimacy had certainly risen in the eyes of the state.

Again, in 1905, yellow fever broke out in Mobile and New Orleans, but the college, reportedly the only institution along the Gulf Coast to open on its scheduled day in September, was unaffected. Once again, the healthy state of the institution kept it in high regard with students and families, although the college did suffer a decrease in students from New Orleans due to an imposed quarantine. On opening day, only 62 students were in attendance; however, the enrollment increased to 162 as quarantines were lifted.[47] As student numbers continued to increase, local support from Mobile's Catholic population was apparent. In 1908, with the student enrollment above 220, members of the Knights of Columbus demonstrated their appreciation for the college with a visit and celebration.[48] However, celebration and support were followed by disaster. For a second time, Spring Hill College was decimated by fire.

On the morning of January 16, 1909, a fire was discovered in the chapel stairwell. Before the fire could be doused, it had spread throughout the main building and leapt to the roof of the campus church. Before the fire was finally subdued, the main building had once again been destroyed, along with the church and dormitories. The Jesuit fathers and brothers sacrificed their own rectory to house many of the junior and senior college students and held classes that same afternoon in the campus infirmary. With the loss of approximately two thousand volumes from the library and the majority of the campus in ruins, the Jesuits made up their mind that they would, once again, rebuild. This time it was the citizens of Mobile who rose to the aid of the institution. The public donated $12,500 and the insurance company awarded the Spring Hill College Jesuits $35,000. Rebuilding began at once, and new structures, again resembled the old. By the start of the fall term, the college opened with a larger set of facilities than before, and soon a new church was finished that complemented the architecture of the college buildings. This time, the church and college buildings were joined by a series of breezeways, enclosing a central quadrangle.[49] After the college was rebuilt, it was the new president, Father Edward. E. Cummings, who opened the doors of the institution to the public for spiritual retreats in accordance with *The Spiritual Exercises*. At the first public laymen's retreat, there were thirty Mobile residents in attendance.[50] As religious functions for the community were expanded, it was decided in 1915 by order of the Jesuit superior general, Father Xavier Wernz, to establish a Sodality of the Blessed Virgin at Spring Hill College. The purpose of the sodality was to spread instruction about the mother of Jesus throughout the parish and to other Jesuit colleges in the New Orleans Province. Subsequently, the sodality helped fortify the Catholic identity and mission of the college.[51]

At this point in the history of Spring Hill College, the institution had suffered disease, fire, and war but had enjoyed steady enrollment, a consistently reinforced institutional identity and mission, and strong support from the local populace. The need now was for increased academic legitimacy from accrediting agencies. The Spring Hill College vice president's house diary indicates that on January 7, 1922, Spring Hill College was formally admitted into the Southern Association of Colleges and Schools (SACS).[52] Letters of assistance from Tulane and Vanderbilt University accompany this entry and demonstrate the college's academic acceptance by peer institutions. In the years that followed, the college was admitted to the Catholic Education Association (CEA). This connection with a larger religious accrediting organization secured Spring Hill College's legitimate standing among other Catholic institutions. The acceptance letter reads:

> To the Registrar:
>
> It gives me great pleasure to inform you that your college was placed upon the standard list of accredited colleges of the Department of Colleges and Secondary Schools of the Catholic Educational Association at a meeting of the Commission on Standardization which took place in Chicago on December 13th.
>
> Yours very Sincerely,
> J. W. R. Maguire C.D.V.
> Sec. Commission on Standardization,
> Catholic Educational Association.[53]

Even after Spring Hill College had received the confirmation of legitimacy from peer institutions and accrediting agencies, other forms of peer acknowledgment resulted. One such example took place in 1930, when Spring Hill College was asked to host the annual convention of the Southern Intercollegiate Athletic Association. Representatives from forty colleges and universities were in attendance, and a banquet was held in the college dining room welcoming guests to the convention and to Spring Hill College.[54] Even though the college was becoming widely accepted by secular entities, the Holy See in Rome questioned the Catholic nature of Spring Hill College.

In 1931, a letter arrived at the Jesuit college from the Sacred Congregation of Seminaries and Universities in Rome and posed a series of questions regarding the Catholic nature of Spring Hill College. The letter demanded answers to questions regarding what precautions were being taken concerning the mixture of Catholic and non-Catholic students, what advantages Spring Hill College gleaned from admitting non-Catholic students, what harm would be done if the college only admitted Catholic students, what danger existed to the faith of Catholic students in integrating them with non-Catholic students, what criteria were used in the selection of non-Catholic instructors, what precautions were taken to keep non-Catholics from corrupting the faith of Catholic students, and whether non-Catholic students participated in Catholic religious services.[55] This letter was, in essence, a way of ensuring the Catholic alignment of the college to the Holy See. In response to the Sacred Congregation's letter, the president of Spring Hill College, Father Joseph Walsh, explained that the college's state charter forbade the exclusion of students based on religion and that the mixture of Catholic and non-Catholic students had never caused any harm but had instead served as a method to decrease bigotry and prejudice toward Catholics in the surrounding communities. In particular, Walsh states that the mixing of students of diverse religious backgrounds aided in the development of "support . . . against attacks through non-Catholic men educated in [the] College."[56] Also, the financial support from Catholics, Protestant, and Jewish students had been helpful during previous financial difficulties. Walsh goes on to explain that in admitting only Catholic students, the state charter would be forfeited, and the good will of the community that the Society of Jesus had worked so hard to foster over the years would be lost.[57]

In his reply to the Sacred Congregation of Seminaries and Universities, Walsh also explains that non-Catholic students were not required to attend Catholic religious services but were free to do so if they chose, and most did. Regarding instructor selection, several lay professors had been hired to aid in teaching, and these non-Catholic individuals were employed only when Catholic instructors of excellent quality were not available. Walsh concludes his letter by explaining that the addition of non-Catholic instructors had served the college well and had strengthened the relationship between the college, Mobile, and surrounding communities.[58] Rome seemed pleased with these answers and allowed the Jesuits to continue their work unabated. Spring Hill College persisted on its path, enrolling greater numbers and continued to garner support from the City of Mobile, as well as the State of Alabama.

At the centennial celebration of Spring Hill College, several notable persons presented their views on the college. Speakers included Dr. B. L. Parker from Peabody College, Governor Bibb Graves, and Father Albert Biever, founder and first president of Loyola University New Orleans. Governor Graves presented some cause for concern due to his connection with the Ku Klux Klan. The Klan's anti-Catholic stance was notorious across the South; however, Graves praised the college and the educational work of the Society of Jesus. The governor spoke about the importance of religious education in the South. He presented Spring Hill as "our oldest daughter of education" in Alabama and stated that the college was "one of God's lighthouses on the shores of time, a beacon conscientiously fingering the turbulent seas of time showing men the way to God."[59] Such positive remarks from Governor Graves probably eased tensions on the part of the Jesuits despite his Klan connections.

With the inclusion of Spring Hill College into SACS and the CEA as well as the apparent approval of the college's educational merits from Rome, the New Orleans Province continued to align the Mobile institution with American college and high school requirements. In 1936, Spring Hill High School, the remnants of the college's preparatory department, was closed to better enhance the image of Spring Hill College as an institution of higher education only.[60] As the city of Mobile grew, other institutions of higher education were established, such as the University of South Alabama and the University of Mobile, but Spring Hill College maintained a steady enrollment with a large percentage of students who claimed the Roman Catholic faith. The college, beautifully adorned with religious symbols, statues, and the iconic Jesuit IHS, reflects its Catholic and Jesuit heritage, a heritage of which all enrolled students and alumni are aware. Adjoining the campus is one of the two New Orleans Province cemeteries. There, and on the surrounding hillside, students stroll and study in the midst of the oldest institution for higher learning in Alabama and the third oldest Catholic college in America.

Mobile, Alabama, with a historically strong Catholic population, was an apt location for a Catholic college. As such, Bishop Portier sought to establish a center for Catholic education in the Mobile area that would support the religious mission of the Vicariate Apostolic Territory of Florida. Despite wavering between the names Spring Hill College (based on locale) and St. Joseph's College Spring Hill (overtly Catholic and relevant to the institution's patron saint), the institution was promoted as a religious college with the purpose of moral training for young men. Enrollment was not exclusive to Catholics; Protestant and Jewish students were also admitted. Clearly, the college did not discriminate along religious lines even though its identity as a Jesuit-administered Catholic institution was heavily promoted in published materials, Catholic symbols, and a physical connection between the college and church.

This case also indicates that after the Society of Jesus accepted governance of Spring Hill College, there was a degree of difficulty aligning the curricular mission with that of the Jesuit *Ratio Studiorum*. Perhaps this difficulty was due to the slow adaptation of the Jesuits to their social surroundings or a result of the language barrier between French-speaking Jesuits and English-speaking students. As the years passed, the institutional mission was enhanced as the methods of the *Ratio Studiorum* were adapted and applied. Also, the Catholic identity and mission of the institution was publicly accepted and promoted via lay retreats, as well as the incorporation of religious student organizations. This increased promotion of Spring Hill College's Catholic identity and mission did not seem to dampen enrollment and perhaps strengthened the bond between the institution and the local Catholic community despite the hindrance of war, disease, and fire.

The geographic location of Spring Hill College must be taken into account in order to understand communal interactions between town and gown. By placing the college near the Pascagoula Highway, which connected Mobile to Washington, DC, and New Orleans, Bishop Portier intended for the institution to remain in the public eye. Thus attracting students from across the American South. Also, such a connection allowed the Jesuit college to stay in close contact with Jesuit superiors in New Orleans, as well as providing some form of access to St. Charles College in Grand Coteau, Louisiana. This college connection was incredibly important when Spring Hill College burned and the student population was transferred to the Louisiana college. As the relationship strengthened between the institution and the surrounding community, student enrollments increased, as did public support. Also, the case of Spring Hill College contains several examples of community support through gifts, acceptance of the college via local and regional organizations, and festivities generated by the public in honor of the Jesuits and their educational efforts in south Alabama.

Unlike several New Orleans Province institutions, Spring Hill College managed to survive for several reasons. First, the Mobile Jesuits relied heavily on a relatively large and supportive Catholic population to provide for the college. Second, as the case indicates, Spring Hill College drew students from Mobile, surrounding states, and from abroad. Third, Spring Hill College, like its peer Jesuit institutions, relied on the preparatory department to keep the college open during the Civil War. Also, networks between the Jesuits and Confederate officials aided in keeping army solicitors from recruiting students and staff. This dependence on strong community relations through an established Catholic identity and Jesuit educational mission not only provided for the needs of the institution but also allowed for its continued subsistence. Fourth, the survival of Spring Hill College was fortified by enhanced legitimacy through its acceptance into the accrediting agencies of SACS and the CEA. Such inclusion demonstrates that the Jesuits were adapting curricula to meet changing educational practices, and with the removal of the high school department from the college division, the institution managed to increase its perception as a modern form of Catholic higher education.

Finally, the response to the Sacred Congregation of Seminaries and Universities in Rome concerning the Catholic nature of Spring Hill College was overt: the Catholic identity and mission of the college had been strenuously retained. However, severing ties with Protestant students would infringe upon the college's state-issued charter. As well, refusing to admit non-Catholic students might have damaged longstanding positive relationships between the college and multiple denomination communities. In short, Spring Hill College was widely accepted, and its Catholic and Jesuit identity and mission were upheld. To deny the admittance of Protestant students might have dissolved positive town and gown relationships and hindered alumni protection from anti-Catholic sentiment.

With the 1921 realignment of Jesuit higher education in the New Orleans Province, it was determined that all colleges, with the exception of Loyola University New Orleans, should close; however, Spring Hill College was allowed to remain open as it was highly supported by surrounding communities, maintained a strong Catholic and Jesuit identity but remained adaptable to changing educational practices, and consistently enrolled a significant number of students. With the continued presence of Spring Hill College in Mobile, Catholic higher education progressed alongside several secular colleges and universities and continues to remain one of the two surviving Jesuit institutions of higher education in the American South.

Loyola University in New Orleans, Louisiana

In 1911, a printed public announcement from the Society of Jesus proclaimed that the Jesuits of the New Orleans Province were to begin construction of a strong religious university in a region populated with secular forms of higher education, a move that would service the Catholic population of New Orleans and fulfill Archbishop James Hubert Blenk's wish for a legitimate American Catholic university in the city.[61] This new Jesuit institution would award a Bachelor of Arts or a Bachelor of Science degree to its graduates. Also, the Society of Jesus announced that those students who were not Catholic would be respected and would not be reproached or chastised for their beliefs. Furthermore, any student with a high school diploma could apply for enrollment, and individuals who wished to attend schools of law or medicine were strongly encouraged to attain a baccalaureate degree at the university before pursuing a professional course of study, as it would better equip them for graduate education.[62] The ultimate purpose behind this new university was the education of the people of New Orleans, Catholic or not.[63]

In order to increase public support, Father Albert Biever, rector of Loyola College, spoke at various events around the city to promote the need for a Catholic university in New Orleans equal to that of other American universities. Biever, chosen by the New Orleans Province to lead the foundation and administration of the new university, solicited his plans for the new university to the Marquette Association for Higher Education and Ladies Auxiliary.[64] In order to closely link the identity of the new university with the Catholic Church, Biever put forth plans for a large church on the new campus facing St. Charles Avenue. Motivated by the prospect of future success, Father Biever stated: "the Jesuits, as well as the Marquette Association and Ladies Auxiliary, feel encouraged with the remarkable progress thus far made, and there are the brightest prospects for the building to go on until the goal of their ambition is reached."[65] New Orleans newspapers reported that the Marquette Association and Ladies' Auxiliary had been created with the sole intent to raise funds for Loyola College and would now do the same for the new university.[66] In fact, this new university, would be built on the grounds of old Loyola College. With the aid of the Marquette Association and Ladies' Auxiliary, $100,000 was raised prior to the onset of construction.[67]

But what would the Jesuits call this new university? According to Albert Biever, the naming process was rather difficult. The New Orleans Province superior, Father William J. Power, insisted that the university's title include "the most Holy Name." However, several Jesuits objected out of a concern that "defeated parties at football or baseball games" might be tempted to profane and besmirch the religious phrase in retaliation.[68] Biever and his colleagues suggested "Marquette University"; however, "the Jesuit Fathers of Marquette University at Milwaukee vigorously objected to this through very Rev. Father General as having prior right to this name."[69] Following the command of Father General Xavier Wernz, the New Orleans Province Jesuits dropped the aforementioned title. Finally, the name of Loyola was proposed and when no objections were received, the institution's title was set as "Loyola University."[70]

With the institution's title in place, several New Orleans residents gave in abundance. Colonel William G. Vincent left in his will the sum of $500,000 in real estate to the Marquette Association for the betterment of Loyola University.[71] Father Biever describes another substantial gift for the new church to be joined with the university: "A handsome Catholic church edifice, costing $100,000, the gift of Miss Kate McDermott, will be erected on the Loyola University grounds, in memory of Miss McDermott's late brother, Thomas McDermott. . . . Miss McDermott's gift is the largest ever received by the Jesuit Fathers in this city."[72] It was planned that this new church would be adorned in Tudor Gothic architecture so as to closely resemble the university buildings and establish a perceptible tie between the church and university. With the inclusion of college divisions from the College of the Immaculate Conception and Loyola College in 1912, Loyola University became the sole Jesuit institution of higher education in New Orleans.[73]

Prior to its opening, New Orleans residents witnessed the groundbreaking ceremony for the new Loyola University on July 31, 1910, the feast of St. Ignatius. Archbishop Blenk shoveled out the first spade of earth, and Father John O'Shanahan, the Jesuit Provincial Father John O'Connor, and Martin Behrman, the mayor of New Orleans, gave speeches. The mayor spoke on the need for a Catholic university in the city and the important work of the Jesuits in the South. Behrman continued by expressing his high hopes for the future of the new university and wished it well in its ability to educate the citizens of New Orleans. Archbishop Blenk concurred with the mayor, indicating that a religious institution would be of great use to the city, and along with the mayor and the Society of Jesus, Blenk had great expectations for the future of Loyola University.[74]

In the presence of papal delegate Archbishop Diomede Falconio and eleven other bishops, the cornerstone of Loyola University was laid in 1911. An estimated 3,500 individuals attended the ceremony. As the first pile drivers steamed into action, thanks and praise were given to Father Albert Biever, congratulating him on his efforts to establish the new university. Those present who personally thanked Biever included Louisiana governor Jared Sanders, New Orleans's Mayor Behrman, as well as Jesuit Provincial O'Connor.[75] Several New Orleans newspapers chronicled the event. The *Times Democrat* reported the supportive speech of Governor Sanders:

> Higher education is the use to which the structure you are to erect here will be dedicated, and higher education means better citizenship. . . . The time is ripe for such an institution, and it is with special pleasure that I join you on so momentous an occasion. The Exposition movement to celebrate the opening of Panama [the Panama Canal], will today have a more logical point added to the reasons why such a celebration should take place here. South America, which is peopled by those of the Catholic faith, will soon be looking in our direction, not only for trade, but for social relationship. The youth of the many Republics to the south of us will desire to know our language

> and to study at our institution. What better vehicle can we offer than [a] University cared for by Jesuit Scholars and equipped with all that science offers, to instruct and fit these boys for the future of American citizenship, which will be theirs in their own countries patterned after the United States, and peopled in the future years by our kind of citizenship. . . . A gathering, such as we have here today, is a great moment to Louisiana. Distinguished prelates, clergymen and laymen from all over our country and from Europe are all come together for this great event and I take much pleasure in officially welcoming this representative body of gentlemen of Louisiana and in extending the felicitations of a State two-thirds of whose citizens are of the Catholic Faith.[76]

Other speakers echoed Sanders's aspirations for the future of Loyola University. Hopes were high that the Jesuits would develop an institution that would serve the public, garner attention from the nation and around the world, and further the guiding Catholic mission directed by the Jesuit motto "for the greater glory of God."[77]

It was announced that the new university would open in the coming weeks and that "its opening will mark the disappearance of Loyola College which it absorbed."[78] Advertisements explained that the downtown Jesuit institution, the College of the Immaculate Conception, "which for more than half a century has furnished educational facilities for many men who have been prominent in local, State and national life," would become a formal high school and serve as a feeder institution for Loyola University.[79] In addition to the new high school, newspapers reported that the Jesuits planned to inaugurate graduate courses in law, medicine, and engineering at Loyola University. The *Times Democrat* reported the following regarding the new university's academic progress: "It is intended to make Loyola University in this city the equal of Georgetown University at Washington, DC, which is now considered the foremost Catholic university in the United States and which also is operated under the auspices of the Jesuit order."[80] Such newspaper articles circulated throughout New Orleans, making the educational plans of the Society of Jesus well known.

Despite proclamations of Loyola University's potential, it was soon discovered that the new university could not confer degrees under the old cooperation act used by the College of the Immaculate Conception, as the former Loyola College had done. This act did not fill the particular description of the new university. Despite the ability of the Jesuits to convince neighboring Tulane University that conferring Loyola College degrees under the Catholic Society for Religious and Literary Education, this new university would have to forgo the old cooperation and vie for a formal, state-authorized charter. In response, the Marquette Association moved to establish a new charter for the university in 1912 that allowed for the granting of degrees in all areas of learning.[81] According to Father Patrick Ryan:

> Since Loyola did not receive its state charter until March 1912, one may ask by what authority was the A.B. degree conferred. The degree was conferred by virtue of the charter which the College of the Immaculate Conception on Baronne St. was supposed to have from 1847 on. This charter was never challenged until 1911 when George Michel, A.B. graduate of the Immaculate Conception, applied for a position as teacher in the public schools of New Orleans. He sent in his diploma with his application and soon he, as well as the Jesuit Fathers, were amazed to learn that the College of the Immaculate Conception was never empowered to confer degrees. It seems that the Jesuits when they returned to New Orleans in 1837 applied for a business charter only but with the understanding that this charter could be later amended as their work and activities grew. But, as often happens, later Superiors never were alerted to the fact that their charter was merely a business charter.[82]

The Louisiana House of Representatives approved the charter for Loyola University; however, the senate moved the act on to the Committee for Education. Once there, the chairman, Mr. Butler, who, according to Father Biever, "though representing Houma a Catholic Constituency was not favorably disposed towards the Jesuits. As a result the act was killed in the Committee."[83] It was not long before news of the charter's denial reached the Jesuits in New Orleans.

After learning of the committee's failure to approve the charter, Father Biever, now president of Loyola University, contacted local supporters, as well as Archbishop Blenk. Blenk, in support of Loyola University, contacted Senator Robert Broussard in Washington, DC, and other senators in Baton Rouge to rally support for the young institution. Biever and other Loyola University supporters boarded a train in New Orleans bound for Baton Rouge to attend a hearing on the university's charter. Finally, the charter was established under the condition that the new university match curricular and instructional standards of other recognized American institutions of higher education.[84] During this tumult, Archbishop Blenk expressed his continued interest in the success of Loyola University. In a letter from Blenk to Father Biever, the archbishop indicates that he is eager to witness the university rise and aid the South. "It is high time for the South to awake from her long inglorious silence," Blenk stated, and he certainly meant for the Jesuit institution to play its part in rousing the slumbering region.[85] With the encouragement of Blenk and his political contacts, the way was made smoother for Loyola to receive its charter.[86] The new charter was indeed granted, and the Jesuits made sure to indicate its longevity over the previous antebellum corporation act that had sustained the College of the Immaculate Conception and Loyola College. This replacement of the old corporation with the new charter is represented in the following statement: "the parties [Jesuits of the New Orleans Province] . . . declare that, availing themselves of the laws of this State, relative to the organization of Corporations for Literary, Scientific, Religious and Charitable Purposes, they, the said parties, have covenanted and agreed . . . to form themselves . . . into a Corporation [Loyola University]."[87] With the state charter secured, the higher education departments of the College of the Immaculate Conception and Loyola College were officially merged into Loyola University.[88]

After the passage of the university charter, Archbishop Blenk's enthusiasm did not diminish. Blenk pushed for newspaper articles to be written about Catholic education, in particular Loyola University, in the *Morning Star*, the Catholic newspaper of New Orleans. Blenk explained to the New Orleans Jesuits that he saw great advantage in advertising Loyola as much as possible.[89] As a result, the following passage was printed: "Loyola University, the Benjamin [Franklin] of our great American Universities, yet an institution which, in a short space of a few years, has risen to a prominence which might well excite envy among many others of decades of growth. . . . Loyola . . . is known not only throughout the length and breadth of our own great republic, but has acquired world-wide celebrity, by reason of the remarkable series of reports that have been sent forth from its seismographic observatory, which is already one of the most noted in the world."[90] Such positive reports were echoed in other newspapers: "Loyola in her new development is young and formative, but behind its growth is strength, and in its development there is purpose."[91] Media support was high, and local residents were receptive. The Jesuits of Loyola University made strides to fortify educational claims with meritorious acts. The Jesuits stocked classrooms and labs with modern scientific equipment such as an X-ray, a telegraph, and telephones. They also offered an expansive science curriculum, including botany, biology, chemistry, and physics, all with lab components that provided more than the theory of the lecture hall. Finally, there was the university's prize apparatus: "the seismograph, the wizard machine . . . which registers an earth shock though it happens 12,000 miles away."[92] The Jesuits spared no effort in advertising their contemporary New Orleans university far and wide.

Such heralds of success were followed by curricular competition with peer institutions. The Jesuit administrators of Loyola University had become aware that other colleges were allowing high school graduates to forgo a formal four-year college education and enter into professional fields of law or medicine without a background of university study. In 1913, the *Times Democrat* reported the following: "Loyola's faculty desires a distinct advance of standard. The faculty would create a sentiment in favor of a college education before entering the professional schools. At present this is not required. A young high school graduate may step directly into the law school or the medical college. The fathers do not believe that a high school graduate is properly equipped."[93] The Jesuits had redeveloped their method of education, adapted it to new American standards, and saw with a certain annoyance that their secular peers in New Orleans had not done the same. In addition, the Jesuits held fast to their curricular mission and fortified their revised regional system of religious higher education.

As the public took greater notice of the university, the Jesuits continued to advertise its identity as a Catholic institution and its mission to spread religion through moral education. A reporter for the *Times Democrat* posed this question to the administration of Loyola University: "Then religion is emphasized?" The Jesuit response was as follows: "A non-Catholic might spend a year here and not feel disturbed by the religious element. . . . We have boys who are not Catholic. What religious features we have can do harm to no one. It is mostly a matter of surroundings and atmosphere."[94] So important was the religious atmosphere of the institution that when Loyola University's president, Albert Biever, was invited to join the New Orleans Academy of Science, he declined in objection to the election of the academy's president, Benjamin Smith, who had published a book containing offensive material to the Catholic faith. Biever, not wanting his association with Smith to negatively affect either the Catholic faith or the educational endeavors of the new university, declined the membership offer from the Academy of Science.[95] Following his disassociation from the New Orleans science academy, Biever began to promote graduate courses at Loyola University.

In 1913, Loyola University New Orleans conferred Master of Arts, Master of Science, and Doctor of Philosophy degrees.[96] In 1914, schools of law and dentistry were opened. These programs were originally housed at the downtown campus of the College of the Immaculate Conception but soon moved to Loyola University.[97] At the start of the law school, classes were offered at night. This course schedule made it possible for many working individuals to advance through the program, an advantage that enhanced graduate enrollment numbers.[98] The first dean of the law school was Judge John St. Paul, a graduate of the College of the Immaculate Conception and a devout Catholic. A report in the *Woodstock Letters* regarding the nature of the law school reads as follows: "With a staff of distinguished jurists whose names are eminent in the history of law in Louisiana among its faculty, the launching of the law school of Loyola University on Monday evening, October 5, 1914, was an event of immense importance in law and educational circles. That this importance is recognized by the community was evident by the splendid audience of prominent men and women who attended the formal opening ceremonies, which were held in Alumni Hall. . . . Mayor Behrman's presence lent civic dignity to the occasion, and a cordial greeting was sent by Governor [Luther Egbert] Hall."[99] The following day, October 6, saw similar celebrations as the university opened the new dental department. The entire fourth floor and a large portion of the fifth of the main building, Marquette Hall, was allocated for the dental program and fitted with the required appliances to best suit the training of students.[100]

In that same year, Chief Justice Edward Douglas White of the US Supreme Court visited Loyola University and recounted his boyhood spent at the College of the Immaculate Conception. White's fondness for the Society of Jesus, support of the Jesuits, and pride in the education he received in his younger years is evident in the following statement: "You know not how great was the consolation drawn by the feeling that, although many who were dear to me had gone to their reward, the [Jesuit] Community remained unchanged in its kindness."[101] Alumni of the College of the Immaculate Conception often expressed positive sentiments regarding the Society of Jesus's educational efforts in New Orleans. In conclusion, White announced his hopes for the continued success of the new university. City leaders and local educational administrators greatly respected the Jesuits and their method of college administration, and this, over time, led to the merger of additional college and professional programs with Loyola University.

In 1913, Loyola University and the New Orleans College of Pharmacy became affiliated. The amalgamation of the thirteen-year-old pharmacy college with Loyola was the first step in a planned wave of professional education expansion. The pharmacy college, once located at St. Charles Avenue and Terpischore Street, eventually moved to the main campus of Loyola University and brought with it a host of students. The name of the pharmacy college was retained, as well as its faculty.[102] According to Biever, "the success of the College of Pharmacy . . . is due to its splendid staff of teachers and we of Loyola have not only the hope, but the conviction, that it will soon be the best not only in the South, but also the best in the entire country. . . . The College of Pharmacy . . . never had a parent and now, after thirteen years of parentless existence, Loyola said to it 'Come, I will be a mother and father to you.' The college came bringing with it ninety-nine students."[103] The course of study at the pharmacy school originally lasted two years, but in an attempt to increase the program's standing among other pharmacy programs, the curriculum was increased to span three years in 1925 and then four in 1932.[104] In 1915, with the increased success of the pharmacy department, and the law and dental programs comfortably affixed in Marquette Hall, Loyola University opened a medical department. Despite slight damages to the campus from a hurricane, the Jesuits of Loyola University felt that the progression of their professional programs, as well as the whole of the university, appeared positive. That same year, preparations were made to begin construction of the church that would enhance the university's externally perceived religious affiliation. The new church took the same name as the original wooden church of Loyola College: the Church of the Most Holy Name.[105]

From the start of Loyola University, the Jesuit fathers and brothers attempted to adapt and expand the university campus and professional curricula. Premedical courses began in 1912 and were soon followed by a graduate school of medicine in 1916, administered by Dr. Joseph A. Dana; however, this program was dissolved in 1925. A wireless telegraph program was begun in 1913 but closed at the onset of the First World War. As well, a department of oration was opened but only lasted three years. While functioning, the graduate school of medicine offered a certificate in midwifery to eliminate dangerous birthing conditions in Louisiana, but the course was discontinued in 1917. In 1918, colleges of nautical sciences, marine architecture, and marine engineering were established as well as a school of mechanics and a school of commerce and finance. These divisions eventually failed, but as a result of the diversified curriculum, an evening division was established to offer late afternoon courses to the public. This "night school" was eventually known as City College. In the final attempts to establish successful forms of professional education, schools of civil engineering and architecture were established in 1920; however, both were closed in 1922.[106]

Passing through the First World War and the Great Depression, the Jesuits claimed that Loyola University's ability to survive depended in large part on night courses offered to the general public who worked during the day.[107] Indeed, public support for the Jesuit university was high during this period of national upheaval. During the First World War, a student speech was given at a Loyola University commencement with the intent of venerating Catholic men who were fighting overseas. The speech also applauded Catholic women who were serving in Red Cross hospitals in Louisiana and abroad. A tertiary intent of the speech was to promote Loyola University by celebrating its evening courses, its adherence to American patriotic ideals, and its impact on those men who were instructed by the Jesuits to sacrifice what was required for God and country.[108] Despite war, economic depression, and the opening and closing of so many academic programs, the 1920s and 1930s seemed to be a relatively stable time for Loyola University. Operating four professional schools in arts and sciences, dentistry, law, and pharmacy, the university continued to meet student academic needs. As the institution's student population outgrew the facilities, the Jesuit administrators of Loyola University began a solicitation campaign in 1921 to raise approximately $1.5 million. These funds would be used to expand the campus by constructing five new buildings. The buildings were intended to house the departments of chemistry, dentistry, physics, engineering, pharmacy, and a gymnasium. Such new structures would improve the university by replacing older buildings. The building campaign was solicited via letters, newspaper advertisements, tracts, and radio announcements, as well as social networks between the university and various businesses and city social groups.[109] Growth in enrollment and successful academic courses attracted not only the attention of the public but also of Jesuits around the world. In 1921, Father Visitor Norbert de Boynes, encouraged the New Orleans Province of the Society of Jesus to pursue academic accreditation and strengthen the teaching staff of Loyola University:

> A cordial parting letter addressed by Father Visitor [Norbert de Boynes], October 23, 1921, to all members of the Province carried significant counsel. While lamenting the then lack of vocations that restricted and overburdened college teachers, he urged biennium and special study years so as "to raise" schools and colleges "to the standard acquired by the Ratio Studiorum and the College Associations," and he asked "why could not Loyola University be the center and focus of all such activities." Accordingly Loyola and all our eligible schools accepted the requirements of the Southern Association of Colleges and High Schools and obtained entrance.[110]

The New Orleans Jesuits took heed and shouldered the suggestions of de Boynes, but the need for campus expansion still existed. The Jesuits hoped that a crafty campaign slogan would encourage the public to donate.

In an attempt to devise a motto for the university building campaign, students from New Orleans city schools were allowed to compete for a $25 cash prize awarded to the creator of the best advertisement slogan. Margaret Hart, a seventeen-year-old, penned the phrase "Loyola University will be big enough if your heart is." The campaign administrators congratulated Margaret and implemented her slogan with the hopes that financial contributions would follow.[111] In fact, Hart's slogan adorned the Knights Templar archway on Carondelet Street, which spanned the streetcar line. The Masonic Lodge converted the archway into a large public notice that illustrated the building campaign's progress. The Masonic emblems were removed and replaced with the founding and current year of Loyola University. As well as university symbols and the campaign slogan, a large clock was constructed to cover the iconic horse that topped the archway. This clock indicated monetary sums in thousands that the campaign had generated thus far.[112]

Advertisements continued to circulate throughout New Orleans, several of which featured female students in professional courses. Pictured in the *New Orleans Item* was Catherine Tomeny, one of the students enrolled in the dental program at Loyola University, stooped over a patient, examining his teeth. The university issued many such publications announcing the enrollment of women into the professional programs.[113] The *Times Picayune* also advertised the growing participation of women in the building campaigns of Loyola University, indicating that "social activities given by women workers for the benefit of Loyola University in its $1,500,000 building campaign are netting large sums, and plans are underway to continue the gatherings through the summer and fall."[114] So much solicitation, coupled with the continued progress of the university, led Father Edward Cummings, president of Loyola University and former president of Spring Hill College, to proclaim that Loyola was "the wonder school of the South. . . . With a meteoric rise in scholastic and athletic activities, Loyola University is the most discussed university in America."[115] Whether Cummings's statement regarding nationwide discussion was factual or not is up for debate, nevertheless, his excitement for the institution was communicated throughout New Orleans.

The Jesuit fathers, brothers, and lay leaders were optimistic that the general public would willingly respond to their various calls for financial support; however, little over $300,000 was donated. Reasons for the lack of support were never recorded. In response to the failure of the building campaign, Father Cummings released a public statement detailing his disappointment with New Orleans citizens to faithfully support the cause for Loyola University. Instead of the grand construction project, a smaller plan, consisting of one building, was outlaid and completed.[116] As the building campaign came to a close, Father Cummings turned his attention to the institution's graduate and professional programs.

Having garnered praise from the American Dental Council for the school of dentistry, the administration of Loyola University hoped that lay support would increase for the dentistry program, however, few financial donations were made. As such, the program relied on tuition dollars alone. In a letter to the Carnegie Corporation in New York, Father Cummings acknowledged that "the South is poor, and the needs of education are very great." Cummings was keen to question the Carnegie Corporation about monetary support to offset the cost of dental instructors' salaries.[117] According to Cummings: "What we need chiefly now is help to support our faculty by adequate salaries. At present we have wonderful services for so small a reward, that it is practically volunteer services; and perhaps [we are] better and higher for being so. But this is not stable enough, and we are faced with the alternative of asking for outside support or leaving the dental field."[118] Although no evidence has been found to indicate whether or not the Carnegie Corporation provided assistance, we do know that the dental program lasted fifty-seven years.[119] Beginning in 1968, Loyola's dental program was transferred to the Louisiana State University School of Dentistry in New Orleans and formally closed in 1971 as a result of financial difficulties.[120]

Despite the failure of the Loyola University building campaign, several supporters remained dedicated to the institution as the Jesuits attempted to expand course offerings. In 1927, following the plans to reorganize curriculum in the New

Orleans Province coupled with the need for a new school to replace the New Orleans business district campus of the College of the Immaculate Conception, Jesuit High School was opened on Carrolton Avenue and Bank Street. In celebration of the new Loyola University and Jesuit High School facilities, Judge St. Paul of the Louisiana Supreme Court gave a speech detailing the entry of the Jesuits into the American South, as well as their work in education. Judge St. Paul announced to a large crowd of local residents that "the Jesuits rendered immense service to civilization, partly by organizing a system of education far superior to any yet seen in Europe. In no university could there be found a scheme of instruction so comprehensive as theirs, and certainly was there displayed nowhere such skill in the management of youth or such insight into the general operation of the human mind."[121] After the comments of Judge St. Paul, the celebration continued with additional speakers, all heralding the educational work of the Jesuits in the American South.

Such celebrations became commonplace and incorporated a variety of speakers. In fact, lists of commencement speakers for Loyola University included community and regional leaders such as bishops, archbishops, attorneys, medical doctors, lawyers, judges, congressmen, senators, professors from secular universities, academic deans from other Jesuit institutions, and, in 1928, Louisiana governor Huey P. Long.[122] The crowning achievement for the Jesuits of Loyola University in their attempt to establish their institution as a legitimate Catholic university, was Loyola's acceptance into the Southern Association of Colleges and Schools on December 5, 1929. As well, in 1930, Father Percy A. Roy, president of Loyola University, was elected as the president of SACS, thus more deeply establishing the institution's identity as an American Jesuit institution among peer religious and secular colleges and universities.[123]

During the annual convention of SACS held in Lexington, Kentucky, on December 7, 1929, Loyola University was introduced as a new member of the accrediting body. This admission carried with it a rating that guaranteed universal acceptance of the degrees awarded from the Jesuit university. A second recognition, which held special significance to the Society of Jesus, took place that same year. The North Central Association of Colleges and Schools convened in Chicago, Illinois, and proclaimed that "the extensive training of Catholic priests, especially the Jesuits, was given formal recognition. In its legislation, the association interprets this training in terms of a PhD degree, 'that all Jesuits had training equivalent to a PhD at least for the purpose of teaching evidences of religion and subjects of a philosophical and ethical character.'"[124] Such academic acknowledgments further steeped southern Jesuits in academic legitimacy.

The Jesuits admitted the importance of Loyola University receiving legitimate standing in SACS but also upheld the historic development and mission of Jesuit higher education. The *Junior's Newsletter*, a publication for Jesuit novices, informed the New Orleans Province that "although the degrees of our University had already been recognized almost unanimously prior to the securing of membership, nevertheless this admission carries with it a technical rating, which [guar] antees universal acceptance and places Loyola upon an equal basis . . . with every university in the country."[125] Along with the promotion of the new SACS membership, Loyola University administrators embarked on a series of program initiatives to further increase enrollment and propagate the ideals of the Society of Jesus. In an attempt to maintain positive associations between college students and the Jesuit identity and mission of Loyola University, a "freshman week" was established for incoming students. In 1931, this program prompted students to join such religious organizations as the Sodality of the Blessed Virgin Mary, reminded students of their required courses in religion, encouraged students to attend spiritual retreats and chapel exercises, and advised Catholic students to attend worship services and receive the Sacraments at least once a month. The intended outcome was quite possibly threefold: the freshman program would give students an increased sense of the university's institutional identity, provide a deeper understanding of its Catholic mission, and serve as an attempt to increase student retention. In addition, extracurricular activities were solicited to students, including drama, band, music, and glee club, all of which incorporated Catholic ideals.[126]

As New Orleans residents plied for enrollment, new academic necessities arose and were met. To address the growing need for teachers and social workers, a school of social services and a school of education were initiated at Loyola. Neither school succeeded, as student interest turned out to be low. But efforts to create an accredited department of medical technology were successful, and in 1935, this new department was added to the university's College of Arts and Sciences and accredited by the Council on Medical Education and Hospitals of the American Society of Clinical Pathologists. In 1932, the New Orleans Conservatory of Music and Dramatic Arts became affiliated with the university.[127] The conservatory later became the College of Music, and in 1936 it was recognized by the National Association of Music Schools.[128] Many such departments and programs would ultimately close due to lack of student interest or the loss of students to competing programs such as those developed by Tulane University and Louisiana State University.[129]

Despite many academic program inceptions and closures, the Jesuits continued to enhance Loyola's emphasis on learning and the propagation of Jesuit identity and mission. By the close of the 1930s, Loyola University had become an established presence in the city of New Orleans. To further the Jesuit identity of Loyola, the university's administration created and issued a seal for the institution that reflected its Catholic, Jesuit, Basque, and Louisiana heritage. The seal not only contains symbols relevant to the Society of Jesus, such as the IHS, but it also displays symbols from the family crest of Ignatius Loyola, including wolves and a cauldron.

Also, the seal displays the regional icon of the fleur-de-lis and the Louisiana state symbol of a pelican feeding chicks blood drawn from her breast, an image that doubles as a Catholic representation of sacrifice.[130] In 1937, the *Times Picayune* reported that Loyola University celebrated its silver jubilee. Institutions such as Holy Cross College, Louisiana State University, Spring Hill College, and Ursuline College paid for large print sections in New Orleans newspapers in order to offer their congratulations to Loyola University on its twenty-fifth anniversary.[131]

During the twentieth century, the institution witnessed the enrollment of an increasing number of female students and the racial integration of New Orleans colleges and schools. Today, Loyola University continues to promote Jesuit educational ideals and has embarked on the creation of a Jesuit center for the enhancement of institutional identity and mission. Tom Benson, owner of the New Orleans Saints professional football team, endowed the university with $8 million for the creation of the aforementioned center. Currently, the financial gift is being used to convert the original campus library into the new Jesuit center.[132]

Building on the foundation of Jesuit education in the New Orleans Province, Loyola University learned from its peer Jesuit institutions, sacrificed programs when such needs arose, and managed to survive by adapting curricula. With a heavy reliance on Jesuit educational ideals and a dependence on supportive communal relations to raise funds and supply students, Loyola University New Orleans has progressed into the twenty-first century. Its success is recognized nationally and internationally through its incorporation in secular and religious accrediting societies and through the support of the global Catholic order of the Society of Jesus.

Potentially the most important move made by the Jesuits of the New Orleans Province was announcing that Loyola University would allow for the enrollment of students stemming from all religions. Even though New Orleans was, and remains, a highly Catholic city, there was a substantial population of non-Catholics. With the inclusion of students outside of the Catholic faith, Loyola University allowed for a broader range of student enrollments that increased yearly. It is possible that this inclusion provided a sense of welcome that was felt among the citizens of New Orleans and beyond. Even with the enrollment of non-Catholic students, the Jesuit institution maintained its Catholic identity.

In descriptions and photographs of Loyola University's campus, religious and Catholic symbols adorn the facilities. From crucifixes, religious icons, and statues of Jesuit saints, the campus is dotted with signs that resonate with the institution's Jesuit identity. From the first published announcement of a new Jesuit university in New Orleans to academic catalogues, the mission listed for Loyola University was that of an Americana Catholic institution of higher education. Similarly, newspaper articles detailed interviews with Jesuit administrators concerning the identity of the university. As such, the Jesuits communicated to New Orleans readers that the university was firmly rooted in religious and moral education though students would not be imposed with overt Catholic doctrine.

Through the promotion of Loyola University's Catholic identity and mission, the educational history of the Society of Jesus, and an adaptable curricular structure, the Jesuits of the New Orleans Province were able to draw upon the city's Catholic and Protestant populations to supply students, garner support, and bolster financial resources. Though New Orleans residents failed to supply funds for the university's building campaign, it was substantial monetary gifts from wealthy New Orleans Catholics that aided in the construction of the main iconic campus building, Marquette Hall, and the brick Church of the Most Holy Name that is connected to and architecturally resembles Loyola University. Along with the identity of the institution, newspapers chronicled the mission of the Catholic institution as "for the greater glory of God," a Jesuit theme that has lasted since the sixteenth-century educational and religious life of St. Ignatius Loyola.

With the public's acceptance of Loyola University's Jesuit identity and mission, support increased and the university survived, despite the struggle to obtain a state charter. When the institution was in need of social aid to secure the charter, New Orleans Catholics, as well as Archbishop Blenk, encouraged state legislators to approve the act of incorporation, thus promoting the university's longevity. Town and gown relationships were strengthened through the efforts of the Marquette Association and advertisements that solicited public support for the university. Such, positive town and gown relationships ultimately led to the progression and survival of the institution. When the university received accreditation from SACS, it was academically legitimized and peer support increased. The continued financial support of Loyola University from the citizens of New Orleans, regional Catholic populations, and city and state officials kept the institution in the public eye, communicating its purpose and adaptability to educational trends.

Loyola University New Orleans profited from the amalgamation of Loyola College and the higher education courses from the College of the Immaculate Conception. As well, positive town and gown relationships between former Loyola College, the College of the Immaculate Conception, and the city of New Orleans enhanced social relationships for Loyola University. With the inclusion of the aforementioned college departments, Loyola University was able to adapt its curricular structure to better match educational trends and become an institution strong enough to win the admiration of the New Orleans archbishop, local and regional residents, and Father Visitor Norbert de Boynes. In 1921, de Boynes asked,

"Why could not Loyola University be the center and focus of intellectual Catholic activity, advantageous both for Catholics and non-Catholics alike?"[133] The recommendations of de Boynes strengthened Loyola University, as all other Jesuit institutions in the New Orleans Province, with the exception of Spring Hill College were closed or repurposed as high schools. By following father visitor's suggestions, substantial human resources were reallocated to aid in the development of Loyola. This cooperation between the internal Jesuit identity and mission of obedience and higher education adaptability proved successful, as it promoted the survival of Loyola University and the persistence of southern Jesuit higher education.

Institutional Survival in Review

Similarities abound in the cases of Spring Hill College and Loyola University. Despite the age difference between the two Jesuit institutions, each case demonstrates that the potential for survival relies on community acceptance of institutional identity and mission and curricular adaptability to social environments. Both Loyola University and Spring Hill College share similar institutional identities comprised of Catholic and Jesuit characteristics. Both institutions are adorned with Catholic symbols and are connected to a Catholic church with architectural features matching each campus. Finally, both institutions adapted their curricular structures and were accredited by SACS. The perceived identity of both institutions seems to have been well accepted by their immediate environments, as well as the larger Society of Jesus. Only in the case of Spring Hill College did the Jesuits have to justify the institution's Catholic identity to the Holy See in Rome due to the enrollment of Protestant students and the hiring of non-Catholic staff. The institutional mission of Loyola University and Spring Hill College, to provide holistic curricula imbued with religion, are marked by trends of adaptability. These adaptations, although taking longer to enact in the case of Spring Hill College, allowed both institutions some means of flexibility in their curricular offerings. The institutional mission of each institution, though adapted to changing educational trends, remained true to overarching aspects of Jesuit educational ideologies; however, curricular adaptations made each institution much more competitive with peer colleges and universities resulting in increased student enrollments and strong alumni support.

The microhistories of Loyola University and Spring Hill College demonstrate how southern Jesuit higher education adapted to changing educational trends to better suit the curricular expectations of students. For example, Loyola University accommodated students by offering night courses so that full-time workers could enroll in classes. Furthermore, the Jesuits of the New Orleans Province required students to obtain an undergraduate degree prior to enrolling in graduate or professional programs. This increased academic rigor, along with enhanced academic legitimacy garnered via state charters and SACS accreditation, made both Loyola University and Spring Hill College viable educational entities that not only extended educational opportunities to Catholics but also propagated an inclusive model of enrollment regardless of religious preference. In reviewing the social acceptance of Jesuit institutional identity and mission, these two cases illustrate several important details. The large Catholic populations of Mobile, Alabama, and New Orleans, Louisiana, provided a pool of individuals willing to support Jesuit higher education. The support of local clergy, bishops, and archbishops also seems to have played in favor of Jesuit educational efforts at both institutions. In addition, it could be argued that the preexisting Jesuit educational presence in New Orleans (that is, Loyola College and the College of the Immaculate Conception) provided a foundational base of support for Loyola University, whereas Spring Hill College developed its own social support over the span of its existence in a geographic region largely accepting of Catholicism as well as the Society of Jesus. As such, it is evident that both institutions enjoyed positive town and gown relationships that allowed for the continued growth and survival of each institution.

Conclusion

Adapting to the South

> It is . . . evident that a few colleges or schools, furnished with an able faculty and the necessary equipment, and measuring up to the recognized standards, will be much better fitted for the good formation of Catholic boys and young men, and at the same time reflect greater credit on the Society [of Jesus], than many colleges and schools that are deficient in teachers and in equipment.
>
> —Father Norbert de Boynes

In probing the history of Jesuit higher education in the American South, this study has formulated an understanding of how some Jesuit institutions failed to survive while others adapted and thrived. This book presents a possible explanation as to how institutional identity, mission, and town and gown relationships work together to either promote or inhibit institutional survivability. As such, it has been necessary to investigate the various responses of southern Jesuit colleges and universities to historically hostile or hospitable social environments in order to determine whether the relationship between a college or university and its social surroundings contribute to its ability to persist. Ultimately, an examination of these factors through historic case examples, especially through close analysis of the town and gown relationship, has shown that institutional identity and mission do indeed play a role in the survival of colleges and universities.

Given the identity and mission of the Society of Jesus and its Catholic educational institutions founded in a highly Protestant region of America, coupled with periods of unrest concerning anti-Catholic and anti-Jesuit sentiment, it was certainly difficult for Jesuits to maintain viable institutions. More important, the ability to enroll sufficient numbers of students who identified with a Jesuit college or university offering liberal arts curricula to financially sustain these institutions was difficult, unless the institution was located in a heavily Catholic or socially supportive environment. A major factor concerning the identity and mission of these institutions was the ability to adapt without losing the characteristics of Jesuit higher education. Such, characteristics (identity, mission) are, according to Alice Brown, guiding elements of effective administrative planning that "ensure[s] the sustainability of the institution."[1]

As has been expressed, the identity and mission of these Jesuit institutions played a major role in their survival primarily through adaptability. In each case, adapting curricula to address social needs was imperative for sustainability. The need to provide practical education and to culturally alter the methods of the *Ratio Studiorum*, which Ignatius himself had emphasized, were of great importance to both Catholic and non-Catholic students. Not only was curricular adaptation needed, religious inclusion was essential. Indeed, advertisements from Loyola University and Spring Hill College proclaimed the acceptance of non-Catholic students and emphasized respect for individual religious preferences. This open and adaptive stance of Jesuit higher education created an atmosphere centered on the development of the whole student—mind, body, and soul—not simply Catholic higher education for Catholics alone.

Also important, the separate identity and mission of the Society of Jesus as a supervisorial organization, as opposed to those of each individual Jesuit college or university, played a significant role in the failure or survival of each institution in the New Orleans Province. As an organization, the guiding principles of the Society of Jesus often trumped those of individual higher education administrators and instructors. A prime example of the role of identity and mission within the Society of Jesus itself is the vow of obedience all Jesuit priests and brothers take. For this study, the recommendations of Norbert de Boynes serve as the ultimate example of the effect of obedience on Jesuit identity, mission, and, in due course, institutional survival. When de Boynes recommended the closure of colleges so as to fortify Jesuit education in the New Orleans Province, the only exception to his verdict was Spring Hill College. Due to the influence of Father Cummings and his conversations with de Boynes, Spring Hill College was spared, whereas St. Charles College and St. Mary's University were shut down. Despite Cummings's success at saving Spring Hill College from father visitor's recommendations, other direct orders to close institutions were followed. Superior General Wlodimir Ledóchowski's 1917 order to close the College of the Sacred Heart in Augusta, Georgia, was obeyed. Such obedience typified the culture of the Society of Jesus. This factor of obedience is transparent throughout the Jesuit college and university cases presented in this book and influenced each institution's administrative actions and reactions to local environs.

As such, the ability to sacrifice particular colleges and universities in order to focus on Loyola University and Spring Hill College allowed for the survival and maintenance of Jesuit higher education in the South via refocused human resources and adapted curricular structures. Thus, the southern system of Jesuit higher education was reduced, but survived and flourished in Mobile, Alabama, and New Orleans, Louisiana. Even as Loyola University was fortified and Spring Hill College was allowed to continue, these institutions were eventually forced to face aspects of academic legitimacy through their application and acceptance into the CEA and SACS. With this inclusion, both institutions expanded their course offerings to better suit the needs of students. These issues, pertaining to institutional retrenchment and the academic legitimacy of southern Jesuit higher education, are further supported by the research of Kathleen Mahoney. Mahoney argues that academic retrenchment was a positive and progressive act for the American Assistancy of the Society of Jesus that sustained their educational mission nationwide. Mahoney states that "despite the Jesuits' slow, often begrudging responses to the rise of a new academic order, the history of Jesuit higher education in the twentieth century is not one of decline . . . but one rather of substantial growth and gradual improvement. By aligning their colleges more closely with American standards and practices during the century's early decades, the move toward academic respectability and institutional viability commenced."[2] Mahoney's statement rings true with the southern Jesuits and their colleges and universities; however, adaptation to increase viability required system reconstruction and human resource retrenchment through the closure of several institutions and the relocation of Jesuit fathers and brothers to Loyola University and Spring Hill College.

In addition to institutional retrenchment, as the data and case analyses attest, other factors that contributed to the longevity of Jesuit higher education in the American South include the relationships of the Jesuits with secular clergy, archbishops, female religious orders, lay-communities, and Jesuits working in tandem with other Jesuits throughout the New Orleans Province and abroad. These three relational bonds—Jesuits to lay community, Jesuits to external clergy and female religious orders, and Jesuits to Jesuits—were at the heart of extended associations that shaped southern Jesuit higher education. Examples of such bonds are clear in the case of St. Charles College and the financial aid provided by the Sisters of the Sacred Heart. Similarly, the College of the Immaculate Conception case demonstrates the support provided by the Ursuline Sisters. Regarding external clergy: in almost every case, including the invited return of the Society of Jesus to the American South, each Jesuit college or university began with a request from a bishop or archbishop. Such an example is the former Jesuit university in Galveston, Texas. Following the appeal of Bishop Gallagher, the Society of Jesus assumed control of St. Mary's University. Despite the 1900 hurricane, which caused depleted city populations, the Jesuits were intent on rebuilding their institution. These relationships between peer religious groups and Catholic leaders contributed to supportive institutional bonds through mutual Catholic identities and desires to provide regional religious higher education.

Even though peer Catholic organizations provided support, local lay environments were not always in favor of the establishment of a Jesuit college or university. Concerning hostile environments, the strongest examples come from the College of the Sacred Heart and St. Charles College. Although the immediate vicinage of St. Charles College was indeed supportive of the institution, communities outside of Grand Coteau were not. Due to this regional hostility, it was difficult for the Jesuit fathers and brothers to attract students external to Grand Coteau. If students came to St. Charles College from beyond Grand Coteau, they typically came from other states or countries. In the case of the College of the Sacred Heart, the surrounding population was highly Protestant and often opposed to Catholics. Wealthy Protestant families enrolled their sons in college courses due to the academic nature of the liberal arts curricula. On the other hand, local Catholics were uninterested in a liberal education and preferred more practical, job-related training. In addition, anti-Catholic sentiment was high in Augusta, and the Jesuits were careful in expressing the Catholic nature of their college. In advertisements for the College of the Sacred Heart, the Catholic identity of the institution is not overtly promoted. Instead, the college's methods are described as rooted in moral instruction, not Catholic doctrine. In contrast, other southern Jesuits institutions issued advertisements that detailed their Catholic nature of instruction. The difficult social environment in Augusta led to the deterioration of Sacred Heart's college curriculum, eventual closure of the college department, and finally the complete failure of the institution.

From the micro-histories presented in this book, we can hypothesize that the roles of institutional identity, mission, and town and gown relationships can be applied to the larger field of higher education, particularly small religious institutions of higher education. As Thomas Bender states, "it may well be, however, that the demands of the comparative and interactive study . . . [of] the university and the city, may prompt the piecemeal development of such theory."[3] In essence, this study does just what Bender claims. It presents the argument that a college's or university's internally and externally perceived identity and mission can affect its ability to survive by triggering the development of supportive or destructive relationships with surrounding locales. This triggering then leads to other models of institutional survival, such as those presented by Jeffrey Pfeffer and Gerald Salancik in their book *The External Control of Organizations*.[4] Ultimately, if an institution's identity and mission are negatively perceived by external communities, then the ability to develop positive social relationships, and thereby gain financial support and student enrollment, is hindered, whereas a college or university with a preexisting identity and mission that is positively supported from its inception can acquire strong communal bonds that engender positive public support. More specifically, a college or university has both an internally established and externally perceived identity, as well as both an externally projected and internally enacted mission. This combination of perceived, projected, and internalized concepts of identity and mission has a distinct influence on social environs, thereby creating a positive or negative set of relationships. Positive relationships allow colleges and universities to garner resources that contribute to their viability and livelihood, whereas negative relationships deny institutions resources and detrimentally affect their ability to survive.

The cases in this book illustrated many factors that contributed to the failure or survival of southern Jesuit colleges and universities, including but not limited to societal interactions, changing educational trends, and the hierarchy of the Society of Jesus. This study has demonstrated that the development of positive relationships between the town and gown was at times difficult for the Society of Jesus due to anti-Catholic and anti-Jesuit sentiment. In addition, the inability of French Jesuits to communicate with students in English and nativism amplified difficulties. With the replacement of French Jesuits with Irish Jesuits, language barriers diminished in the New Orleans Mission. In addition, the number of Jesuits teaching in the South had a resounding effect on institutional perseverance, as the lack of Jesuit instructors made it difficult to administer each institution. The small number of Jesuits throughout the South resulted in a myriad of decisions based on total numbers of priests and brothers. When the New Orleans Mission was separated from the administration of Lyons, southern Jesuits became responsible for training local Catholic men in the ways of the cloth. However, due to low Catholic populations and non-Catholics' inability to fully understand the identity and mission of the Society of Jesus, the growth of the New Orleans Mission was inhibited and subsequently influenced the longevity of Jesuit higher education in the New Orleans Province.

Academic research on institutional survival is of extreme importance as the current field of higher education is witnessing the closure of colleges and universities across the nation and abroad. Small colleges and several religious institutions in particular are struggling to survive in the economic climate of the early twenty-first century. Despite research that examines institutional success and subsistence, there is very little literature regarding institutional survival and virtually no research that examines what causes institutions of higher education to completely shut down. With this deficit in mind, researchers have an opportunity to direct their attentions to scholarly inquiry regarding institutional failure and survivability. This study has attempted to examine components that catalytically affect survivability, particularly as it has applied to the Society of Jesus in the American South. Even so, larger studies need to be undertaken to chart the overarching process of institutional decline, failure, and warning signs pertaining to college and university atrophy. By reconstructing the histories of closed colleges and universities, higher education administrators, researchers, and instructors can profit through an understanding of what may cause institutions to close and potential means to avert college or university failure.

It is important to remember that this study is not an investigation of something long dead, as Jesuit higher education still exists in the American South. Even now, when exploring the websites of Loyola University New Orleans and Spring Hill College, viewers are inundated with Catholic symbols and subsections containing substantial information on Jesuit identity. Such advertisements aid in the public promotion of Jesuit ideals and educational missions present on each campus. Like the electronic promulgation of Jesuit identity and mission through the aforementioned websites, older, closed southern Jesuit institutions promoted their educational endeavors through print media; however, as the cases in this study have illustrated, mission statements alone do not always communicate the entire purpose of an institution. Researchers must dig deep; they must analyze symbols, curricula, administrative records, and founding documents in order to determine the true educational mission of any college or university.

One has but to walk onto the campuses of Loyola University and Spring Hill College to be transported to a religious realm of learning quite different from secular college campuses. A large Catholic church crowns each Jesuit campus; buildings and walkways are adorned with religious art, statues of Catholic saints, and engravings of Jesuit mottoes and phrases. Each campus—Loyola University with its Tudor-Gothic architectural style of red brick and Spring Hill College combining a Neo-Renaissance and Gothic Revival style with a pale-yellow façade—conveys to faculty, staff, students, and visitors that both institutions have a unique place in the history of the South. Such visible aspects of Jesuit and Catholic identity create atmospheres where the overall mission of religious higher education can be conveyed. Likewise, when visiting the Jesuit novitiate at St. Charles College in Grand Coteau, Louisiana, it is impossible to detach the Jesuit identity from the physical campus, which is covered with large religious statues and Catholic images. Each campus is a living, breathing historical record: a monument to southern Jesuit higher education, an artistic rendering of Catholic ideology, and a working institution of higher education and spiritual contemplation. Such historic remnants of the Jesuit presence in the American South serve as cultural repositories for the study of Jesuit and Catholic higher education. To lose these remaining Jesuit institutions would be the loss of critical pieces of southern history and Catholic educational culture. Even though the American South hosts a variety of Catholic colleges and universities, Loyola University and Spring Hill College embody the remaining elements of a once expansive system of higher education. Collectively, this system, including the college efforts at Shreveport, Louisiana; Tampa, Florida; and Baton Rouge, Louisiana, consisted of ten institutions that spanned the South. Each institution embodied the formative elements of Jesuit education, and each survived or failed in accordance with the proposed theory of institutional survivability in this text. With the closure of so many Jesuit institutions in mind, it becomes imperative that scholars of higher education focus on particular systems of American higher education that maintain formative identities and missions and consider the role of adaptation as it has and will apply to institutional survival. Such research not only aids in understanding what sustains a college or university but allows us to better comprehend important catalytic factors that may ultimately cause institutional death if not addressed in a timely manner.

Appendix

LETTER
ADDRESSED TO THE FATHERS, SCHOLASTICS AND BROTHERS
OF THE NEW ORLEANS PROVINCE
BY
REV. Fr. NORBERT de BOYNES, S.J.
AT THE CLOSE OF THE VISITATION
OCT. 23rd., 1921.

Reverend Fathers and dear Brothers:

The Visitation of the Province has come to a close. Before leaving you and promulgating the Memorial which must be first approved by Fr. General, I wish to express my keen appreciation of your hearty welcome, your filial charity and the good will shown in your cooperation with my efforts. May God bless and reward you!

It will certainly be agreeable to you to know, at the end of this Visitation, some of the conclusions I have arrived at, and to hear a few suggestions that I deem helpful for the good of your own souls and the success of your apostolic endeavors for the greater glory of God.

In going over the history of the Province and viewing actual conditions of the same, it was most gratifying to see that there has been and still is a generous effort to develop among you the interior life, and to be faithful to religious discipline as found in our Constitutions and Rules. In order to direct your efforts in the future, let me briefly recall to your memory your chief duties as religious of the Society of Jesus, and encourage you to adhere more and more closely to the high principles laid down by St. Ignatius in the Constitutions.

A true Jesuit, trained in the school of the Spiritual Exercises, is a man of prayer, ever faithful to his daily spiritual duties and united by the bonds of the closest friendship to our divine Lord. Such a man's aim in life is summed up in our motto: "Ad Majorem Dei Gloriam". He is determine to fulfill, according to the measure of God's grace imparted to him, the solemn obligations he took upon himself on the day of his vows.

A true Jesuit observes his rules and carries out the orders of his superiors; nay more, he obeys their least wish, cost what it may. He fights incessantly against his own sensuality and the spirit of the world; and in the words of the "Summa et Scopus nostrarum Constitutionum", he is a man crucified to the world and to whom the world itself is crucified.

To the world that bows down before the rich and worships at the shrine of wealth, he opposes the real spirit of poverty and his love for the poor who are the favorites of his apostolate.

To the world which is pleasure-mad and sunken deep in the mire of sensuality, he shows his contempt for all that it holds dear and his love for heavenly things. He finds in the practice of continual mortification more delight than in worldly recreations and amusements.

To the world which proclaims aloud its independence, he proves that submission for God's sake makes the religious freer than the worldly man who is often the slave of his own passions and prejudices.

To the world which is always longing for honors, he shows by his example that humility and humiliations possess a sweetness and a charm compared to which mere human praise and distinction pale and fade away into nothing.

A true Jesuit is imbued with the spirit of the Constitutions and the Institute, and in their perusal he finds light, encouragement and inspiration.

When we read the evangelical counsels as proclaimed by our Lord in the Gospel and incorporated by St. Ignatius into the Constitutions, we are compelled to confess that the life of a Jesuit is not one of ease and comfort, but one of self-sacrifice, self-denial and hard work undertaken out of love for Christ our Lord. He who looks for mere human pleasure and happiness in the Society, is on the wrong road, and is following a path that leads to disappointment and failure. He, on the contrary, who joined the Society in order that he might, as we read in the "Examen Generale", practice obedience and humility, is on the way which leads to perfection and to heaven. To be a true Jesuit means to be after Christ's example, a crucified man.

If I have laid so much stress on the great principles of the interior life, it is because we absolutely need them to advance in the way of perfection, and to dispel the illusions suggested by the spirit of the world which nowadays insinuates itself even into religious communities. It is also because the apostolic and the spiritual life are so closely linked together. All over the world the work of the Society for the salvation of souls will succeed if the members of the Society are holy and worthy of their holy Founder. In our apostolate we are not looking for that exterior display which attracts the human eye and elicits praise and applause. We want to reach the souls of men to convert or better them, to give them the pure light of Faith and to inspire them with a burning, undying love for the Master. This work of God is done by men of God; by men of prayer who freely draw from the Divine Heart the graces which transform the soul. Consequently the chief and indispensable preparation and most powerful instrument of our apostolic life will always be our own perfection.

I said the CHIEF preparation and instrument, because it is not the only one. Divine Providence and our Constitutions bid us employ in our apostolic undertakings, natural means which are also necessary, though secondary in importance and efficiency.

This leads me to speak about apostolic works in your Province.

Since its foundation, the one time Mission, now Province of New Orleans has accomplished great things for the glory of God in part of the Lord's vineyard that is fraught with difficulties peculiarly its own. It covers an immense territory of some 1,000,000 square miles, with the newly added part of the New Mexico and Colorado Mission. It contains, in round numbers, some 25,700,000 inhabitants the greater part of whom, or about 60%, have no church affiliation at all. Of the remainder about 1,600,000 are Catholics, the rest are Protestants. The Catholics, except in southern Louisiana, and in the Spanish-speaking part of the Province, are scattered over a large area and live in the midst of non-Catholics and Protestants who are prejudice against, not to say overtly hostile to the Catholic Church. Outside of the larger cities they as a rule have few facilities for the practice of their religion.

The apostolate of the Society must needs be greatly influenced by the conditions of Catholicity in the South. It has to adapt itself to such conditions and it has done so.

As a devoted instrument of the Catholic Church, the Society took the brunt of the pioneer work and is still actively engaged in extending it far and wide. This is real missionary labor which will last as long as there is dearth of secular priests.

In such an immense territory where Catholics are so few and far between, there are not many cities in which a strong Catholic influence can be exercised on a large scale. As a matter of fact, if we lay aside the Mexican population of the Province, there is now but one important Catholic center in your Province, New Orleans itself and Southern Louisiana. This is the reason why it is so difficult to find suitable cities for flourishing day-schools and colleges.

It is only just and right to take these special conditions into account when judging the present work of the Province, or that of the whole Catholic Church in the South.

Having gone over the matter most carefully and with great sympathy for those who are cultivating this portion of Christ's vineyard, it immediately became patent to me that everybody, priest, scholastic and lay brother, is working strenuously for the glory of God. Moreover I could not help noticing a few are overworked. There is no proportion between the amount of work done and the number of men who do it. Consequently the Province has not been able for long years, to prepare specialists either for the class room or the pulpit. Good will, generosity and earnest study are not sufficient in many instances to make up for the lack of preparation. This condition of the Province is serious but not hopeless or without remedy. It can be adjusted by superiors planning the work of the Province more and more in accordance with the direction of the Institute and our Father

General, and in making the most of the men whom God has given the Society. It will come by the unselfish cooperation of each college and residence for the common good of the Province, by the earnestness of each one in following the guidance given him by superiors, and by taking all the initiative compatible with holy obedience.

Our Father General has often expressed his views concerning the apostolate of the Society, and reminded the different provinces of the high principles laid down by St. Ignatius. He has often repeated these short and expressive words: "Non multa sed multum". The Society in truth, is expected to accomplish everywhere solid and far-reaching results not looked for from secular priests whose time is taken up for the most part with parochial work.

St. Ignatius founded the Society to promote the greater glory of God, and consequently, as is clear from the Constitutions, to carry on an intellectual apostolate. He wanted his sons to give a thorough college training to their students and impart an education that will form leaders. His intention was that his sons, some of them at least, should be specialists in ecclesiastical sciences, so that they might help the Church to strengthen the faith of her members against the attacks of enemies. His plan was to do this through preachers, lecturers and writers who would be perfect masters in their respective lines. It is clear that a few men who are thoroughly prepared for such work will do more good for the glory of God than a host of men who have all the good will in the world, but are lacking in the necessary preparation and knowledge. It is also evident that a few colleges or schools, furnished with an able faculty and the necessary equipment, and measuring up recognized standards, will be much better fitted for the good formation of Catholic boys and young men, and at the same time reflect greater credit on the Society, than many colleges and schools that are deficient in teachers and equipment.

To realize this ideal to its full extent, your Province needs more men, and that means, first of all, more vocations of young men endowed with the qualities required by St. Ignatius in prospective members of the Society. When speaking of the lack of vocations, I do not intend to cast the slightest reflection on the Province; for a thorough study of statistics shows the proportion of vocations, obtained from your colleges and schools during the past decade, in relation to the number of boys that they contain, is practically the same, as in the other provinces of your assistancy. But you have neither as many colleges, nor as many boys in your colleges and schools as they have, and only one million Catholics scattered over a large territory to draw from.

Procuring vocations to the religious life is a problem all over the world. Is it more difficult in the South? Some say that it is. Be that as it may, there is only one logical conclusion. With courage and constancy you have to take the means to get them.

A vocation to the religious life is the choicest favor and most precious gift of God. You have therefore to beg Him to inspire with this holy calling young men who will make good novices of the Society. You did so this year; you did not spare prayers and penances, and the Sacred Heart of Jesus and the Blessed Virgin have had mercy on your Province. But remember that the efficacy of your prayers will depend of your faithfulness to God as religious and on your devotedness to His cause in your apostolic life. If you really are, as you ought to be, the faithful friends of our Lord, your prayers are bound to move His Sacred Heart.

But prayer is not the only means of inspiring vocations. There is need moreover of universal cooperation on the part of every member of the community especially in the schools and colleges. Without any doubt this work belongs first and foremost to the spiritual fathers and confessors of the boys and the prefects of the Sodalities. But it is at the same time the work of all others, teachers and prefects alike, who come in constant contact with the boys. As far as lies in their power, they should leave no stone unturned to lift the minds and hearts of boys to the service of God. They must preserve them against the spirit of the world, that archenemy of all piety and generosity, and consequently of the religious life. They have to impart to them a high esteem for a calling to the Society of Jesus. This can be done by showing in their own lives and conduct what happens there is in the religious state. We know from the history of the Society how many young men have been moved to enter the religion by the example of fervent religious, priests, scholastics and lay brothers.

Parish priests in their parishes, especially by their influence with the alter boys, and preachers in the pulpit, have many occasions of making boys and young men think of the priesthood or the religious life, and of instilling a more exalted idea of the sublime vocation into the minds of the faithful. If God does not require of them the sacrifice of one of their sons for the service of the alter, they might at least be willing to help in the education of boys destined for the religious life. And why not prudently and discreetly, when the occasion offers itself, as for the cooperation of friendly priests and sisters in finding vocations?

While speaking of vocations, I can not help deploring the absence of vocations of lay brothers, who by their fidelity, their love for prayer and work, their devotedness and their charity are so important to the welfare of a community. In other provinces the spreading of literature suitable to make this vocation better known met with real success.

But let these suggestions suffice, for I do not intend to enumerate here all the different means of obtaining vocations. I wish merely to make an earnest appeal to your love for the Society, to your gratitude for your holy vocation, and I beg you to do your utmost, in your particular sphere of action to procure vocations of scholastics and lay brothers for your dear Province.

However, good and numerous vocations are not sufficient to endow the works of the Province with their full apostolic power. It is necessary also to give our young men the thorough formation of the Society. It has always been the wise tradition of the Society to devote its best men to the spiritual and intellectual formation of its novices and scholastics. Moreover it is a strict duty on the part of superiors to study the special abilities of their subjects, and not to allow any extraordinary gift of God to lie fallow. This is especially important for those who have a very special capacity for some branch of knowledge or talent for preaching or writing. Is not this right and judicious use of talents given by God to the Province one of the best means of obtaining from His Goodness more excellent vocations?

I cannot be too insistent in exhorting the scholastics to earnestly carry out the wishes of the Society by acquiring as great a store-house of knowledge and literary lore as they possibly can during their scholasticate and regency. Let them with simplicity and frankness make known to their superiors any special talents they may have, and make every effort to develop and perfect them. All this, of course, means constancy and earnestness in their studies, seriousness in their reading, the proper use of their time and fidelity in following the direction given them. Let them all remember that the glory of God and the salvation of many souls are at stake. If they are careful as scholastics to realize in their spiritual life and in their studies the end and aim of the Society, their apostolic undertakings will be later on abundantly blessed by God. If not, they will be responsible for many shortcomings in their apostolic efficiency.

When a Province has vocations and well equipped men, it becomes its duty to distribute their activities and direct their zeal in accordance with the spirit of the Constitutions and the necessities of its own field of apostolate. The principles which guide our apostolate are taken from the 7th part of the Constitutions. There we are told that we must strive to procure the greater glory of God and the greater good of souls. To attain this end it is necessary in all our ministries to do work that is solid and lasting.

Now your Province, as a consequence of the lack of vocations, has not men enough for its colleges and for its other important works. The good will and the generosity of all, which I acknowledge publicly is most gratifying, are not a sufficient remedy for your difficulties. Overwork lesssens our efficiency, injures our health, hinders our intellectual formation and weakens our spiritual life. Professors who are too much taken up with ministerial activities, can not but neglect one or other of their duties, and perhaps at times both. Moreover, this would necessitate preaching or teaching without due preparation, a thing detrimental to the reputation of the Society. Under these conditions it is impossible to raise the studies of your colleges and schools to the standard required by the Ratio Studiorum and the College Associations. Hence in spite of great efforts you can not bring about proper development in your educational activities, nor make them, as they should be, models for the other colleges of the South to imitate.

In the line of preaching you have the same aim in view and employ the same methods. Your preachers should receive during their studies a solid formation, but they should never be deprived of serious immediate preparation especially when they are starting out. Moreover it would be very beneficial, at least for some of them, to get a biennium destined to prepare them for preaching. It is now one of my most earnest wishes that you may, as soon as possible, build up a strong missionary band, as missions are a work that is essential for the glory of God and the credit of the Province.

It seems to me also that your apostolate should little by little broaden out. Your duty is to work first of all for the Catholics living in the territory of the Province; but at the same time you should not forget the 24 millions of non-Christians and Protestants who surround you. It is true that one of the best means to correct some of them of their false notions is to form strong and fervent Catholic congregations that will by their example be a living proof of the divinity of the Roman Catholic Church. But could not also your apostolate be *actively* exercised among your non-Catholic fellow citizens? Why should not men well equipped with a deep knowledge of their religion and of ecclesiastical history be able both by word and by pen to make the Catholic truth shine before their eyes and dispel their prejudices, so that gradually they may be brought to the full knowledge of the truth? Such work, accomplished in a kind and sympathetic way, would certainly be most helpful to the salvation of so many souls that are deprived of the wonderful gift of Faith. And to express my thought completely, why could not Loyola University be the center and focus of intellectual Catholic activity, advantageous both for Catholic and non-Catholic alike?

As to your apostolate among the Catholics, I thoroughly appreciate what you are doing in your parishes and churches. I exhort you to give greater attention to the Sodalities of the Blessed Virgin, especially for men and boys; and I heartily approve of your plan of establishing a house of retreats for men near New Orleans. This is a work very dear to the Society, because it fits in with her purpose of training leaders among Catholics. It has been a great consolation to me to find among the priests, scholastics and lay brothers of your Province so many applications for the foreign Missions, and expressions of regret that you have not yet, as other Provinces, your own Mission to take care of. Such wishes and regrets manifest the true Spirit of the Society, and encourage me to hope that the day is not far distant when your Province, well supplied with solid vocations, will have some foreign field of apostleship committed to its zeal.

Meanwhile have you not a splendid opportunity of doing real missionary work among the Mexicans of El Paso and Albuquerque, the Cubans of Florida, and the colored people where they are entrusted to your care?

Moreover is not the labor of propagating the Catholic religion among unbelievers and Protestants, which has already been spoken of, that of genuine missionaries? Be certain that our Devine Savior who reads your hearts will bless your generous desires and make them efficacious for the salvation of souls.

I have spoken to you, reverend Fathers and dear Brothers, plainly and frankly with nothing else in view but the improvement of your apostolic work and the spreading of the influence of the Province for the greater glory of God. I know that you all have cheerfully consecrated your lives to this great cause, and that you will generously follow the directions which I am giving you before leaving the Province.

To improve your work you may with profit look at the apostolic activities of other Provinces. This will be suggestive of valuable ideas. But it would be a great mistake to copy indiscriminately all that is done elsewhere. The reason is that your Province, as is evident, has some characteristic traits which make it different from all others.

Consequently you should adapt your plans and your work to the possibilities and the needs of the South, and not dream impossible things or build castles in the air. Your share of work, such as we find it in the South, is splendid when we consider either the ordinary ministries of the Society among Catholics, or the hard work of spreading the Faith among non-Catholics. It has been assigned to you by God Himself; do your work therefore with courage and zeal, and love it as you love the will of God. Love, as such as they are with their good points and their shortcomings, the souls of Catholics entrusted to you, and those of non-Catholics who will obtain the pure light of Faith through your apostolate. If you meet with difficulties and hardships, if at times consolations are rare and disappointments are abundant, thank our Lord who shares the sufferings of His passion with you. Remember that souls are saved by the sacrifice of the Cross.

The double duty of tending to religious perfection and working for the salvation of souls has never been and never will be an easy undertaking. On the contrary it requires constant and generous efforts and self-sacrifice, and consequently great love for our Lord and invincible trust in Him. These virtues you will draw from the Sacred Heart of Jesus who has promised to help His faithful servants in the work of their perfection and in their apostolate. May that divine Heart grant you this priceless favor, and may He so bless the visitation that it may have a lasting influence for the good of your dear Province.

Commending myself to your holy Sacrifices and prayers, I am,
Your devoted servant in Christ,
N. de Boynes, S.J.
VISITOR OF THE PROVINCE OF NEW ORLEANS[1]

Notes

Introduction

Epigraph: Lawrence Stone, *The Past and the Present, Revised* (London and New York: Routledge and Kegan Paul Ltd., 1987), 261–62.

1. James L. Bess and Jay R. Dee, *Understanding College and University Organization: Theories for Affective Policy and Practice* (Sterling, VA: Stylus, 2008), 127.

2. Harold T. Shapiro, *A Larger Sense of Purpose: Higher Education and Society* (Princeton: Princeton University Press, 2005), xii.

3. John Aubrey Douglas, *The California Idea and American Higher Education: 1850 to the 1960 Master Plan* (Stanford: Stanford University Press, 2000), xi.

4. Alice W. Brown and contributors, *Cautionary Tales: Strategy Lessons from Struggling Colleges* (Sterling, Virginia: Stylus Publishing, LLC., 2012), xiii–2.

5. Ray Brown, *List of Colleges that Have Closed, Merged, or Changed Their Names.* http://www2.westminster-mo.edu/wc_users/homepages/staff/brownr/closedcollegeindex.htm, accessed August 10, 2012.

6. Donald G. Tewksbury, *The Founding of American Colleges and Universities before the Civil War* (New York: Bureau of Publication, Teachers College, Columbia University, 1932), v.

7. Colin B. Burke, *American Collegiate Populations: A Test of the Traditional View* (New York and London: New York University Press, 1982), 11–52.

8. Alice W. Brown and contributors, *Cautionary Tales: Strategy Lessons from Struggling Colleges* (Sterling, Virginia: Stylus Publishing, LLC., 2012), 212.

9. Brown, *List of Colleges that Have Closed, Merged, or Changed Their Names.* Ray Brown's database of colleges and universities that have closed, merged, or changed their names is extensive; however, it is periodically updated when new data is discovered.

10. Oliver P. Carriere, *A Sketch of the History of Jefferson College and Manresa House of Retreats Convent, Louisiana* (Convent, Louisiana: Manresa House of Retreats, 1974), 6.

11. William D. Reeves, *Manresa on the Mississippi: For the Greater Glory of God* (Convent, Louisiana: Manresa House of Retreats, 1996), 26.

12. R. Bentley Anderson, *Black, White, and Catholic: New Orleans Interracialism, 1947–1956* (Nashville, TN: Vanderbuilt University Press, 2005), 192, 129.

13. Albert Biever, *Diary and Notes on the Church of the Most Holy Name, Loyola College, and Loyola University New Orleans, 1904–1914*, Albert Biever Papers, Archives of the New Orleans Province, Society of Jesus, Monroe Library, Loyola University New Orleans, p. 163.

14. Albert Biever, *Diary and Notes on St. Charles College, Grand Coteau, 1837–1915*, Albert Biever Papers, Archives of the New Orleans Province, Society of Jesus, Monroe Library, Loyola University New Orleans, p. 34.

15. Anderson, *Black, White, and Catholic.*

16. Albert H. Biever, *The Jesuits in New Orleans and the Mississippi Valley: Jubilee Memorial* (New Orleans, 1924), 74.

17. Charles J. Boyle, *Gleanings from the Spring Hill College Archives* (Mobile, Alabama: Friends of Spring Hill College Library, 2004), 1; Michael Kenny, *The Torch on the Hill: Centenary Story of Spring Hill College, 1830–1930* (New York: The American Press, 1931), 48.

18. Jean Delanglez, "The Jesuits and Education in Louisiana during the Eighteenth Century," *Jesuit Educational Quarterly* 7 no. 1 (June 1944): 14.

19. Ignatius Loyola, *A Pilgrim's Journey: The Autobiography of Ignatius Loyola*, trans. Joseph N. Tylenda, S.J. (San Francisco: Ignatius Press, 2001), 108.

20. *New Advent Catholic Encyclopedia*, "IHS," New Advent, http://www.newadvent.org/cathen/07649a.htm, accessed June 15, 2010.

21. Dominic J. Balestra, "Where Loyalties Lie?," *Conversations on Jesuit Higher Education* (Fall 2003): 10.

22. Stringfellow Barr, "The Republic of Letters: Town and Gown," *Journal of Higher Education* 34, no. 6 (June 1963): 301.

23. Jeffrey Pfeffer and Gerald R. Salancik, *The External Control of Organizations: A Resource Dependence Prospective* (New York: Harper and Row, 1978), 1, 3.

24. James A Perkins, *The University in Transition* (Princeton: Princeton University Press, 1966), 24.

25. Bharti Venkatesh, "Leadership Transitions: The Key to Organizational Success," *Academic Leadership* (August 2008): 1, http://www.academicleadership.org/empirical_research/476_printer.shtml, accessed June 16, 2010.

26. Michael A. Diamond, *The Unconscious Life of Organizations: Interpreting Organizational Identity* (Westport, CT: Quorum Books, 1993), 77–78.

27. John R. Thelin, *Higher Education and Its Useful Past: Applied History in Research and Planning* (Rochester, VT: Schenkman, 1982), 47.

28. Francisco Marmolejo, "Higher Education Facilities: Issues and Trends," *Organization for Economic Co-Operation and Development* PEB Exchange 1 (2007): 1.

29. John W. Meyer and Brian Rowan, "Institutional Organization: Formal Structure as Myth and Ceremony," *American Journal of Sociology* 83, no. 2 (September 1977): 352.

30. Pfeffer and Salancik, *The External Control of Organizations*, 2.

31. James L. Bess and Jay R. Dee, *Understanding College and University Organization: Theories for Affective Policy and Practice* (Sterling, Virginia: Stylus Publishing, LLC.), 88.

32. M. Allen, *The Goals of Universities* (Milton Keyes, UK: SRHE and Open University Press, 1988), 7.

33. Lin Lerpold, David Ravasi, Johan van Rekom, and Guillaume Soenen "Identity, Strategy, and the Environment," in *Organizational Identity in Practice*, ed. Lin Lerpold, David Ravasi, Johan van Rekom, and Guillaume Soenen (New York: Routledge, 2007), 1.

34. Penelope Eckert and Etienne Wenger, "From School to Work: An Apprenticeship in Institutional Identity," *Institute for Research on Learning* 1 (1994): 2.

35. Dennis A. Gioia, Majken Schultz, and Kevin G. Corely, "Organizational Identity, Image, and Adaptive Instability," *Academy of Management Review* 25, no. 1 (2000): 64, 76.

36. Lerpold, Ravasi, van Rekom, and Soenen, "Identity, Strategy, and the Environment," 6.

37. S. Albert and D. A. Whetten, "Organizational Identity," quoted in *Organizational Identity in Practice*, ed. Lerpold, Ravasi, van Rekom, and Soenen, 3.

38. Ibid.

39. *2011 Catalog of the Provinces of Jesus in the United States of America* (Jesuit Conference, 2010), 241–42, 245–46.

40. Office of Mission and Ministry, "Welcome to University Ministry," Loyola University New Orleans, 1996–2010, http://mm.loyno.edu/university-ministry, accessed November 25, 2010.

41. Albert and Whetten, "Organizational Identity," 3.

42. Lerpold, Ravasi, van Rekom, and Soenen, "Identity, Strategy, and the Environment," 17.

43. Ibid., 17–18.

44. Ibid., 13.

45. Dennis A. Gioia, Majken Schultz, and Kevin G. Corely, "Organizational Identity, Image, and Adaptive Instability," *Academy of Management Review* 25, no. 1 (2000): 65.

46. Ibid., 63.

47. John C. Scott, "The Mission of the University: Medieval to Postmodern Transformations," *Journal of Higher Education* 77, no. 1 (January–February 2006): 1.

48. Richard Chait, "College Mission Statements," *Science* 205, no. 4410 (September 1979): 957.

49. Nancey Fjortoft and John C. Smart, "Enhancing Organizational Effectiveness: The Importance of Culture Type and Mission Agreement," *Higher Education* 27, no. 4 (June 1994): 431.

50. Ibid., 442.

51. Fjortoft and Smart, "Enhancing Organizational Effectiveness," 432.

52. H. G. Good, "Historical Research in Education," *Educational Research Bulletin* 9, no. 1 (January 1930): 10.

53. Ignatius Loyola, *The Constitutions of the Society of Jesus*, trans. George E. Ganss, S.J. (St. Louis: Institute of Jesuit Sources, 1970), 281.

54. Pfeffer and Salancik, *The External Control of Organizations*, 3.

55. Paul L. Dressel, "Mission, Organization, and Leadership," *Journal of Higher Education* 58, no. 1 (January–February 1987): 105–9.

56. Pfeffer and Salancik, *The External Control of Organizations*, 43.

57. American Academy of Arts and Sciences, "Town and Gown: The Urban Community and the University Community," *Bulletin of the American Academy of Arts and Sciences* 22, no. 6 (April 1969): 2, 6.

58. Ibid.

59. Edward Shils, "The University, the City, and the World: Chicago and the University of Chicago," in *The University and the City: From Medieval Origins to the Present*, ed. Thomas Bender (New York, Oxford: Oxford University Press, 1988), 211.

60. Bruce W. Leslie. *Gentlemen and Scholars: College and Community in the "Age of the University," 1865–1917* (University Park: Pennsylvania State University Press, 1992), 11.

61. Paul Claval, "Politics and the University," in *The Urban University and Its Identity: Roots, Locations, Roles*, ed. Herman van der Wusten (Boston: Kluwer Academic, 1998), 29.

62. Pfeffer and Salancik, *The External Control of Organizations*, 193.

63. Ibid., 26.

64. Ibid., 194, 202.

65. Thomas G. Dyer, "Higher Education in the South since the Civil War: Historiographical Issues and Trends," quoted in *The Web of Southern Social Relations: Women, Family, and Education*, ed. Walter J. Fraser Jr., R. Frank Saunders Jr., and Jon L. Wakelyn (Athens: University of Georgia Press, 1987), 127.

Chapter 1

Epigraph: Ignatius Loyola, *The Constitutions of the Society of Jesus*, trans. George E. Ganss (St. Louis: Institute of Jesuit Sources, 1970), 210–11.

1. Philip Gleason, *Contending with Modernity: Catholic Higher Education in the Twentieth Century* (New York, Oxford: Oxford University Press, 1995), vii.

2. Thomas Clancy, *An Introduction to Jesuit Life: The Constitutions and History through 435 Years* (St. Louis: Institute of Jesuit Sources, 1976), 23.

3. Christopher Hollis, *The Jesuits: A History* (New York: Macmillian, 1968), 8.

4. James Brodrick, *The Origins of the Jesuits* (Chicago: Loyola Press, 1997), 2.

5. Hugo Rahner, *The Spirituality of St. Ignatius Loyola: An Account of Its Historical Development*, trans. Francis John Smith, S.J. (Westminster, MD: Newman Press, 1953), 6–7.

6. Brodrick, *The Origins of the Jesuits*, 7–8.

7. Ibid., 9.

8. Ibid., 10.

9. Rahner, *The Spirituality of St. Ignatius Loyola*, 18–19.

10. Brodrick, *The Origins of the Jesuits*, 15.

11. William V. Bangert, *A History of the Jesuits* (St. Louis: Institute of Jesuit Resources, 1972), 7–9.

12. William A. Barry, "Prayer as Conscious Relationship," quoted in *An Ignatian Spiritual Reader*, ed. George W. Traub (Chicago: Loyola Press, 2008), 122.

13. Brodrick, *The Origins of the Jesuits*, 21–22.

14. Ibid., 21.

15. Chris Lowney, *Heroic Leadership: Best Practices from a 450-Year-Old Company that Changed the World* (Chicago: Loyola Press, 2003), 121.

16. Ignatius Loyola, *A Pilgrim's Journey: The Autobiography of Ignatius Loyola*, trans. Joseph N. Tylenda, S.J. (San Francisco: Ignatius Press, 2001), 86–101.

17. Daniel Bartoli, *History of the Life and Institute of St. Ignatius De Loyola, Founder of the Society of Jesus* (New York: Edward Dunigan and Brother, 1855), 109.

18. Brodrick, *The Origins of the Jesuits*, 34–35.

19. Simon Decloux, *The Ignatian Way*, trans. Cornelius M. Buckley (Chicago: Loyola Press, 1983), 8.

20. Hollis, *The Jesuits: A History*, 14–16.

21. Ronald Modras, "The Spiritual Humanism of the Jesuits," *America* (1995), quoted in *An Ignatian Spiritual Reader*, ed. George W. Traub (Chicago: Loyola Press, 2008), 7.

22. George Ganss, *Saint Ignatius' Idea of a Jesuit University* (Milwaukee: Marquette University Press, 1956), 18.

23. Clancy, *An Introduction to Jesuit Life*, 45.

24. Loyola, *The Constitutions of the Society of Jesus*, 210–11.

25. Ibid., 213–14.

26. Ibid., 215.

27. Allan P. Farrell, trans., *The Jesuit Ratio Studiorum of 1599* (Washington, DC: Conference of Major Superiors of Jesuits, 1970), i–iii.

28. John W. O'Malley, *The First Jesuits* (Cambridge: Harvard University Press, 1993), 226–27

29. Pedro Arrupe, "The Jesuit Apostolate in Education," *Jesuit Educational Quarterly* 29, no. 1 (June 1966): 5, 6; and quoted in William F. Kelley, S.J., *The Jesuit Order and Higher Education in the United States: 1789–1966* (Milwaukee: Wisconsin Jesuit Province, 1967), 9–10.

30. William P. Leahy, *Adapting to America: Catholics, Jesuits, and Higher Education in the Twentieth Century* (Washington, DC: Georgetown University Press, 1991), x.

31. Ibid., x.

32. Ibid.

33. Jean-Marc Laporte, "Ignatian Identity and Mission: Beyond GC 35," workshop on communal apostolic discernment (Rome, 2009), www.jesuits.ca/orientations/ignat%20jes.pdf, accessed October 9, 2010.

34. Loyola, *The Constitutions of the Society of Jesus*, 292.

35. Miguel Bartllori, "Some International Aspects of the Activity of the Jesuits in the New World," *Americas* 14, no. 4 (April 1958): 434.

36. Albert H. Biever, *The Jesuits in New Orleans and the Mississippi Valley: Jubilee Memorial* (New Orleans, 1924), 12.

37. William V. Bangert, *A History of the Jesuits* (St. Louis: Institute of Jesuit Resources, 1972), 261.

38. Edna Kenton, *The Jesuit Relations and Allied Documents: Travels and Explorations of the Jesuit Missionaries in North America, 1610–1791* (Whitefish, MT: Kessinger, 2006), xlix.

39. Bangert, *A History of the Society of Jesus*, 261–64.

40. Biever, *The Jesuits in New Orleans and the Mississippi Valley*, 14.

41. Thomas Clancy, *Our Friends*, 3rd ed. (New Orleans: Jesuit Provincial Residence, 1998), 3.

42. Donald A. Howkins, S.J., "Pioneer Jesuits in the South—1566 to 1763,"in *Jesuits of the South Celebrate 75 Years as a Province (1907–1982), Apostolic Ministry in the South Since 1837, Early Jesuits Missions in the South (1566–1763)* 2, no. 1 (August 1982): 5.

43. Biever, *The Jesuits in New Orleans and the Mississippi Valley*, 17.

44. Ibid., 17–19.

45. Ibid., 20–21.

46. Clancy, *Our Friends*, 3.

47. Albert James Pickett, *History of Alabama and Incidentally Georgia and Mississippi, from the Earliest Period* (Birmingham, AL: Robert and Son, 1878), 176.

48. Roger Baudier, *The Catholic Church in Louisiana* (New Orleans, 1939; repr., Louisiana Library Association Public Library Section, 1972), 139.

49. Biever, *The Jesuits in New Orleans and the Mississippi Valley*, 32–35.

50. Ibid., 33.

51. Emily Clark, *Voices from an Early American Convent: Marie Madeleine Hachard and the New Orleans Ursulines, 1727–1760* (Baton Rouge: Louisiana State University Press, 2007), 12–13.

52. Biever, *The Jesuits in New Orleans and the Mississippi Valley*, 34.

53. Ibid., 37–39.

54. Emily Clark, *Masterless Mistresses: The New Orleans Ursulines and the Development of a New Society, 1727–1834* (Williamsburg, VA: University of North Carolina Press, 2007), 46–47.

55. Ibid.

56. Edwin Whitfield Fay, *The History of Education in Louisiana* (Washington, DC: Government Printing Office, 1898), 10.

57. Adam Otis Hebert Jr., "History of Education in Colonial Louisiana," (master's thesis, Louisiana State University, 1958), quoted in Michael G. Wade, ed., *The Louisiana Bicentennial Series in Louisiana History: Volume XVIII, Education in Louisiana* (Lafayette: Center for Louisiana Studies, 1999), 10–12.

58. Ibid.

59. Ibid., 13–15.

60. Fay, *The History of Education in Louisiana*, 11.

61. Jean Delanglez, "The Jesuits and Education in Louisiana during the Eighteenth Century," *Jesuit Educational Quarterly* 7, no. 1 (June 1944): 17–18.

62. Clancy, *An Introduction to Jesuit Life*, 173–75.

63. Hollis, *The Jesuits: A History*, 148–53.

64. Ned Sublette, *The World That Made New Orleans: From Spanish Silver to Congo Square* (Chicago: Lawrence Hill Books, 2008), 87.

65. Howkins, "Pioneer Jesuits in the South—1566 to 1763," 7.

66. Edward Hardin, "Record of the Jesuit Expulsion from Louisiana," *Journal of the Louisiana Historical Association* 9, no. 2 (Spring 1968): 108.

67. Biever, *The Jesuits in New Orleans and the Mississippi Valley*, 60–61.

68. Hollis, *The Jesuits: A History*, 159.

69. *Go Forth and Teach: The Characteristics of Jesuit Education* (Washington, DC: Jesuit Secondary Education Association, 1987), 65.

70. Raymond A. Schroth, *The American Jesuits: A History* (New York: New York University Press, 2007), 58–59.

71. Bangert, *A History of the Society of Jesus*, 425.

72. Gilbert J. Garraghan, *The Jesuits of the Middle United States*, vol. 3 (New York: American Press, 1938), 129–32.

73. Ibid., 132–34.

74. Biever, *The Jesuits in New Orleans and the Mississippi Valley*, 73.

75. Benjamin H. Trask, *Fearful Ravages: Yellow Fever in New Orleans, 1796–1905* (Lafayette, Louisiana: Center for Louisiana Studies, 2005), 1.

76. Biever, *The Jesuits in New Orleans and the Mississippi Valley*, 73–74.

77. Thomas Clancy, "The Antebellum Jesuits of the New Orleans Province, 1837–1861," *Journal of the Louisiana Historical Association* 34, no. 3 (Summer 1993): 329–30.

78. Andrew H. M. Stern, *Southern Crucifix, Southern Cross: Catholic-Protestant Relations in the Old South* (Tuscaloosa: University of Alabama Press, 2012), 104.

79. Donald E. Crosby, "Jesuits Go Home: The Anti-Jesuit Movement in the United States, 1830–1860," *Woodstock Letters* 97, no. 1 (1968): 225.

80. William P. Leahy, *Adapting to America: Catholics, Jesuits, and Higher Education in the Twentieth Century* (Washington, DC: Georgetown University Press, 1991), 3.

81. Crosby, "Jesuits Go Home," 229.

82. Ibid., 239–40.

83. Leahy, *Adapting to America*, 227.

84. Howkins, "Pioneer Jesuits in the South—1566 to 1763," 12–13.

85. Maria Monk, *The Awful Disclosures of Maria Monk*, revised ed. (New York: D. M. Bennett Literal and Scientific Publishing House, 1878), iv.

86. Ibid., iii–vii.

87. Ray Allen Billington, "Maria Monk and Her Influence," *Catholic Historical Review* 22, no. 3 (October 1936): 289, 292.

88. Albert Biever, *Diary and Notes on Spring Hill College, Mobile, 1878–1885*, Albert Biever Papers, Loyola University New Orleans, Monroe Library, Archives of the New Orleans Province, Society of Jesus, p. 149.

89. Michael Kenny, *Jesuits in Our Southland, 1566–1946: Origin and Growth of New Orleans Province*, Kenny Papers, Archives of the New Orleans Province, Society of Jesus, Loyola University, Monroe Library, New Orleans, 125–26.

90. Baudier, *The Catholic Church in Louisiana*, 379.

91. Ibid., 379–80.

92. M. Veronica Kelly, "A Century of Catholic Education in Baton Rouge (1847–1947)," (MA Thesis, Catholic University of America, 1947), 13.

93. Kenny, *Jesuits in Our Southland, 1566–1946*, 53.

94. Ibid., 53.

95. Frank M. Uter, *A History of the Catholic Church in Baton Rouge* (Baton Rouge: Privately Published, 1992), 26, 28.

96. Ibid., 27, 31,33.

97. W. C. Widman, "Spring Hill (1830–1898.)," *Woodstock Letters* 27, no. 3 (1898): 273.

98. Cornelius M. Buckley, *A Frenchman, A Chaplain, A Rebel: The War Letters of Pere Louis-Hippolyte Gache, S.J.* (Chicago: Loyola University Press, 1981), 201, 203.

99. Leahy, *Adapting to America*, 5–6.

100. Ibid., 7, 13, 14.

101. Father General Xavier Wernz to the Fathers and Brothers of the New Orleans Province, June 7, 1907, Loyola University New Orleans, Monroe Library, Archives of the New Orleans Province, Society of Jesus.

102. Leahy, *Adapting to America*, 15, 156.

103. Ibid., 21–22.

104. Ibid., 23, 25, 33, 34.

Chapter 2

Epigraph: Carnegie Foundation for the Advancement of Teaching, *More Than Survival: Prospects for Higher Education in a Period of Uncertainty* (San Francisco, Washington, London: Jossey-Bass, 1975), 72, 77.

1. Peter McDonough, *Men Astutely Trained: A History of the Jesuits in the American Century* (New York: Free Press, 1992), 206.

2. George Ganss, *Saint Ignatius' Idea of a Jesuit University* (Milwaukee: Marquette University Press, 1956), 162.

3. Ibid., 63.

4. John L. McKenzie, "Theology as an Integrating Factor in Jesuit Education," *Jesuit Educational Quarterly* 21, no. 1 (1958): 25.

5. Judith Kelleher Schafer, "Life and Labor in Antebellum Louisiana," in *Louisiana: A History*, 5th ed. (Wheeling, IL: Harlan Davidson, 1990), 169.

6. Robert Schwickerath, *Jesuit Education: Its History and Principles Viewed in the Light of Modern Educational Problems* (St. Louis: B. Herder, 1904), 118, 130.

7. Ganss, *Saint Ignatius' Idea of a Jesuit University*, 33.

8. Allan P. Farrell, "Notes on Jesuit Teaching Procedures," *Jesuit Educational Quarterly* 5, no. 4 (1943): 238, 241–42.

9. Albert Biever, *Diary and Notes on Spring Hill College, Mobile, 1878–1885*, Albert Biever Papers, Loyola University New Orleans, Monroe Library, Archives of the New Orleans Province, Society of Jesus, p. 143.

10. William D. Ryan, "Is There Anything Distinctive about Jesuit Education?," *Jesuit Educational Quarterly* 28, no. 1 (1965): 59, 60.

11. Eugene J. Devlin, "Character Formation in the *Ratio Studiorum*," *Jesuit Educational Quarterly* 15, no. 4 (1953): 222.

12. Schwickerath, *Jesuit Education*, 280, 281, 285.

13. Jean Delanglez, "The Jesuits and Education in Louisiana," *Jesuit Educational Quarterly* 7, no. 1 (1944): 18.

14. Miguel A. Bernard, "The Class of 'Humanities' in the *Ratio Studiorum*," *Jesuit Educational Quarterly* 15, no. 4 (1953): 205.

15. Albert H. Biever, *The Jesuits in New Orleans and the Mississippi Valley: Jubilee Memorial* (New Orleans, 1924), 132.

16. Ibid., 101.

17. Rodney Cline, *Pioneer Leaders and Early Institutions in Louisiana Education* (Baton Rouge: Claitor's Publishing Division, 1969), 224.

18. Biever, *The Jesuits in New Orleans and the Mississippi Valley*, 134.

19. Ibid., 139–40.

20. McDonough, *Men Astutely Trained*, xvii.

21. Michael Kenny, *Jesuits in Our Southland, 1566–1946: Origin and Growth of New Orleans Province*, 1946, Kenny Papers, Archives of the New Orleans Province, Society of Jesus, Loyola University, Monroe Library, New Orleans, La., 120.

22. John E. Wise, "The College Boards in Jesuit Schools," *Jesuit Educational Quarterly* 7, no. 1 (1944): 25.

23. Thomas H. Clancy, *The Last 150 Years*, http:/norprove.org/identity/last150yrs .htm, accessed November 24, 2009.

24. Kathleen Mahoney, *Catholic Higher Education in Protestant America: The Jesuits and Harvard in the Age of the University* (Baltimore: Johns Hopkins University Press, 2003), 235–36.

25. Ibid.

26. Philip Gleason, "What Made Catholic Identity a Problem," in *The Challenge and Promise of a Catholic University*, ed. Theodore M. Hesburgh (Notre Dame: University of Notre Dame Press, 1994), 93.

27. Michael Kenny, *The Torch on the Hill: Centenary Story of Spring Hill College, 1830–1930* (New York: American Press, 1931), 270.

28. Melanie M. Morey and John J. Piderit, *Catholic Higher Education: A Culture in Crisis* (New York: Oxford University Press, 2006), 21.

29. Ganss, *Saint Ignatius' Idea of a Jesuit University*, 117.

30. Timothy J. O'Leary, "The Role of Science in Jesuit Colleges," *Jesuit Educational Quarterly* 15, no. 4 (1953): 223, 228.

31. Gustave A. Weigel, "The Heart of Jesuit Education—The Teacher," *Jesuit Educational Quarterly* 20, no. 1 (1957): 9.

32. William J. Byron, "A Religious-Based College and University Perspective," in *Civic Responsibility and Higher Education*, ed. Thomas Ehrlich (Phoenix, Arizona: Oryx Press, 2000), 281–82.

33. George E. Ganss, "St. Ignatius' Constitutions and the Spirit of the *Ratio*," *Jesuit Educational Quarterly* 17, no. 2 (1954): 73.

34. Ganss, *Saint Ignatius' Idea of a Jesuit University*, 176–177.

35. Biever, *The Jesuits in New Orleans and the Mississippi Valley*, 133.

36. Harold W. Attridge, "Reflections on the Mission of a Catholic University," in *The Challenge and Promise of a Catholic University*, ed. Theodore M. Hesburgh (Notre Dame, Indiana: University of Notre Dame Press, 1994), 19.

37. Ganss, *Saint Ignatius' Idea of a Jesuit University*, 137–138.

38. Mahoney, *Catholic Higher Education in Protestant America*, 6, 7, 14.

39. Ibid., 53.

40. Ibid., 53, 59, 97–98.

41. Biever, *The Jesuits in New Orleans and the Mississippi Valley*, 93.

42. Mahoney, *Catholic Higher Education in Protestant America*, 22, 37, 52.

43. Schwickerath, *Jesuit Education*, 264–65.

44. Ibid., 239.

45. Ibid., 89.

46. Kenny, *The Torch on the Hill*, 226–27.

47. Roger Baudier, *The Catholic Church in Louisiana* (New Orleans: Louisiana Library Association Public Library Section, 1939), 357.

48. Thomas Clancy, *List of Jesuits Whose Names Appear in the Jesuit Catalogs 1837–1861 as Serving in the New Orleans Province*, n.d., Clancy Papers, Loyola University New Orleans, Monroe Library, Archives of the New Orleans Province, Society of Jesus.

49. Peter Beck, "Decree of Father General Becker," AR Files: 66, Loyola University New Orleans, Monroe Library, Archives of the New Orleans Province, Society of Jesus.

50. Thomas Clancy, Georgetown Speech, June 1989, Clancy Papers, Loyola University New Orleans, Monroe Library, Archives of the New Orleans Province, Society of Jesus.

51. William F. Kelley, *The Jesuit Order and Higher Education In the United States, 1789–1966* (Milwaukee: Wisconsin Jesuit Province, 1966), 34.

52. *Catalogus Sociorum Et Officiorum Provinciae Lugdunensis Societatis Jesu, IMEUNTE ANNO MDCCCLXXX* (Lugduni: Ex Typis Catholicis, 1880); *Missio Neo-Aurelianensis Societatis Jesu, Ineunte Anno 1898* (Woodstock: Typis Collegii SS. Cordis, 1898); *Catalogus Provinciae Neo-Aurelianensis Societatis Jesu, Ineunte Anno 1908* (New Orleans, Louisiana: Perry and Buckley, 1908); *Catalogus Provincia Neo Aurelianensis Societatis Jesu, Ineunte Anno MCMXXIII* (El Paso: Ex typis "Revosfa Catolica," 1923).

53. Minister's Diary, Sacred Heart Church and College, Augusta, Georgia, December 2, 1900–December 31, 1913, Loyola University New Orleans, Monroe Library, Archives of the New Orleans Province, Society of Jesus.

54. Edward John Power, *A History of Catholic Higher Education in the United States* (Milwaukee, Wisconsin: The Bruce Publishing Company, 1958), 172.

55. Biever, *The Jesuits in New Orleans and the Mississippi Valley*, 161.

56. Mahoney, *Catholic Higher Education in Protestant America*, 2.

57. Baudier, *The Catholic Church in Louisiana*, 372.

58. Byron, "A Religious-Based College and University Perspective," 280.

59. Ganss, *Saint Ignatius' Idea of a Jesuit University*, 33.

60. Allan P. Farrell, "Four Hundred Years of Jesuit Education," *Jesuit Educational Quarterly* 3, no. 2 (1940): 125.

61. McDonough, *Men Astutely Trained*, 315.

62. Biever, *The Jesuits in New Orleans and the Mississippi Valley*, 83.

63. Baudier, *The Catholic Church in Louisiana*, 371.

64. Bruce W. Leslie. *Gentlemen and Scholars: College and Community in the "Age of the University," 1865–1917* (University Park: Pennsylvania State University Press, 1992), 255.

65. Biever, *The Jesuits in New Orleans and the Mississippi Valley*, 91–92.

66. Baudier, *The Catholic Church in Louisiana*, 470.

67. *The Catholic Church in the United States of America: To Celebrate the Golden Jubilee of His Holiness, Pope Pius X* (New York: Catholic Editing Company, 1908), 195.

68. Attridge, "Reflections on the Mission of a Catholic University," 13–14.

69. F. H., "The Ratio Studiorum and the American College," *Woodstock Letters* 26, no. 3 (1897): 369–77.

70. Chairman, Committee on University Objectives and Goals to Chairman of all Self-Study Committee, April 15, 1963, Loyola University New Orleans, Monroe Library, Archives of the New Orleans Province, Society of Jesus.

71. Mahoney, *Catholic Higher Education in Protestant America*, 147–48, 203, 226.

72. Letter from Thomas Clancy to Mike Alchediak reviewing the Provincial Correspondence concerning the closure of St. Mary's University, March 29, 1978, Clancy Papers, Loyola University New Orleans, Monroe Library, Archives of the New Orleans Province, Society of Jesus.

73. Ibid.

74. Norbert de Boynes, *Letter Addressed to the Fathers, Scholastics and Brothers of the New Orleans Province by Rev. Fr. Norbert de Boynes, S.J. At the Close of the Visitation, October 23rd., 1921*, 1921, Box, Fr. Norbert de Boynes, S.J.: Visitation to New Orleans Province, Feb. 11–Oct. 23, 1921, Loyola University New Orleans, Monroe Library, Archives of the New Orleans Province, Society of Jesus.

75. Kenny, *Jesuits in Our Southland, 1566–1946*, 134.

76. Thomas Clancy to Mike Alchediak, Archives of the New Orleans Province, Society of Jesus.

77. *Memorial of the Visitation of the New Orleans Province Left by the Very Rev. Norbert de Boynes Visitor of the Same Province from February 11, 1921 to October 23, 1921*, Box, Fr. Norbert de Boynes, S.J.: Visitation to New Orleans Province, Feb. 11–Oct. 23, 1921, Loyola University New Orleans, Monroe Library, Archives of the New Orleans Province, Society of Jesus.

78. *Report of the Meeting of Inter-Province Committee on Studies with the Decisions of the Provincials of the American Provinces on Each Number of the Report*, April 20, 1921, Loyola University New Orleans, Monroe Library, Archives of the New Orleans Province, Society of Jesus.

79. Ibid.

80. *Report of the Proceedings of a Meeting On Studies: Held at Spring Hill College*, August 1906, Loyola University New Orleans, Monroe Library, Archives of the New Orleans Province, Society of Jesus.

81. F. H., "The Ratio Studiorum and the American College (Second Paper)," *Woodstock Letters* 22, no. 2 (1898): 183.

82. *Report of the First Meeting of the Committee on Studies of the New Orleans Province*, September 1, 1921, Loyola University New Orleans, Monroe Library, Archives of the New Orleans Province, Society of Jesus

83. *The Catholic Educational Association, Department of Colleges and Secondary Schools, Commission on Standardization*, Spring Hill College, Burke Library, Spring Hill College Archives and Special Collections, 1–2.

84. *Report of the Committee on the Revision of Studies*, n.d., Loyola University New Orleans, Monroe Library, Archives of the New Orleans Province, Society of Jesus

85. W. Ledóchowski, *General of the Society of Jesus to the Fathers and Scholastics of the American Assistancy*, August 15, 1934, Loyola University New Orleans, Monroe Library, Archives of the New Orleans Province, Society of Jesus.

86. Kenny, *Jesuits in Our Southland, 1566–1946*, 196.

87. Morton A. Hill, "Twentieth Century Thought on the *Ratio Studiorum*," *Jesuit Educational Quarterly* 14, no. 4 (1952): 239.

88. Ibid.

89. *Woodstock Letters*, undated insert in the *Woodstock Letters* on the private nature of the *Letters*, Archives of the New Orleans Province, Society of Jesus, Loyola University New Orleans, Monroe Library, New Orleans.

90. Pedro Leturia, "Why the Society of Jesus Became a Teaching Order," *Jesuit Educational Quarterly* 4, no. 1 (1941): 54.

Chapter 3

Epigraph: Thomas Clancy to Mike Alchediak, March 29, 1978, Clancy Papers, Loyola University New Orleans, Monroe Library, Archives of the New Orleans Province, Society of Jesus.

1. J. Maitrugues, "St. Charles' College, Grand Coteau, La.," *Woodstock Letters* 5, no. 1 (1876): 17–29.

2. Albert Biever, *Diary and Notes on St. Charles College, Grand Coteau, 1837–1915*, Albert Biever Papers, Archives of the New Orleans Province, Society of Jesus, Monroe Library, Loyola University New Orleans, p. 57.

3. Trent Angers, *Grand Coteau: The Holy Land of South Louisiana* (Lafayette, Louisiana: Acadian House Publishing), 27.

4. Michael Kenny, *Jesuits in Our Southland, 1566–1946: Origin and Growth of New Orleans Province*, 1946, Kenny Papers, Loyola University New Orleans, Monroe Library, Archives of the New Orleans Province, Society of Jesus, 34.

5. Angers, *Grand Coteau: The Holy Land of South Louisiana*, 37, 69.

6. Kenny, *Jesuits in Our Southland*, 35.

7. Jean Baptiste Maisounabe, *Diary, 1847*, Maisounabe Papers, Loyola University New Orleans, Monroe Library, Archives of the New Orleans Province, Society of Jesus.

8. Kenny, *Jesuits in Our Southland, 1566–1946*, 35.

9. Biever, *Diary and Notes on St. Charles College, Grand Coteau, 1837–1915*, p. 59.

10. Ibid.

11. P. F. O'Donnell, "Digest of Land History of Catholic Property in Grand Coteau of Consequence to the Jesuit Fathers From 1837 to 1930," ca. 1950, AR Files, Loyola University New Orleans, Monroe Library, Archives of the New Orleans Province, Society of Jesus.

12. Biever, *Diary and Notes on St. Charles College, Grand Coteau, 1837–1915*, pp. 59–62.

13. Ibid., 64.

14. Maitrugues, "St. Charles' College, Grand Coteau, La.," 17–29.

15. Biever, *Diary and Notes on St. Charles College, Grand Coteau, 1837–1915*, p. 36.

16. Ibid., 62–63.

17. Margaret Humphreys, *Yellow Fever and the South* (Baltimore and London: The Johns Hopkins University Press, 1992), 3–4.

18. Prospectus of St. Charles College, n.d., Grand Coteau Early Photos (A-1), Loyola University New Orleans, Monroe Library, Archives of the New Orleans Province, Society of Jesus.

19. "St. Charles' College, Grand Coteau, LA," *Woodstock Letters* 5, no. 1 (1876): 20.

20. Kenny, *Jesuits in Our Southland, 1566–1946*, 36.

21. Ibid.

22. *Constitution of the Catholic Society of Religious and Catholic Literary Education*, 1847, AR Files, Loyola University New Orleans, Monroe Library, Archives of the New Orleans Province, Society of Jesus.

23. Ibid.

24. "Graduates' Day at St. Charles College," *Daily Picayune*, June 22, 1913.

25. Charter of Saint Charles College of Grand Coteau, 1852, St. Charles College Box:

Varia, Loyola University New Orleans, Monroe Library, Archives of the New Orleans Province, Society of Jesus.

26. C. M. Widman, "Grand Coteau College in War Times, 1860–1866," *Woodstock Letters* 30, no. 1 (1901): 35.

27. Biever, *Diary and Notes on St. Charles College, Grand Coteau, 1837–1915*, pp. 28, 32.

28. Jean Baptiste Maisounabe, *Diary, 1847.* Maisounabe Papers. Archives of the New Orleans Province, Society of Jesus, Monroe Library, Loyola University New Orleans, LA.

29. Ibid.

30. J. Jourdant to Abbadie, October 8, 1847, AR Files: 1049-E, Loyola University New Orleans, Monroe Library, Archives of the New Orleans Province, Society of Jesus.

31. Kenny, *Jesuits in Our Southland, 1566–1946:*, 45, 47.

32. "Grand Coteau," *Woodstock Letters* 30, no. 2 *Varia* (1901): 319.

33. Kenny, *Jesuits in Our Southland, 1566–1946*, 42, 46.

34. Ralph J. Smith to Jesuit Fathers, St. Charles College, 1853, AR Files: 71, Loyola University New Orleans, Monroe Library, Archives of the New Orleans Province, Society of Jesus.

35. Henry J. Millard, *An Account of a Meeting Held in Grand Coteau on the Occasion of Its [St. Charles College] Suppression*, October 29, 1853, AR Files: 71, Loyola University New Orleans, Monroe Library, Archives of the New Orleans Province, Society of Jesus.

36. "The Society and Her Martyrs Honored," *Woodstock Letters* 55, no. 2 (1926): 308.

37. L. H. Gache, "Our College at Baton Rouge, Louisiana," *Woodstock Letters* 27, no.1 (1898): 1–5.

38. Kenny, *Jesuits in Our Southland, 1566–1946*, 60–62.

39. Ibid., 36–37.

40. Ibid., 38.

41. Ibid., 37.

42. Ibid., 39–41.

43. Ibid., 42–43.

44. Ibid.

45. "St. Charles' College, Grand Coteau, LA," *Woodstock Letters* 5, no. 1 (1876): 20.

46. Kenny, *Jesuits in Our Southland, 1566–1946*, 48–49.

47. Ibid., 124.

48. Biever, *Diary and Notes on St. Charles College, Grand Coteau, 1837–1915*, p. 118.

49. P. J. K., "Louisiana: A Short Account of the Society in New Orleans," *Woodstock Letters* 14, no. 3 (1885): 327.

50. "Grand Coteau," *Woodstock Letters* 30, no. 2 *Varia* (1901): 319.

51. Biever, *Diary and Notes on St. Charles College, Grand Coteau, 1837–1915*, p. 34.

52. Minister's Diary, St. Charles College, 1891–1917, Loyola University New Orleans, Monroe Library, Archives of the New Orleans Province, Society of Jesus.

53. "Grand Coteau. St. Charles' College," *Woodstock Letters* 36, no. 1 (1907): 406–8.

54. Sanders to Maring, telegram, March, 23, 1909, AR Files, Loyola University New Orleans, Monroe Library, Archives of the New Orleans Province, Society of Jesus.

55. "Commencement at End: St. Charles Alumni Form Association," *Daily Picayune*, June 23, 1913.

56. "Grand Coteau," *Woodstock Letters* 42 no. 1 Varia (1913): 123.

57. J. P. Conniff to M. A. Grace, September 22, 1916, AR Files, Loyola University New Orleans, Monroe Library, Archives of the New Orleans Province, Society of Jesus.

58. "St. Charles' College," *Woodstock Letters* 46 no. 1 Varia (1917): 137.

59. St. Charles College, Grand Coteau, La.: 1919–20, *St. Charles College Catalogue, R.O.T.C. Reserve Officer's Training Corps Unit* (1919), Loyola University New Orleans, Monroe Library, Archives of the New Orleans Province, Society of Jesus.

60. Ibid.

61. Ibid.

62. Ibid.

63. Ibid.

64. "New Orleans: Grand Coteau—*St. Charles College Wins High Honor in Victory Loan Drive—R.O.T.C. Wins Fourth Place Among All Other Units in the United States,*" *Woodstock Letters* 48 no. 2 *Varia* (1919): 434.

65. Ibid.

66. "Grand Coteau. St. Charles' College. Retreats for Lay-men," *Woodstock Letters* 45 no. 3 *Varia* (1916): 448.

67. "Grand Coteau. St. Charles' College. Ours of the Secular Clergy," *Woodstock Letters* 44 no. 1 *Varia* (1915): 130.

68. Biever, *Diary and notes on St. Charles College, Grand Coteau, 1837–1915*, 65.

69. Kenny, *Jesuits in our Southland 1566–1946: Origin and Growth of New Orleans Province*, 187.

70. Thomas Clancey to Mike Alchediak, March 29, 1978, Clancey Papers.

71. James D. Carroll, "The Mississippi Flood Disaster," *Woodstock Letters* 57 no. 1 (1928): 52–53.

72. *University of St. Mary, Galveston, Texas: Souvenir Volume of the Silver Jubilee of the College Under Jesuit Administration, 1884–1909*, Clark & Courts (MFG. Stationers, Galveston 1909), Loyola University New Orleans, Monroe Library, Archives of the New Orleans Province, Society of Jesus, 8.

73. Ibid., 9.

74. Ibid., 7.

75. John B. Quinlan, "Galveston, Texas," *Woodstock Letters* 16 no. 1 (1887): 282–283.

76. *University of St. Mary, Galveston, Texas*, 18.

77. M. K., "Galveston. St. Mary's University, Galveston, Texas, New Year's Day, 1890," *Woodstock Letters* 19 no. 1 (1890): 75.

78. *University of St. Mary, Galveston, Texas*, 10–15.

79. Ibid., 10.

80. J. A. Hogan, "Reminiscences of the Galveston Storm," *Woodstock Letters* 29 no. 3 (1900): 430.

81. Quinlan, "Galveston, Texas," 282–283.

82. *University of St. Mary, Galveston, Texas*, 47.

83. Ibid, 18.

84. Kenny, *Jesuits in our Southland 1566–1946: Origin and Growth of New Orleans Province*, 132.

85. Ibid.

86. *University of St. Mary, Galveston*, 7.

87. Ibid., 16.
88. Ibid., 18.
89. Ibid., 19.
90. "Galveston," *Woodstock Letters* 23 no. 1 *Varia* (1894): 187–188.
91. *University of St. Mary, Galveston*, 19.
92. Ibid., 42.
93. Ibid., 20.
94. Ibid., 41.
95. "New Orleans Mission, St. Mary's College, Galveston," *Woodstock Letters* 27, no. 2 *Varia* (1898): 403.
96. *University of St. Mary, Galveston, Texas*, 16.
97. Albert Biever, *Diary and Notes on the New Orleans Province Mission Band, 1913–1932*, Albert Biever Papers, Loyola University New Orleans, Monroe Library, Archives of the New Orleans Province, Society of Jesus, p. 292.
98. Ibid., 293.
99. Ibid., 300–301.
100. Ibid., 301.
101. Biever, *Diary and Notes on the New Orleans Province Mission Band, 1913–1932*, p. 301.
102. Hogan, "Reminiscences of the Galveston Storm," 428–32.
103. Hogan to New Orleans Province, 1900, AR Files: 56, Loyola University New Orleans, Monroe Library, Archives of the New Orleans Province, Society of Jesus.
104. Kenny, *Jesuits in Our Southland, 1566–1946*, 135.
105. Hogan, "Reminiscences of the Galveston Storm," 430–40.
106. Kenny, *Jesuits in Our Southland, 1566–1946*, 135.
107. Biever, *Diary and Notes on the New Orleans Province Mission Band, 1913–1932*, p. 303.
108. Hogan, "Reminiscences of the Galveston Storm," 430–40.
109. Account of the Galveston Flood by James J. O'Brien, 1900, AR Files: 84, Loyola University New Orleans, Monroe Library, Archives of the New Orleans Province, Society of Jesus.
110. Hogan, "Reminiscences of the Galveston Storm," 430–40.
111. Hogan to New Orleans Province, 1900, AR Files: 56, Loyola University New Orleans, Monroe Library, Archives of the New Orleans Province, Society of Jesus.
112. *University of St. Mary, Galveston, Texas*, 21.
113. "Galveston, Tex.," *Woodstock Letters* 30, no. 2 *Varia* (1901): 320.
114. *University of St. Mary, Galveston, Texas*, 24–26.
115. "Galveston," *Woodstock Letters* 31, no. 3 *Varia* (1902): 483.
116. "Galveston," *Woodstock Letters* 33, no. 2 *Varia* (1904): 254.
117. Kenny, *Jesuits in Our Southland, 1566–1946*, 133.
118. *St. Mary's University, College Catalogue, 1906–1907*, Knap Bros. (Galveston, Texas: Stationers and Print, 1906), Loyola University New Orleans, Monroe Library, Archives of the New Orleans Province, Society of Jesus.
119. "New Orleans Mission. Galveston. Jubilee of the Parish and the University," *Woodstock Letters* 38, no. 3 *Varia* (1909): 440.

120. *University of St. Mary, Galveston, Texas*, front cover.

121. Ibid., 66–81.

122. "Galveston. St. Mary's University. Refugees from Mexico," *Woodstock Letters* 44, no. 1 *Varia* (1915): 130.

123. "New Orleans Mission: St. Mary's Church, Galveston," *Woodstock Letters* 34, no. 1 (1905): 110.

124. *University of St. Mary, Galveston, Texas*, 44.

125. Thomas Clancy to Mike Alchediak, Archives of the New Orleans Province, Society of Jesus.

126. Kenny, *Jesuits in Our Southland, 1566–1946*, 187.

127. Thomas Clancy to Mike Alchediak, Archives of the New Orleans Province, Society of Jesus.

128. Sacred Heart Church, postcard, 1977, Galveston Photograph Drawer, Loyola University New Orleans, Monroe Library, Archives of the New Orleans Province, Society of Jesus.

129. "New Orleans Province. Augusta. Sacred Heart College," *Woodstock Letters* 36, no. 1 *Varia* (1907): 405.

130. F. William to New Orleans Mission Superior S.J., March 1, 1874, AR Files: 1043-K, Loyola University New Orleans, Monroe Library, Archives of the New Orleans Province, Society of Jesus.

131. J. M. Salter, "Our College at Augusta, Georgia," *Woodstock Letters* 34, no. 3 (1905): 382.

132. Kenny, *Jesuits in Our Southland, 1566–1946*, 129.

133. Ibid.

134. Edward J. Cashin, *The Story of the Sacred Heart* (Augusta: Sacred Heart Cultural Center, Streeter Printing and Graphics, 1987), 15–16.

135. Salter, "Our College at Augusta, Georgia," 381–82.

136. "New Orleans Mission, Augusta Ga. The New College," *Woodstock Letters* 30, no. 1 *Varia* (1901): 157.

137. Salter, "Our College at Augusta, Georgia," 384–85.

138. Edward J. Cashin, Peter S. Knox, Spyro Meimarides, Alexandra Ross Fenstermacher, and Roger H. Finch, *The Story of the Sacred Heart Cultural Center: 1874–1998, Augusta, Georgia* (Augusta: Manhattan Source Publishing, 1998), 11.

139. *Catalogue of the Officers and Students of the College of the Sacred Heart: Augusta, GA., 1903–1904* (Augusta: Richards and Shaver Co., Printers and Lithographers, 1904), Loyola University New Orleans, Monroe Library, Archives of the New Orleans Province, Society of Jesus.

140. Salter, "Our College at Augusta, Georgia," 383.

141. L. G. Bashnal, "The Flood at Augusta Ga. Sacred Heart College," *Woodstock Letters* 38, no. 1 (1909): 65–72.

142. Ibid.

143. Ibid.

144. *Augusta College Essay*, 1914, AR Files: 247, Loyola University New Orleans, Monroe Library, Archives of the New Orleans Province, Society of Jesus.

145. Cashin, *The Story of Sacred Heart*, 16.

146. "New Orleans Province. Augusta. Sacred Heart College," *Woodstock Letters* 36, no. 1 (1907): 406.

147. *Catalogue of the Officers and Students of the College of the Sacred Heart: Augusta, GA., 1912–1913* (Augusta, Georgia: Chronicle Job Print, 1913), Loyola University New Orleans, Monroe Library, Archives of the New Orleans Province, Society of Jesus

148. J. M. Salter, August 15, 1915, Account of the Closing of Augusta College, AR Files: 248, Loyola University New Orleans, Monroe Library, Archives of the New Orleans Province, Society of Jesus.

149. History of Sacred Heart Cadets of the Sacred Heart Parish, Augusta, GA. Folder: Sacred Heart, Augusta; Sacred Heart Cadets; Box: Sacred Heart, Augusta, Loyola University New Orleans, Monroe Library, Archives of the New Orleans Province, Society of Jesus.

150. Sacred Heart Cadets. Constitution and By-Laws. 1895. Folder: Sacred Heart, Augusta; Sacred Heart Cadets; Box: Sacred Heart, Augusta, Loyola University New Orleans, Monroe Library, Archives of the New Orleans Province, Society of Jesus.

151. Felicitas Powers, "Prejudice, Journalism, and the Catholic Laymen's Association of Georgia," *US Catholic Historian*, 8, no. 3 (1989): 201.

152. Rita H DeLorme, "Recalling an Epic Battle: Bishop Keiley, Sisters, and the Layman's Association versus the Veazey Law," *Southern Cross* (2006), 3.

153. Rose Margaret Scheers, "On Tom Watson and the Veazey Bill," Letter to the editor, the *Southern Cross* [Savanah, Georgia] March 18, 1999, 4.

154. Powers, "Prejudice, Journalism, and the Catholic Laymen's Association of Georgia," 205.

155. Ibid.

156. Scheers, "On Tom Watson and the Veazey Bill," 4.

157. "Augusta. Sacred Heart College," *Woodstock Letters* 45, no. 3 (1916): 447–48.

158. Thomas Shields, "Novitiate at Macon Destroyed by Fire" *Woodstock Letters* 51, no. 3 (1922): 348–50.

159. DeLorme, "Recalling an Epic Battle: Bishop Keiley, Sisters, and the Layman's Association versus the Veazey Law," 3.

160. Cashin, *The Story of Sacred Heart*, 16–17.

161. "Sacred Heart Cultural Center: Celebrating History, Art and Architecture." Accessed July 27, 2013. http://www.sacredheartaugusta.org/

Chapter 4

Epigraph: Albert Biever, *Diary and Notes on the Church of the Most Holy Name, Loyola College, and Loyola University New Orleans, 1904–1914*, Albert Biever Papers, Loyola University New Orleans, Monroe Library, Archives of the New Orleans Province, Society of Jesus, p. 158.

1. College of the Immaculate Conception, letterhead, January 18, 1862, Loyola University New Orleans, Monroe Library, Archives of the New Orleans Province, Society of Jesus.

2. Jean Baptiste Maisounabe, *Diary, 1847,* Maisounabe Papers, Loyola University New Orleans, Monroe Library, Archives of the New Orleans Province, Society of Jesus.

3. I. Timmreck and Francis L. Janssen, "Loyola University New Orleans: A Compen-

dium of Historical Information to Approximately 1974" (unpublished manuscript, 1974), Loyola University New Orleans, Monroe Library, Archives of the New Orleans Province, Society of Jesus, 12.

4. J. J. Obrien, Account of the Ursuline Loans to Jesuit Fathers, AR Files: 245, Loyola University New Orleans, Monroe Library, Archives of the New Orleans Province, Society of Jesus.

5. Michael Kenny, *Jesuits in Our Southland, 1566–1946: Origin and Growth of New Orleans Province,* 1946, Kenny Papers, Archives of the New Orleans Province, Society of Jesus, Loyola University Monroe Library, New Orleans, 50.

6. Albert Biever, *Diary and Notes on St. Charles College, Grand Coteau, 1837–1915,* Albert Biever Papers, Loyola University New Orleans, Monroe Library, Archives of the New Orleans Province, Society of Jesus, pp. 27–28.

7. Kenny, *Jesuits in Our Southland, 1566–1946,* 67.

8. *College of the Immaculate Conception: Corner of Common and Baronne Streets, New Orleans, 1910/1911,* catalogue, Jesuit High School Archives, New Orleans.

9. James F. Whelan, "Loyola University, New Orleans, Louisiana," *Southern Association Quarterly* 11 no. 4 (November 1946): 3.

10. Kenny, *Jesuits in Our Southland, 1566–1946,* 130.

11. Sherry, "Our Southern Houses During the Yellow Fever," *Woodstock Letters* 27, no. 1 (1898): 53.

12. "New Orleans Mission, College of the Immaculate Conception, N. Orleans," *Woodstock Letters* 30, no. 2 *Varia* (1901): 318–19.

13. Ned Hémard, "Taft Visits New Orleans," *New Orleans Nostalgia,* 2009, hrrp://www.neworleansbar.org/documents/TaftVisitsNewOrleansArticle.11–4.pdf, accessed October 16, 2012.

14. Timmreck and Janssen, "Loyola University New Orleans," 13.

15. "New Orleans Mission. College of the Immaculate Conception," *Woodstock Letters* 33, no. 1 *Varia* (1904): 408–9.

16. "New Orleans Mission. College of the Immaculate Conception," *Woodstock Letters* 31, no. 1 *Varia* (1902): 154.

17. "New Orleans Mission, New Orleans," *Woodstock Letters* 32, no. 2 *Varia* (1903): 278.

18. Whelan, "Loyola University, New Orleans, Louisiana," 2.

19. Ibid., 3.

20. *College of the Immaculate Conception: Corner of Common and Baronne Streets, New Orleans, 1910/1911,* catalogue, Jesuit High School Archives, New Orleans.

21. Ibid.

22. "New Orleans Mission. College of the Immaculate Conception, New Orleans," *Woodstock Letters* 31, no. 3 *Varia* (1902): 483.

23. "New Orleans Mission, College of the Immaculate Conception," *Woodstock Letters* 29, no. 1 *Varia* (1900): 188.

24. "New Orleans Mission: College of the Immaculate Conception, New Orleans," *Woodstock Letters* 34, no. 1 (1905): 108–9.

25. "Immaculate Conception College, New Orleans, New Villa," *Woodstock Letters* 34, no. 3 *Varia* (1905): 447.

26. "Immaculate Conception College," *Woodstock Letters* 35, no. 1 *Varia* (1906): 262.

27. "Burning of St. Charles' College," *Woodstock Letters* 36, no. 1 *Varia* (1907): 408.

28. Biever, *Diary and Notes on the Church of the Most Holy Name, Loyola College, and Loyola University New Orleans, 1904–1914*, Albert Biever Papers, Archives of the New Orleans Province, Society of Jesus, Monroe Library, Loyola University New Orleans, p. 157.

29. Ibid.

30. "The College, An Important Change," *Woodstock Letters* 41, no. 1 *Varia* (1912): 126–27.

31. Biever, *Diary and Notes on the Church of the Most Holy Name, Loyola College, and Loyola University New Orleans, 1904–1914*, p. 158.

32. *College of the Immaculate Conception: Corner of Common and Baronne Streets, New Orleans, 1911/1912*, catalogue, Jesuit High School Archives, New Orleans.

33. Ibid.

34. Timmreck and Janssen, "Loyola University New Orleans," 15, 31.

35. William Woods, "A New Jesuit High School," *Woodstock Letters* 56, no. 2 (1927): 329–30.

36. Ibid.

37. Fred W. Rickert to Rev. Harry L. Crane, S.J., Provincial, New Orleans, April 9, 1946, Loyola University New Orleans, Monroe Library, Archives of the New Orleans Province, Society of Jesus.

38. John Eaton, *Special Report by the Bureau of Education: Educational Exhibits and Conventions at the Worlds Industrial and Cotton Centennial Exposition* (Washington, DC: Government Printing Office, 1886), 5.

39. Ibid., 85–142.

40. Herbert S. Fairall, *Iowa at the Worlds Industrial and Cotton Centennial and the North Central and South American Expositions: New Orleans, 1884–6* (Des Moins: Geo. E. Roberts, State Printer, 1885), 26.

41. Eaton, *Special Report by the Bureau of Education*, 151–52.

42. Thomas Ruys Smith, *Southern Queen: New Orleans in the Nineteenth Century* (New York: Continuum International Publishing Group, 2011), 135.

43. Wogan and Bernard, *The Story of the Jesuits' Church Baronne St., 1847–1928* (New Orleans: Church of the Immaculate Conception, 1928), 18–19.

44. Albert Biever, *Diary and Notes on the Church of the Most Holy Name, Loyola College, and Loyola University New Orleans, 1904–1914*, p. 10.

45. Ibid., 2.

46. John O'Shanahan, Account of the Purchase of the Uptown Property, December 19, 1904, AR Files: 253, Loyola University New Orleans, Monroe Library, Archives of the New Orleans Province, Society of Jesus.

47. Biever, *Diary and Notes on the Church of the Most Holy Name, Loyola College, and Loyola University New Orleans, 1904–1914*, p. 2.

48. Ibid., 10.

49. Ibid.

50. Kenny, *Jesuits in Our Southland, 1566–1946*, 155.

51. "New Orleans Mission, A New College," *Woodstock Letters* 33, no. 2 *Varia* (1904): 253–254.

52. Ibid.

53. Biever, *Diary and Notes on the Church of the Most Holy Name, Loyola College, and Loyola University New Orleans, 1904–1914*, p. 2.

54. "A New Jesuit College Opposite Audubon Park," *Daily Picayune*, July 2, 1904.

55. Biever, *Diary and Notes on the Church of the Most Holy Name, Loyola College, and Loyola University New Orleans, 1904–1914*, p. 43.

56. Timmreck and Janssen, "Loyola University New Orleans," 21–22.

57. "New Orleans Mission, A New College," *Woodstock Letters* 33, no. 2 *Varia* (1904): 253–54.

58. Judge McGloin's Property, 1902, AR Files: 166, Loyola University New Orleans, Monroe Library, Archives of the New Orleans Province, Society of Jesus.

59. A. Morgan Brian, "Loyola 25th Anniversary: Founded in 1912 by Father Biever, Now Teaches 1800," *Action YMBC: Official Publication of the Young Men's Business Club of New Orleans* 6, no. 29 (March 1937): 13.

60. "New Orleans Mission, A New College," *Woodstock Letters* 33, no. 2 *Varia* (1904): 253–54.

61. Whelan, "Loyola University, New Orleans, Louisiana," 4.

62. "Auction Sales," *Daily Picayune*, May 1, 1904.

63. Biever, *Diary and Notes on the Church of the Most Holy Name, Loyola College, and Loyola University New Orleans, 1904–1914*, pp. 90–93.

64. *Loyola College: St. Charles Avenue Audubon, Park, 1904*, Loyola University New Orleans, Monroe Library, Archives of the New Orleans Province, Society of Jesus.

65. Biever, *Diary and Notes on the Church of the Most Holy Name, Loyola College, and Loyola University New Orleans, 1904–1914*, p. 64.

66. Ibid., 51–53.

67. Ibid

68. *Loyola College Catalogue*, Archives of the New Orleans Province, Society of Jesus.

69. Biever, *Diary and Notes on the Church of the Most Holy Name, Loyola College, and Loyola University New Orleans, 1904–1914*, p. 43.

70. Timmreck and Janssen, "Loyola University New Orleans," 24, 26.

71. P. A. Ryan, *An Eye Witness Account of Loyola University's First Beginnings and Pioneer Days*, October 28, 1956, AR Files: 292, Loyola University New Orleans, Monroe Library, Archives of the New Orleans Province, Society of Jesus.

72. *Loyola College Catalogue, St Charles Avenue Opposite Audubon Park, New Orleans, Louisiana, 1905–1906*, Box, Loyola University New Orleans, *Varia*, Loyola University New Orleans, Monroe Library, Archives of the New Orleans Province, Society of Jesus.

73. Ibid.

74. Ibid.

75. Charter of the Marquette Association for Higher Education, 1907, Box, Loyola University New Orleans, *Varia*, Loyola University New Orleans, Monroe Library, Archives of the New Orleans Province, Society of Jesus.

76. Biever, *Diary and Notes on the Church of the Most Holy Name, Loyola College, and Loyola University New Orleans, 1904–1914*, p. 72.

77. Ibid., 73.

78. Ibid., 76.

79. Ibid., 62.

80. Timmreck and Janssen, "Loyola University New Orleans," 29.

81. P. A. Ryan, journal, c.a. 1960, Box, Early Beginnings of Loyola University, Journal of Rev. P. A. Ryan, Loyola University New Orleans, Monroe Library, Archives of the New Orleans Province, Society of Jesus.

82. Ibid.

83. Thomas Clancy to Mike Alchediak, Archives of the New Orleans Province, Society of Jesus.

84. "The Progress of Twenty Five Years," *Woodstock Letters* 51, no. 1 (1922): 90.

85. *Catalogus Sociorum Et Officiorum Provinciae Lugdunensis Societatis Jesu, IMEUNTE ANNO MDCCCLXXX* (Lugduni: Ex Typis Catholicis, 1880); *Missio Neo-Aurelianensis Societatis Jesu, Ineunte Anno 1898* (Woodstock: Typis Collegii SS. Cordis, 1898); *Catalogus Provinciae Neo-Aurelianensis Societatis Jesu, Ineunte Anno 1908* (New Orleans, Louisiana: Perry & Buckley Co., 1908); *Catalogus Provincia Neo Aurelianensis Societatis Jesu, Ineunte Anno MCMXXIII* (El Paso, Texas: Ex typis "Revosfa Catolica," 1923).

86. *St. John's College: Vice Pres. Diary—1912–1930*, Archives of the New Orleans Province, Society of Jesus, Loyola University Monroe Library.

87. *St. John Berchman's Co-Cathedral, Diamond Jubilee 1902–1977*, Archives of the New Orleans Province, Society of Jesus, Loyola University, Monroe Library, p. 16.

88. *Sacred Heart Parish Centennial, Souvenir Program for Sacred Heart Parish Centennial, February, 21–23, 1960, Tampa Florida*, Archives of the New Orleans Province, Society of Jesus, Monroe Library, Loyola University New Orleans, 21.

89. *Historical Heart, Tampa, 1910–1950*, Sacred Heart College Notes, Box, Archives of the New Orleans Province, Society of Jesus, Monroe Library, Loyola University New Orleans.

90. Ibid.

Chapter 5

Epigraph: Norbert de Boynes, *Letter Addressed to the Fathers, Scholastics and Brothers of the New Orleans Province by Rev. Fr. Norbert de Boynes, S.J. At the Close of the Visitation, October 23rd., 1921*, Box, Fr. Norbert de Boynes, S.J. Visitation to New Orleans Province, Feb. 11–Oct. 23, 1921, Loyola University New Orleans, Monroe Library, Archives of the New Orleans Province, Society of Jesus.

1. C. M. Widman, "Springhill College," *Woodstock Letters* 27, no. 3 (1898): 268–76.

2. Ibid.

3. *Annals of Spring Hill College: Mobile, Alabama, 1830–1914*, Spring Hill College, Burke Library, Spring Hill College Archives and Special Collections, 1–2.

4. Joseph C. Mulhern, "Spring Hill Observes Centennial," *Woodstock Letters* 59, no. 2 (1930): 337.

5. Widman, "Springhill College," 268–76.

6. *Annals of Spring Hill College: Mobile, Alabama, 1830–1914*, 5.

7. Widman, "Springhill College," 268–76.

8. Ibid.

9. *Annals of Spring Hill College: Mobile, Alabama, 1830–1914*, 7.

10. Ibid., 8.

11. Jean Baptiste Maisounabe, *Diary, 1847*, Maisounabe Papers, Loyola University New Orleans, Monroe Library, Archives of the New Orleans Province, Society of Jesus.

12. Widman, "Springhill College," 268–276.

13. Maisounabe, *Diary, 1847*, Archives of the New Orleans Province, Society of Jesus.

14. Widman, "Springhill College," 272.

15. Ibid., 268–72.

16. *Annals of Spring Hill College: Mobile, Alabama, 1830–1914*, 10.

17. Widman, "Springhill College," 272.

18. Michael Portier to the Jesuit Fathers, Spring Hill College, May 31, 1857, AR Files: 1, Loyola University New Orleans, Monroe Library, Archives of the New Orleans Province, Society of Jesus.

19. Albert Biever, *Diary and Notes on Spring Hill College, Mobile, 1878–1885*, Albert Biever Papers, Loyola University New Orleans, Monroe Library, Archives of the New Orleans Province, Society of Jesus, p. 168.

20. Ibid.

21. Ibid., 164, 168.

22. Louis Curioz, Superior's Correspondence, New Orleans Mission, 1859–1862.

23. Michael Kenny, *Jesuits in Our Southland 1566–1946: Origin and Growth of New Orleans Province*, 1946, Kenny Papers, Archives of the New Orleans Province, Society of Jesus, Loyola University Monroe Library, New Orleans, 45.

24. Maisounabe, *Diary, 1847*, Archives of the New Orleans Province, Society of Jesus.

25. Louis Curioz, Superior's correspondence, New Orleans Mission, 1859–1862.

26. Ibid.

27. Joseph C. Mulhern, "Spring Hill Observes Centennial," *Woodstock Letters* 59, no. 2 (1930): 339–42.

28. Louis Curioz, Superior's correspondence, New Orleans Mission, 1859–1862.

29. Michael Kenny, *The Torch on the Hill: Centenary Story of Spring Hill College, 1830–1930* (New York: The American Press, 1931), 90.

30. Ibid., 212.

31. *Annals of Spring Hill College: Mobile, Alabama, 1830–1914*, 7.

32. Louis Curioz, Superior's correspondence, New Orleans Mission, 1859–1862.

33. *Annals of Spring Hill College: Mobile, Alabama, 1830–1914*, 13–15.

34. Biever, *Diary and Notes on Spring Hill College, Mobile, 1878–1885*, p. 169.

35. Widman, "Springhill College," *Woodstock Letters* 27, no. 3 (1898): 268–76.

36. Ibid.

37. "St. Charles' College, Grand Coteau, LA," *Woodstock Letters* 5, no. 1 (1876): 25.

38. Widman, "Springhill College," 273–76.

39. Ibid.

40. John Sherry, "Our Southern Houses during the Yellow Fever," *Woodstock Letters* 27, no. 1 (1898): 61–62.

41. Biever, *Diary and Notes on Spring Hill College, Mobile, 1878–1885*, pp. 142–43.

42. "Spring Hill," *Woodstock Letters* 30, no. 2 *Varia* (1901): 319.

43. "Springhill College, Mobile, Ala.," *Woodstock Letters* 31, no. 1 *Varia* (1902): 154–55.

44. Ibid., 154.

45. "Spring Hill College," *Woodstock Letters* 32, no. 2 *Varia* (1903): 278–79.

46. *Annals of Spring Hill College: Mobile, Alabama, 1830–1914*, 22.

47. "Spring Hill," *Woodstock Letters* 34, no. 3 *Varia* (1905): 447–48.

48. *Annals of Spring Hill College: Mobile, Alabama, 1830–1914*, 26.

49. Ibid., 28.

50. *Annals of Spring Hill College: Mobile, Alabama, 1830–1914*, 30.

51. "Spring Hill Ala.," *Woodstock Letters* 44, no. 1 *Varia* (1915): 128–29.

52. Vice President's House Diary, Spring Hill College, 1911–1943, Spring Hill College, Burke Library, Spring Hill College Archives and Special Collections, 174.

53. J. W. R. Maguire to the Registrar, Spring Hill College, January 7, 1926, Spring Hill College, Burke Library, Spring Hill College Archives and Special Collections.

54. Juniors' Newsletter, January 1930, Loyola University New Orleans, Monroe Library, Archives of the New Orleans Province, Society of Jesus.

55. Sacra Congregatio de Seminariis et Studiorum Universitatibus to the Rector, Spring Hill College, March 20, 1931, Spring Hill College, Burke Library, Spring Hill College Archives and Special Collections.

56. J. M. Walsh to Cajeton Cardinal Bilseti, Sacred Congregation of Seminaries and Universities, Rome, Italy, June 22, 1931, Spring Hill College, Burke Library, Spring Hill College Archives and Special Collections.

57. Ibid.

58. Mulhern, "Spring Hill Observes Centennial," 337

59. Ibid., 345.

60. Kenny, *Jesuits in Our Southland, 1566–1946*, 189.

61. A. Biever and P. A. Ryan, Announcement: Loyola University, New Orleans, August 24, 1911, AR Files: 1372, Loyola University New Orleans, Monroe Library, Archives of the New Orleans Province, Society of Jesus.

62. Ibid.

63. I. Timmreck and Francis L. Janssen, "Loyola University New Orleans: A Compendium of Historical Information to Approximately 1974" (unpublished manuscript, 1974), Loyola University New Orleans, Monroe Library, Archives of the New Orleans Province, Society of Jesus, 3.

64. "Work for University," *Times Democrat*, June 10, 1909.

65. "Marquette Association Plans New Church at Loyola College," *Daily Picayune*, January 26, 1912.

66. "Movement for Great University Launched by Priests and Laymen," *Times Democrat*, March 27, 1907.

67. Biever, *Diary and Notes on the Church of the Most Holy Name, Loyola College, and Loyola University New Orleans, 1904–1914*, p. 80.

68. Ibid., 51.

69. Ibid.

70. Ibid.

71. Ibid., 165.

72. "Miss McDermott Gift of Church to Loyola," *Daily Picayune*, March 12, 1913.

73. "New Orleans. The College. An Important Change," *Woodstock Letters* 41, no. 1 *Varia* (1912): 127.

74. "New Orleans. The New University," *Woodstock Letters* 39, no. 3 *Varia* (1910): 418.

75. "New Orleans Province. New Orleans. Laying of Corner Stone of the New University," *Woodstock Letters* 40, no. 1 *Varia* (1911): 119–120.

76. Albert Biever, *Diary and Notes on the Church of the Most Holy Name, Loyola College, and Loyola University New Orleans, 1904–1914*, pp. 134, 136.

77. "Turns Earth for Great University," *Times Democrat*, August 1, 1910.

78. "Faculties Announced: Corps of Jesuit University and College Determined," *Times Democrat*, August 18, 1911.

79. Ibid.

80. Ibid.

81. Biever, *Diary and Notes on the Church of the Most Holy Name, Loyola College, and Loyola University New Orleans, 1904–1914*, p. 150.

82. P. A. Ryan, journal, c.a. 1960, Box, Early Beginnings of Loyola University, Journal of Rev. P. A. Ryan, Loyola University New Orleans, Monroe Library, Archives of the New Orleans Province, Society of Jesus, 6.

83. Biever, *Diary and Notes on the Church of the Most Holy Name, Loyola College, and Loyola University New Orleans, 1904–1914*, pp. 152–53.

84. Ibid.

85. James Blenk to Albert Biever, March 14, 1912, AR Files: 1431, Loyola University New Orleans, Monroe Library, Archives of the New Orleans Province, Society of Jesus.

86. Ryan, journal, 17.

87. Charter of Loyola University, 1913, Loyola University New Orleans, Monroe Library, Archives of the New Orleans Province, Society of Jesus.

88. James F. Whelan, "Loyola University, New Orleans, Louisiana," *Southern Association Quarterly* 11 no. 4 (November 1946): 5.

89. James Blenk to Albert Biever, May 15, 1912, Loyola University New Orleans, Monroe Library, Archives of the New Orleans Province, Society of Jesus.

90. "Catholic Education in Louisiana," *Morning Star*, June 29, 1912.

91. "Loyola University," *Times Democrat*, October 26, 1913.

92. Ibid.

93. Ibid.

94. "Loyola University," *Times Democrat*, October 26, 1913.

95. Biever, *Diary and Notes on the Church of the Most Holy Name, Loyola College, and Loyola University New Orleans, 1904–1914*, pp. 139–42.

96. Timmreck and Janssen, "Loyola University New Orleans." 209.

97. Ibid., 41.

98. Ryan, journal, 19.

99. "Loyola University. Opening of the Law School," *Woodstock Letters* 44, no. 1 *Varia* (1915): 130–31.

100. Ibid.

101. "New Orleans. Loyola University Annexes the New Orleans College of Pharmacy," *Woodstock Letters* 42, no. 1 *Varia* (1913): 123–24.

102. Ibid.

103. "Loyola Welcomes Pharmacy School: Adds a Hundred Pupils and Department Already Widely Known. Fast Growth Hailed," *Morning Star*, June 29, 1912.

104. Timmreck and Janssen, "Loyola University New Orleans," 41.

105. "Loyola University," *Woodstock Letters* 44, no. 3 *Varia* (1915): 440.

106. Timmreck and Janssen, "Loyola University New Orleans," 42–43.

107. Brian, "Loyola 25th Anniversary: Founded in 1912 by Father Biever, Now Teaches 1800," 12.

108. Charles Duchauf, Speech Given on the Jesuit System of Education and the Participation of American Catholics in the First World War, on June 16, 1918, to the Jesuits of the New Orleans Province, Jesuit Alumni, and Citizens of New Orleans, AR Files: 1063, Loyola University New Orleans, Monroe Library, Archives of the New Orleans Province, Society of Jesus.

109. "Loyola Launches Drive for Funds for 5 Buildings," *Times Picayune*, December 4, 1921.

110. Kenny, *Jesuits in Our Southland, 1566–1946*, 187.

111. "Slogan for Loyola Building Campaign," *New Orleans Item*, April 23, 1922.

112. "The Clock Should Go Fast," *Times Picayune*, May 10, 1922.

113. "Encroaching in Man's Field," *New Orleans Item*, May 14, 1922.

114. "Women Active in Loyola's Aid: Plan to Continue Gatherings in Behalf of Fund for Buildings," *Times Picayune*, May 31, 1922.

115. Timmreck and Janssen, "Loyola University New Orleans." 49.

116. Ibid., 49–52.

117. Regent of the Dental School, Loyola University to Mr. Leonard of the Carnegie Corporation, October 20, 1922, Loyola University New Orleans, Monroe Library, Archives of the New Orleans Province, Society of Jesus.

118. Ibid.

119. Mary Jameson, "Loyola's Dental School Existed for 57 Years," *The Maroon*, http://www.loyolamaroon.com/2.6710/loyola-s-dental-school-existed-for-57-years-1.2728713#.UNt7KYXPa3k, accessed April 12, 2012.

120. "Our History," LSU Health Sciences Center New Orleans, School of Dentistry, http://www.lsusd.lsuhsc.edu/history.html, accessed December 26, 2012.

121. Woods, "A New Jesuit High School," *Woodstock Letters* 56, no. 2 (1927): 329–30.

122. Timmreck and Janssen, "Loyola University New Orleans," 217–18.

123. Ibid., 66.

124. "Recognitions," *Woodstock Letters* 59, no. 2 *Varia* (1930): 279–80.

125. Juniors' Newsletter, January 1930, Loyola University New Orleans, Monroe Library, Archives of the New Orleans Province, Society of Jesus.

126. Timmreck and Janssen, "Loyola University New Orleans," 59–60.

127. Whelan, "Loyola University, New Orleans, Louisiana," 9.

128. Timmreck and Janssen, "Loyola University New Orleans," 66.

129. Whelan, "Loyola University, New Orleans, Louisiana," 62.

130. Seal of Loyola University New Orleans, 1929, Loyola University New Orleans, Monroe Library, Archives of the New Orleans Province, Society of Jesus; Friedrich Rest, *Our Christian Symbols* (Cleveland, Ohio: The Pilgrim Press, 1954), 10.

131. "Silver Jubilee of Loyola University," *Times Picayune*, April 10, 1937.

132. Martha Carr, *Tom Benson Gives Loyola $8 Million for Jesuit Center*, 2010, available from http://www.nola.com/education/index.ssf/2010/09/benson_gives_loyola_8_million.html accessed April 16, 2011.

133. De Boynes, *Letter Addressed to the Fathers, Scholastics and Brothers of the New Orleans Province by Rev. Fr. Norbert de Boynes, S.J. At the Close of the Visitation, October 23rd.,*

1921, Box, Fr. Norbert de Boynes, S.J.: Visitation to New Orleans Province, Feb. 11–Oct. 23, 1921, Loyola University New Orleans, Monroe Library, Archives of the New Orleans Province, Society of Jesus.

Conclusion

Epigraph: Norbert de Boynes, *Letter Addressed to the Fathers, Scholastics and Brothers of the New Orleans Province by Rev. Fr. Norbert de Boynes, S.J. At the Close of the Visitation, October 23rd., 1921*, Box, Fr. Norbert de Boynes, S.J. Visitation to New Orleans Province, Feb. 11–Oct. 23, 1921, Loyola University New Orleans, Monroe Library, Archives of the New Orleans Province, Society of Jesus.

1. Alice W. Brown and contributors, *Cautionary Tales: Strategy Lessons from Struggling Colleges* (Sterling, Virginia: Stylus Publishing, LLC., 2012), 28–29.

2. Kathleen Mahoney, *Catholic Higher Education in Protestant America: The Jesuits and Harvard in the Age of the University* (Baltimore: Johns Hopkins University Press, 2003), 241.

3. Thomas Bender, ed., *The University and the City: From Medieval Origins to the Present* (New York, Oxford: Oxford University Press, 1988), 291.

4. Jeffrey Pfeffer and Gerald R. Salancik, *The External Control of Organizations: A Resource Dependence Prospective* (New York: Harper and Row, 1978), 2.

Appendix

1. Norbert de Boynes, *Letter Addressed to the Fathers, Scholastics and Brothers of the New Orleans Province by Rev. Fr. Norbert de Boynes, S.J. At the Close of the Visitation, October 23rd., 1921*, 1921, Box, Fr. Norbert de Boynes, S.J.: Visitation to New Orleans Province, Feb. 11—Oct. 23, 1921, Loyola University New Orleans, Monroe Library, Archives of the New Orleans Province, Society of Jesus.

Bibliography

Archival Sources

Albert Biever Papers. Archives of the New Orleans Province, Society of Jesus, Monroe Library, Loyola University New Orleans, New Orleans, LA.

Archives of the New Orleans Province, Society of Jesus, Monroe Library, Loyola University New Orleans, New Orleans, LA.

Clancy Papers. Archives of the New Orleans Province, Society of Jesus, Monroe Library, Loyola University New Orleans, New Orleans, LA.

Jesuit High School Archives, New Orleans, LA.

Kenny Papers. Archives of the New Orleans Province, Society of Jesus, Monroe Library, Loyola University New Orleans, New Orleans, LA.

Maisounabe Papers. Archives of the New Orleans Province, Society of Jesus, Monroe Library, Loyola University New Orleans, New Orleans, LA.

Spring Hill College Archives and Special Collections. Burke Library. Spring Hill College, Mobile, AL.

Selected Primary Sources

"Augusta. Sacred Heart College." *Woodstock Letters* 45, no. 3 *Varia* (1916): 447–48.

Bashnal, L. G. "The Flood at Augusta Ga. Sacred Heart College." *Woodstock Letters* 38, no. 1 (1909): 65–72.

Beck, Peter. "Decree of Father General Becker." AR Files: 66. Loyola University New Orleans, Monroe Library, Archives of the New Orleans Province, Society of Jesus.

Brian, Morgan A. "Loyola 25th Anniversary: Founded in 1912 by Father Biever, Now Teaches 1800." *Action YMBC: Official Publication of the Young Men's Business Club of New Orleans* 6, no. 29 (March 1937): 11–14.

"Burning of St. Charles' College." *Woodstock Letters* 36, no. 1 *Varia* (1907): 406–8.

Carroll, James D. "The Mississippi Flood Disaster." *Woodstock Letters* 57, no. 1 (1928): 39–54.

"The College, An Important Change." *Woodstock Letters* 41, no. 1 (1912): 126–27.

Crosby, Donald E. "Jesuits Go Home: The Anti-Jesuit Movement in the United States, 1830–1860." *Woodstock Letters* 97, no. 1 (1968): 225–40.

Gache, L. H. "Our College at Baton Rouge, Louisiana." *Woodstock Letters* 27, no.1 (1898): 1–6.

"Galveston." *Woodstock Letters* 23 no. 1 (1894): 187–88.

"Galveston." *Woodstock Letters* 31, no. 3 *Varia* (1902): 483.

"Galveston." *Woodstock Letters* 33, no. 2 *Varia* (1904): 254.

"Galveston. St. Mary's University. Refugees from Mexico." *Woodstock Letters* 44, no. 1 *Varia* (1915): 129–30.

"Galveston, Tex." *Woodstock Letters* 30, no. 2 *Varia* (1901): 320.

"Grand Coteau." *Woodstock Letters* 30, no. 2 (1901): 319–20.

"Grand Coteau. St. Charles' College." *Woodstock Letters* 36, no. 1 *Varia* (1907): 406–8.

"Grand Coteau." *Woodstock Letters* 42, no. 1 *Varia* (1913): 123.

"Grand Coteau. St. Charles' College. Ours of the Secular Clergy." *Woodstock Letters* 44, no. 1 *Varia* (1915): 130.

"Grand Coteau. St. Charles' College. Retreats for Lay-men." *Woodstock Letters* 45, no. 3 *Varia* (1916): 448.

"Grand Coteau—St. Charles' College Wins High Honor in Victory Loan Drive—R.O.T.C. Wins Fourth Place Among Other Units in United States." *Woodstock Letters* 48, no. 2 *Varia* (1919): 434–35.

Hogan, J. H. "Reminiscences of the Galveston Storm." *Woodstock Letters* 29, no. 3 (1900): 428–47.

"Immaculate Conception College." *Woodstock Letters* 35, no. 1 *Varia* (1906): 262–63.

"Immaculate Conception College, New Orleans, New Villa." *Woodstock Letters* 34, no. 3 Varia; K., M. "Galveston. St. Mary's University, Galveston, Texas, New Year's Day, 1890," *Woodstock Letters* 19 no. 1 (1890): 75–80.

K., P. J. "Louisiana: A Short Account of the Society in New Orleans." *Woodstock Letters* 14, no. 3 (1885): 317–30.

"Loyola University." *Woodstock Letters* 44, no. 3 (1915): 440.

"Loyola University. Opening of the Law School." *Woodstock Letters* 44, no. 1 *Varia* (1915): 130–31.

Maitrugues, J. "St. Charles' College, Grand Coteau, La." *Woodstock Letters* 5, no. 1 (1876): 3–29.

Missio Neo-Aurelianensis Societatis Jesu. Ineunte Anno 1898. Woodstock: Typis Collegii SS. Cordis, 1898.

Mulhern, Joseph C. "Spring Hill Observes Centennial." *Woodstock Letters* 59, no. 2 (1930): 335–46.

"New Orleans: Grand Coteau—*St. Charles College Wins High Honor in Victory Loan Drive – R.O.T.C. Wins Fourth Place Among All Other Units in the United States*." *Woodstock Letters* 48 no. 2 (1919): 434–35.

"New Orleans. Loyola University Annexes the New Orleans College of Pharmacy." *Woodstock Letters* 42, no. 1 *Varia* (1913): 123–24.

"New Orleans Mission, A New College." *Woodstock Letters* 33, no. 2 *Varia* (1904): 253–54.

"New Orleans Mission, Augusta Ga. The New College." *Woodstock Letters* 30, no. 1 *Varia* (1901): 156–57.

"New Orleans Mission, College of the Immaculate Conception." *Woodstock Letters* 29, no. 1 *Varia* (1900): 188.

"New Orleans Mission. College of the Immaculate Conception." *Woodstock Letters* 31, no. 1 *Varia* (1902): 154.

"New Orleans Mission. College of the Immaculate Conception." *Woodstock Letters* 33, no. 1 *Varia (*1904): 408–9.

"New Orleans Mission, College of the Immaculate Conception, N. Orleans." *Woodstock Letters* 30, no. 2 *Varia* (1901): 318–19.

"New Orleans Mission. College of the Immaculate Conception, New Orleans." *Woodstock Letters* 31, no. 3 *Varia* (1902): 482–83.

"New Orleans Mission: College of the Immaculate Conception, New Orleans." *Woodstock Letters* 34, no. 1 (1905): 108–10.

"New Orleans Mission. Galveston. Jubilee of the Parish and the University." *Woodstock Letters* 38, no. 3 *Varia* (1909): 440.

"New Orleans Mission, New Orleans." *Woodstock Letters* 32, no. 2 *Varia* (1903): 278.

"New Orleans Mission: St. Mary's Church, Galveston." *Woodstock Letters* 34, no. 1 (1905): 110.

"New Orleans Mission, St. Mary's College, Galveston." *Woodstock Letters* 27, no. 2 *Varia* (1898): 403.

"New Orleans Province. Augusta. Sacred Heart College." *Woodstock Letters* 36, no. 1 *Varia* (1907): 405–6.

"New Orleans Province. New Orleans. Laying of Corner Stone of the New University." *Woodstock Letters* 40, no. 1 *Varia* (1911): 119–21.

"New Orleans. The College. An Important Change." *Woodstock Letters* 41, no. 1 *Varia* (1912): 126–27.

"New Orleans. The New University." *Woodstock Letters* 39, no. 3 *Varia* (1910): 418.

"The Progress of Twenty Five Years." *Woodstock Letters* 51, no. 1 (1922): 81–98.

Quinlan, John B. "Galveston, Texas." *Woodstock Letters* 16, no. 1 (1887): 282–83.

"The Ratio Studiorum and the American College." *Woodstock Letters* 26, no. 3 (1897): 369–78.

"The Ratio Studiorum and the American College (Second Paper)." *Woodstock Letters* 22, no. 2 (1898): 182–90.

"Recognitions." *Woodstock Letters* 59, no. 2 (1930): 279–80.

Salter, J. M. "Our College at Augusta, Georgia." *Woodstock Letters* 34 no. 3 (1905): 381–385.

Shields, Thomas. "Novitiate at Macon Destroyed by Fire." *Woodstock Letters* 51, no. 3 (1992): 347–51.

Sherry, John. "Our Southern Houses During the Yellow Fever." *Woodstock Letters* 27, no. 1 (1898): 53–63.

"The Society and Her Martyrs Honored." *Woodstock Letters* 55, no. 2 (1926): 307–8.

"Spring Hill." *Woodstock Letters* 30, no. 2 *Varia* (1901): 319.

"Spring Hill." *Woodstock Letters* 34, no. 3 *Varia* (1905): 447–48.

"Spring Hill Ala." *Woodstock Letters* 44, no. 1 *Varia* (1915): 128–29.
"Spring Hill College." *Woodstock Letters* 32, no. 2 *Varia* (1903): 278–79.
"Springhill College, Mobile, Ala." *Woodstock Letters* 31, no. 1 *Varia* (1902): 154–55. "St. Charles' College." *Woodstock Letters* 46, no. 1 *Varia* (1917): 137.
"St. Charles' College, Grand Coteau, LA." *Woodstock Letters* 5, no. 1 (1876): 17–29.
2011 *Catalog of the Provinces of Jesus in the United States of America.* Jesuit Conference, 2010.
Widman, C. M. "Grand Coteau College in War Times, 1860–1866." *Woodstock Letters* 30, no. 1 (1901): 34–49.
———. "Springhill College." *Woodstock Letters* 27, no. 3 (1898): 267–76.
Wogan and Bernard. *The Story of the Church of the Immaculate Conception (Jesuits) Baronne Street, 1847–1928.* New Orleans, Louisiana: Church of the Immaculate Conception, 1928.
Woods, William. "A New Jesuit High School." *Woodstock Letters* 56, no. 2 (1927): 329–30.

Newspapers

New Orleans (LA) *Daily Picayune*
New Orleans (LA) *Maroon*
New Orleans (LA) *Morning Star*
New Orleans (LA) *New Orleans Item*
New Orleans (LA) *Times Democrat*
New Orleans (LA) *Times Picayune*

Secondary Sources

Albert, S., and D. A. Whetten, "Organizational Identity." In *Organizational Identity in Practice*, edited by Lin Lerpold, David Ravasi, Johan van Rekom, and Guillaume Soenen, 1–18. New York: Routledge, 2007.
Allen M. *The Goals of Universities.* Milton Keyes, UK: SRHE and Open University Press, 1988.
American Academy of Arts & Sciences. "Town and Gown: The Urban Community and the University Community." *Bulletin of the American Academy of Arts and Sciences* 22, no. 6 (April 1969): 2–10.
Anderson, James. *The Education of Blacks in the South, 1860–1935.* Chapel Hill: University of North Carolina Press, 1988.
Anderson, R. Bentley. *Black, White, and Catholic: New Orleans Interracialism, 1947–1956.* Nashville: Vanderbilt University Press, 2005.
Angers, Trent. *Grand Coteau: The Holy Land of South Louisiana.* Lafayette: Acadian House Publishing, 2005.
Arrupe, Pedro. "The Jesuit Apostolate in Education." *Jesuit Educational Quarterly* (June 1966): 5–6.
Attridge, Harold W. "Reflections on the Mission of a Catholic University." In *The Challenge and Promise of a Catholic University*, edited by Theodore M. Hesburgh, 13–25. Notre Dame: University of Notre Dame Press, 1994.

Balestra, Dominic J. "Where Loyalties Lie?" *Conversations on Jesuit Higher Education* (Fall 2003): 10.

Bangert, William V. *A History of the Jesuits*. Saint Louis: Institute of Jesuit Resources, 1972.

Barr, Stringfellow. "The Republic of Letters: Town and Gown." *Journal of Higher Education* 34, no. 6 (June 1963): 301–10.

Barry, William A. "Prayer as Conscious Relationship." In *An Ignatian Spiritual Reader*, edited by George W. Traub, 99–103. Chicago: Loyola Press, 2008.

Bartllori, Miguel. "Some International Aspects of the Activity of the Jesuits in the New World." *Americas* 14, no. 4 (April 1958): 432–36.

Bartoli, Daniel. *History of the Life and Institute of St. Ignatius De Loyola, Founder of the Society of Jesus*. New York: Edward Dunigan and Brother, 1855.

Baudier, Roger. *The Catholic Church in Louisiana*. New Orleans: Louisiana Library Association Public Library Section, 1939.

Bender, Thomas, ed., *The University and the City: From Medieval Origins to the Present*. New York: Oxford University Press, 1988.

Bernard, Miguel A. "The Class of 'Humanities' in the *Ratio Studiorum*." *Jesuit Educational Quarterly* 15, no. 4 (1953): 197–205.

Bess, James L., and Jay R. Dee. *Understanding College and University Organization: Theories for Affective Policy and Practice*. Sterling, VA: Stylus Publishing, 2008.

Biever, Albert H. *The Jesuits in New Orleans and the Mississippi Valley: Jubilee Memorial*. New Orleans, 1924.

Billington, Ray Allen. "Maria Monk and Her Influence." *Catholic Historical Review* 22, no. 3 (October 1936): 283–96.

Boyle, Charles J. *Gleanings from the Spring Hill College Archives*. Mobile: Friends of Spring Hill College Library, 2004.

———. *The Origins of the Jesuits*. Chicago: Loyola Press, 1997.

Brown, Alice W & Contributors. *Cautionary Tales: Strategy Lessons from Struggling Colleges*. Sterling, Virginia: Stylus Publishing, LLC., 2012.

Brown, Ray. *List of Colleges that Have Closed, Merged, or Changed Their Names*. http://www2.westminstermo.edu/wc_users/homepages/staff/brownr/closedcollegeindex.htm, accessed August 10, 2012.

Buckley, Cornelius M. *A Frenchman, A Chaplain, A Rebel: The War Letters of Pere Louis-Hippolyte Gache, S.J.* Chicago: Loyola University Press, 1981.

Burke, Colin B. *American Collegiate Populations: A Test of the Traditional View*. New York: New York University Press, 1982.

Byron, William J. "A Religious-Based College and University Perspective." In *Civic Responsibility and Higher Education*, edited by Thomas Ehrlich, 279–94. Phoenix, Arizona: Oryx Press, 2000.

Carnegie Foundation for the Advancement of Teaching. *More Than Survival: Prospects for Higher Education in a Period of Uncertainty*. San Francisco, Washington, London: Jossey-Bass Publishers, 1975.

Carr, Martha. 2010. *Tom Benson Gives Loyola $8 Million for Jesuit Center*. file:///Users/ericplatt/Desktop/Dissertation%20Docs/Dissertation%20Chapter%20Seven/benson_gives_loyola_8_million.html, accessed April 16, 2011.

Carriere, Oliver P. *A Sketch of the History of Jefferson College and Manresa House of Retreats Convent, Louisiana*. Convent, LA: Manresa House of Retreats, 1974.

Cashin, Edward J. *The Story of the Sacred Heart*. Sacred Heart Cultural Center. Augusta, GA: Streeter Printing and Graphics, 1987.

Cashin, Edward J., Peter S. Knox, Spyro Meimarides, Alexandra Ross Fenstermacher, and Roger H. Finch. *The Story of the Sacred Heart Cultural Center, 1874–1998, Augusta, Georgia*. Augusta, GA: Manhattan Source, 1998.

"Cathedral of St. Joseph, Baton Rouge, Louisiana." St. Joseph Cathedral. http://www.cathedralofstjoseph.org/, accessed April 23, 2012.

The Catholic Church in the United States of America: To Celebrate the Golden Jubilee of His Holiness, Pope Pius X. New York: Catholic Editing Company, 1908.

Chait, Richard. "College Mission Statements." *Science* 205, no. 4410 (September 1979): 957.

Clancy, Thomas. *An Introduction to Jesuit Life, The Constitutions and History through 435 Years*. St. Louis: Institute of Jesuit Sources, 1976.

———. "The Antebellum Jesuits of the New Orleans Province, 1837–1861." *The Journal of the Louisiana Historical Association* 34 no. 3 (Summer, 1993): 329–330.

———. *Our Friends*, 3rd ed. New Orleans, Louisiana: Jesuit Provincial Residence, 1998.

———. *The Last 150 Years*. http:/norprove.org/identity/last150yrs.htm, accessed November 24, 2009.

Clark, Emily. *Masterless Mistresses: The New Orleans Ursulines and the Development of a New Society, 1727–1834*. Williamsburg: University of North Carolina Press, 2007.

———. *Voices from an Early American Convent: Marie Madeleine Hachard and the New Orleans Ursulines, 1727–1760*. Baton Rouge: Louisiana State University Press, 2007.

Claval, Paul. "Politics and the University." In *The Urban University and Its Identity: Roots, Locations, Roles*, edited by Herman van der Wusten, 29–46. Boston: Kluwer Academic, 1998.

Cline, Rodney. *Pioneer Leaders and Early Institutions in Louisiana Education*. Baton Rouge: Claitor's Publishing Division, 1969.

Decloux, Simon. *The Ignatian Way*. Translated by Cornelius M. Buckley. Chicago: Loyola Press, 1983.

Delanglez, Jean. "The Jesuits and Education in Louisiana during the Eighteenth Century." *Jesuit Educational Quarterly* 7, no. 1 (June 1944): 14–19.

DeLorme, Rita H. "Recalling an Epic Battle: Bishop Keiley, Sisters, and the Layman's Association versus the Veazey Law." *Southern Cross* (July 2006): 3.

Devlin, Eugene J. "Character Formation in the *Ratio Studiorum*." *Jesuit Educational Quarterly* 15, no. 4 (1953): 213–22.

Diamond, Michael A. *The Unconscious Life of Organizations: Interpreting Organizational Identity*. Westport, CT: Quorum Books, 1993.

"Discover Loyola." Loyola University New Orleans. http://www.loyno.edu/discover/, accessed April 23, 2012.

Douglas, John Aubrey. *The California Idea and American Higher Education: 1850 to the 1960 Master Plan*. Stanford: Stanford University Press, 2000.

Dressel, Paul L. "Mission, Organization, and Leadership." *Journal of Higher Education* 58, no. 1 (January–February 1987): 101–9.

Dyer, Thomas G. "Higher Education in the South since the Civil War: Historiographical Issues and Trends." In *The Web of Southern Social Relations: Women, Family, and Edu-*

cation, edited by Walter J. Fraser Jr., R. Frank Saunders Jr., and Jon L. Wakelyn, 127–45. Athens: University of Georgia Press, 1987.

Eaton, John. *Special Report by the Bureau of Education: Educational Exhibits and Conventions at the Worlds Industrial and Cotton Centennial Exposition.* Washington, DC: Government Printing Office, 1886.

Eckert, Penelope, and Etienne Wenger. "From School to Work: an Apprenticeship in Institutional Identity." *Institute for Research on Learning* 1 (1994): 2–19.

Fairall, Herbert S. *Iowa at the World's Industrial Cotton Centennial and the North Central and South American Exposition*. Des Moines: Geo. E. Roberts, State Printer, 1885.

Farrell, Allan P. "Four Hundred Years of Jesuit Education." *Jesuit Educational Quarterly* 3, no. 2 (1940): 125.

———, trans. *The Jesuit Ratio Studiorum of 1599*. Washington, DC: Conference of Major Superiors of Jesuits, 1970.

———. "Notes on Jesuit Teaching Procedures." *Jesuit Educational Quarterly* 5, no. 4 (1943): 237–42.

Fay, Edwin Whitfield. *The History of Education in Louisiana*. Washington, DC: Government Printing Office, 1898.

Fjortoft, Nancey, and John C. Smart. "Enhancing Organizational Effectiveness: The Importance of Culture Type and Mission Agreement." *Higher Education* 27, no. 4 (June 1994): 429–47.

Ganss, George E. "St. Ignatius' Constitutions and the Spirit of the *Ratio*." *Jesuit Educational Quarterly* 17, no. 2 (1954): 69–82.

———. *Saint Ignatius' Idea of a Jesuit University*. Milwaukee: Marquette University Press, 1956.

Garraghan, Gilbert J. *The Jesuits of the Middle United States,* Vol. 3. New York: American Press, 1938.

Gleason, Philip. *Contending with Modernity: Catholic Higher Education in the Twentieth Century*. New York: Oxford University Press, 1995.

———. "What Made Catholic Identity a Problem." In *The Challenge and Promise of a Catholic University*, edited by Theodore M. Hesburgh, 91–102. Notre Dame: University of Notre Dame Press, 1994.

Gioia, Denniss A., Majken Schultz, and Kevin G. Corely. "Organizational Identity, Image, and Adaptive Instability." *Academy of Management Review* 25, no. 1 (2000): 63–81.

Go Forth and Teach: The Characteristics of Jesuit Education. Washington, DC: Jesuit Secondary Education Association, 1987.

Good, H. G. "Historical Research in Education." *Educational Research Bulletin* 9, no. 1 (January 1930): 7–18.

Hardin, Edward, "Record of the Jesuit Expulsion from Louisiana." *Journal of the Louisiana Historical Association* 9, no. 2 (Spring,1968): 108.

Hebert, Adam Otis. "History of Education in Colonial Louisiana." Master's thesis, Louisiana State University, 1958.

Hémard, Ned. "Taft Visits New Orleans." *New Orleans Nostalgia*. 2009. http://www.neworleansbar.org/documents/TaftVisitsNewOrleansArticle.11-4.pdf, accessed October 16, 2012.

Hill, Morton A. "Twentieth Century Thought on the *Ratio Studiorum*." *Jesuit Educational Quarterly* 14, no. 4 (1952): 197–205.

Hollis, Christopher. *The Jesuits: A History*. New York: Macmillian, 1968.

"Holy Family Parish Worship Spaces." Holy Family Parish of Galviston and Bolivar. http://holyfamilygb.org/AboutUs/OurWorshipSpaces.aspx, accessed April 23, 2012.

Howkins, Donald A. "Pioneer Jesuits in the South—1566 to 1763." In *Jesuits of the South Celebrate 75 Years as a Province (1907–1982), Apostolic Ministry in the South Since 1837. Early Jesuits Missions in the South (1566–1763)* 2, no. 1 (August 1982): 12–13.

Humphreys, Margaret. *Yellow Fever and the South*. Baltimore and London: The Johns Hopkins University Press, 1992.

"Immaculate Conception Church Parish Jesuit Church." Jesuit Church. http://jesuitchurch.net/, accessed April 23, 2012.

Jameson, Mary. "Loyola's Dental School Existed for 57 Years." *Maroon*. April 12, 2012. http://www.loyolamaroon.com/2.6710/loyola-s-dental-school-existed-for-57-years-1.2728713#.UNt7KYXPa3k.

Jaschik, Scott. "Threat to Black Colleges." *Inside Higher Education*, November 17, 2009.

"Jesuit." Jesuit High School, Tampa, Florida. http://www.jesuittampa.org/, accessed April 23, 2012.

"Jesuit New Orleans." Jesuit High School, New Orleans. http://www.jesuitnola.org/cgi-bin/j.pl?i=1296, accessed April 23, 2012.

"The Jesuit Spirituality Center at St. Charles College." Jesuit Spirituality Center, Grand Coteau, LA. http://home.centurytel.net/spiritualitycenter/, accessed April 23, 2012.

Kelley, William F. *The Jesuit Order and Higher Education in the United States, 1789–1966*. Milwaukee: Wisconsin Jesuit Province, 1966.

Kelly, M. Veronica. "A Century of Catholic Education in Baton Rouge (1847–1947)." (MA Thesis, Catholic University of America, 1947).

Kenny, Michael. *The Torch on the Hill: Centenary Story of Spring Hill College, 1830–1930*. New York: The American Press, 1931.

Kenton, Edna. *The Jesuit Relations and Allied Documents: Travels and Explorations of the Jesuit Missionaries in North America 1610–1791*. Whitefish, MT: Kessinger, 2006.

Laporte, Jean-Marc. "Ignatian Identity and Mission: Beyond GC 35" (Workshop on communal apostolic discernment). Rome, 2009. www.jesuits.ca/orientations/ignat%20jes.pdf, accessed October 9, 2010.

Leahy, William P. *Adapting to America: Catholics, Jesuits, and Higher Education in the Twentieth Century*. Washington, DC: Georgetown University Press, 1991.

Lerpold, Lin, David Ravasi, Johan van Rekom, and Guillaume Soenen. "Identity, Strategy, and the Environment." In *Organizational Identity in Practice*, edited by Lin Lerpold, David Ravasi, Johan van Rekom, and Guillaume Soenen, 13–78. New York: Routledge, 2007.

Leslie, Bruce W. *Gentlemen and Scholars: College and Community in the "Age of the University," 1865–1917*. University Park: Pennsylvania State University Press, 1992.

Leturia, Pedro. "Why the Society of Jesus Became a Teaching Order." *Jesuit Educational Quarterly* 4, no. 1 (1941): 31–54.

Lowney, Chris, *Heroic Leadership: Best Practices from a 450-Year-Old Company that Changed the World*. Chicago: Loyola Press, 2003.

"Loyola College Prep, Shreveport, La.: Founded 1902." Loyola Prep. http://www.loyolaprep.org/, accessed April 23, 2012.

Loyola, Ignatius. *The Constitutions of the Society of Jesus*. Translated by George E. Ganss, S.J. St. Louis: Institute of Jesuit Sources, 1970.

———. *A Pilgrim's Journey: The Autobiography of Ignatius Loyola*. Translated by Joseph N. Tylenda, San Francisco: S.J., Ignatius Press, 2001.

Mahoney, Kathleen A. *Catholic Higher Education in Protestant America: The Jesuits and Harvard in the Age of the University*. Baltimore: Johns Hopkins University Press, 2003.

"Manresa House of Retreats, Convent, Louisiana: Society of Jesus USA." Manresa House of Retreats, Convent, LA. http://manresala.org/, accessed April 23, 2012.

Marmolejo, Francisco. "Higher Education Facilities: Issues and Trends." *Organization for Economic Co-Operation and Development* PEB Exchange 1 (2007): 1–14.

McDonough, Peter. *Men Astutely Trained: A History of the Jesuits in the American Century*. New York: Free Press, 1992.

McKenzie, John L. "Theology as an Integrating Factor in Jesuit Education." *Jesuit Educational Quarterly* 21, no. 1 (1958): 19–26.

Meyer, John W., and Brian Rowan. "Institutional Organization: Formal Structure as Myth and Ceremony." *American Journal of Sociology* 83, no. 2 (September 1977): 340–63.

Modras, Robert. "The Spiritual Humanism of the Jesuits." In *An Ignatian Spiritual Reader*, edited by George W. Traub, 4–15. Chicago: Loyola Press, 2008.

Monk, Maria. *The Awful Disclosures of Maria Monk*. Revised ed. New York: D. M. Bennett Literal and Scientific Publishing House, 1878.

Morey, Melanie M., and John J. Piderit. *Catholic Higher Education: A Culture in Crisis*. New York: Oxford University Press, 2006.

New Advent Catholic Encyclopedia. "IHS." New Advent. http://www.newadvent.org/cathen/07649a.htm, accessed June 15, 2010.

Office of Mission and Ministry. "Welcome to University Ministry." Loyola University New Orleans, 1996–2010, http://mm.loyno.edu/university-ministry, accessed November 25, 2010.

O'Leary, Timothy J. "The Role of Science in Jesuit Colleges." *Jesuit Educational Quarterly* 15, no. 4 (1953): 223–28.

O'Malley, John W. *The First Jesuits*. Cambridge: Harvard University Press, 1993.

"Our History." LSU Health Sciences Center New Orleans, School of Dentistry. http://www.lsusd.lsuhsc.edu/history.html, accessed December 26, 2012,

Perkins, James A. *The University in Transition*. Princeton: Princeton University Press, 1966.

Pfeffer, Jeffrey, and Gerald R. Salancik *The External Control of Organizations: A Resource Dependence Prospective*. New York: Harper and Row, 1978.

Pickett, Albert James. *History of Alabama and Incidentally Georgia and Mississippi, from the Earliest Period*. Birmingham: Press of Roberts and Son, 1878.

Pope, Justin. "More Colleges May Close in Ailing Economy." Boston.com. http://articles.boston.com/2008-11-17/news/29272837_1_colleges-university-business-officers-endowments, accessed April 21, 2011.

Power, Edward. *A History of Catholic Higher Education in the United States*. Milwaukee, Wisconsin: The Bruce Publishing Company, 1958.

Rahner, Hugo. *The Spirituality of St. Ignatius Loyola: An Account of Its Historical Development*. Translated by Francis John Smith. Westminster, MD: Newman Press, 1953.

Reeves, William D. *Manresa on the Mississippi: For the Greater Glory of God*. Convent, LA: Manresa House of Retreats, 1996.

Rest, Friedrich. *Our Christian Symbols*. Cleveland, Ohio: The Pilgrim Press, 1954.

Ryan, William D. "Is There Anything Distinctive About Jesuit Education?" *Jesuit Educational Quarterly* 28, no. 1 (1965): 58–60.

"Sacred Heart Cultural Center: Celebrating History, Art, and Architecture." Sacred Heart Cultural Center. http://www.sacredheartaugusta.org/, accessed April 23, 2012.

Schafer, Judith Kelleher. "Life and Labor in Antebellum Louisiana." In *Louisiana: A History*, 5th ed. Wheeling, IL: Harlan Davidson, 1990.

Schroth, Raymond A. *The American Jesuits, A History*. New York and London: New York University Press, 2007.

Schwickerath, Robert. *Jesuit Education: Its History and Principles Viewed in the Light of Modern Educational Problems*. St. Louis: B. Herder, 1904.

Scott, John C. "The Mission of the University: Medieval to Postmodern Transformations." *Journal of Higher Education* 77, no. 1 (January–February 2006): 1–39.

Shapiro, Harold T. *A Larger Sense of Purpose: Higher Education and Society*. Princeton: Princeton University Press, 2005.

Shils, Edward. "The University, the City, and the World: Chicago and the University of Chicago." In *The University and the City: From Medieval Origins to the Present*, edited by Thomas Bender, 210–30. New York: Oxford University Press, 1988.

Smith, Thomas Ruys. *Southern Queen: New Orleans in the Nineteenth Century*. New York: Continuum International Publishing Group, 2011.

"Spring Hill College," Spring Hill College. http://www.shc.edu/, accessed April 23, 2012.

Stern, Andrew, H. M. *Southern Crucifix, Southern Cross: Catholic-Protestant Relations in the Old* South. Tuscaloosa: The University of Alabama Press, 2012.

Stone, Lawrence. *The Past and the Present, Revised*. London and New York: Routledge and Kegan Paul, 1987.

Sublette, Ned. *The World That Made New Orleans: From Spanish Silver to Congo Square*. Chicago: Lawrence Hill, 2008.

Tewksbury, Donald G. *The Founding of American Colleges and Universities Before the Civil War*. New York: Bureau of Publication, Teachers College, Columbia University, 1932.

Thelin, John R. *Higher Education and Its Useful Past: Applied History in Research and Planning*. Rochester, VT: Schenkman, 1982.

Trask, Benjamin H. *Fearful Ravages: Yellow Fever in New Orleans, 1796–1905*. Lafayette, Louisiana: Center for Louisiana Studies, 2005.

Traub, George W., ed. *Ignatian Spiritual Reader*. Chicago: Loyola Press, 2008.

Uter, Frank M. *A History of the Catholic Church in Baton Rouge*. Baton Rouge: Privately published, 1992.

Van der Wusten, Herman, ed. *The Urban University and Its Identity: Roots, Locations, Roles*. Boston: Kluwer Academic, 1998.

Van Dyke, Paul. *Ignatius Loyola: The Founder of the Jesuits*. New York: Charles Scribner's Sons, 1926.

Venkatesh, Bharti. "Leadership Transitions: The Key to Organizational Success." *Academic Leadership* (August 2008): 1, http://www.academicleadership.org/empirical_research/476_printer.shtml, accessed June 16, 2010.

Weigel, Gustave A. "The Heart of Jesuit Education—The Teacher." *Jesuit Educational Quarterly* 20, no. 1 (1957): 7–16.

Whelan, James F. "Loyola University, New Orleans, Louisiana." *Southern Association Quarterly* 11, no. 4 (November 1946): 1–9.

Wise, John E. "The College Boards in Jesuit Schools." *Jesuit Educational Quarterly* 7, no. 1 (1944): 25–29.

Index

Page numbers in italics refer to figures.